A Practical Guide to
Early Childhood Curriculum

Related Titles

Observation and Participation in Early Childhood Settings: A Practicum Guide, Second Edition
Jean Billman and Janice Sherman
ISBN: 0-205-37555-3

The Young Child as Scientist: A Constructivist Approach to Early Childhood Science Education, Third Edition
Christine Chaille and Lory Britain
ISBN: 0-205-36776-3

Engaging Young Children's Academic and Moral Aspirations in School
Joan Goodman and Usha Balamore
ISBN: 0-205-34823-8

Challenging Behavior in Young Children: Understanding, Preventing, and Responding Effectively
Barbara Kaiser and Judy Sklar Rasminski
ISBN: 0-205-34226-4

Completing the Computer Puzzle: A Guide for Early Childhood Educators
Suzanne Thouvenelle and Cynthia Bewick
ISBN: 0-205-26544-8

The Arts, Young Children, and Learning
Susan Wright
ISBN: 0-205-19889-9

For further information on these and other related titles, contact:

Allyn and Bacon
75 Arlington Street
Boston, MA 02116
www.ablongman.com

Second Edition

A Practical Guide to Early Childhood Curriculum

Linking Thematic, Emergent, and Skill-Based Planning to Children's Outcomes

EVELYN A. PETERSEN

Boston   New York   San Francisco
Mexico City   Montreal   Toronto   London   Madrid   Munich   Paris
Hong Kong   Singapore   Tokyo   Cape Town   Sydney

Series editor: Traci Mueller
Editorial assistant: Erica M. Tromblay
Manufacturing buyer: JoAnne Sweeney
Marketing manager: Elizabeth Fogarty
Cover designer: hannusdesign.com
Illustrator: Karin Petersen
Production coordinator: Pat Torelli Publishing Services
Editorial-production service: TKM Productions
Electronic composition: TKM Productions

For related titles and support materials, visit our online catalog at www.ablongman.com.

Library of Congress Cataloging-in-Publication Data

Petersen, Evelyn A.
    A practical guide to early childhood curriculum : linking thematic, emergent, and
skill-based planning to children's outcomes / Evelyn A. Petersen.-- 2nd ed.
        p. cm.
    Rev. ed. of: A practical guide to early childhood planning, methods, and materials. c1996.
    Includes bibliographical references and index.
    ISBN 0-205-33754-6
    1. Early childhood education--Curricula--Handbooks, manuals, etc. 2. Lesson
planning--Handbooks, manuals, etc. I. Petersen, Evelyn A. Practical guide to early
childhood planning, methods, and materials. II. Title.

LB1139.4 .P48 2003
372.21--dc21   2002026008

Printed in the United States of America

Contents

---

4   The Schedule: When Curriculum Happens   50

5 Lesson Plans: How Curriculum Happens   61

6 Individualizing: The Why of Curriculum   74

7 Interest-Based Curriculum: Horizontal Planning   95

10   Classroom Management: Social-Emotional Outcomes   163

11   Trends and Priorities in Early Childhood Education   179

Preface

I am very pleased and excited to bring you the second edition of *A Practical Guide to Early Childhood Curriculum*, in which my mission continues to be to provide early childhood teachers and students with helpful information on curriculum planning. This edition is even more effective in presenting systems to help teachers organize and integrate interest-based and skill-based curriculum ideas and to do effective, individualized planning for young children. New illustrations and diagrams support the practical planning systems in this book and show teachers how to use developmentally sequenced activities to help children achieve expected outcomes gradually and naturally.

This second edition includes *all* topics that have a great impact on curriculum planning—child development, settings, methods, materials, daily schedules, written plans, projects, planning webs, individualized teaching, documentation, outcomes, classroom management/guidance, trends in the field of early childhood education, and the curriculum priorities of literacy, math, and science.

In response to input from programs using this book in the field, information on computers and technology has been included, as have examples of small-group planning. Developmental profiles for children from birth to age 8 and information on infant-toddler curriculum and environments have also been added, as well as a floor plan of an infant-toddler classroom. More lesson plan form examples have been added, along with more learning experiences in literacy, math, and science. Important new information on children's outcomes has been included. In addition, comprehensive information on the what, who, where, when, how, and why of curriculum has been included in this edition, and a new chapter is devoted to classroom management and guidance.

The practical information in this book will help students see how to put learning theories into practice, and will help experienced teachers improve the quality of their curriculum planning. It will make ongoing lesson plans easier to write, implement, and monitor, as well as link lesson planning to curriculum objectives and children's outcomes in all learning domains.

The systems, examples, and ideas presented here are flexible. They support individual choices and teaching styles, and have been field tested in a variety of programs to ensure that they support the diversity and autonomy of programs. In addition, because these systems are not a "curriculum" but a developmental framework and approach to curriculum development, they can be easily and simultaneously used with *any* other curriculum ideas, modules, or assessment tools. By the same token, creative teachers can modify these systems of curriculum development to use with toddlers and 2-year-olds or in kindergartens and primary grades.

Developmentally sequenced skill-based activity examples that mesh with themes are provided in this edition for every learning center and for large-group, small-group, free-choice time, and individualized teaching from September through May. Learning experiences and teacher scaffolding relating to goals and outcomes match the diverse skill levels and changing development of 3- to 5-year-olds, facilitating the children's natural and gradual mastery of skills. (See Chapter 8 and Appendix A.)

In addition to presenting a clear understanding of the ongoing assessment process and the parents' roles in assessment and planning, this book provides a simple, effective system for planning, doing, and documenting individualized teaching for every child. This also helps to document children's outcomes, and is an expected part of best practices in the field.

To summarize, the curriculum planning systems in this book are not only simple and practical but they will also help teachers meet the diverse and changing needs of children throughout the entire year. Lesson planning will be done much more quickly and effectively. Teachers will have more time to observe and enjoy the children, and to share their excitement as they experience the joys of collaboration and discovery learning. With the information in this second edition, you will be able to plan a consistent balance of developmentally appropriate learning experiences, based not only on children's thematic and emergent interests but also on curricular content in all learning domain areas—motor, perceptual, language, memory, and problem solving. You will also be able to individualize your teaching for every child and be able to prove it. In addition, your curriculum planning will lead gradually and naturally toward children's outcomes.

Curriculum development and individualized teaching are such important concepts that the first six chapters of this book will cover the what, who, where, when, how, and why of curriculum. By the time you reach Chapters 7 through 9 you will be ready to learn about the curriculum development systems in this book, and how to use them in your own personal way to develop curriculum and lesson plans throughout the year. Chapters 10 and 11 cover classroom management and early childhood trends and priorities, which also impact curriculum planning. After you read and internalize the concepts and systems of the book, Appendix A, "Skill-Based Learning Experiences" and the Time Blocks you find there may become your most valued resource.

Acknowledgments

This book represents many years of experience with programs and colleagues in the field, all of whom I deeply thank. I could never have shared the range of practical ideas and information in this book without field experiences as a consultant, trainer, and Child Development Associate Representative. These roles have given me opportunities to work with hundreds of children, teachers, and parents in rural and urban areas and in many states as well as in Tribal Nations.

I have especially appreciated my work with the Head Start family, including children, parents, teachers, Head Start Bureau staff, federal specialists, and consultants. Each person I've worked with has been a resource and inspiration to me. One consultant, Roy Pierson, playing the devil's advocate, encouraged me to write the first edition of this book. Elder and consultant Winona Sample, and Dr. Helen Scheirbeck, of the Smithsonian Institute and former Chief of the Head Start Bureau's American Indian and Alaskan Native Program Branch, inspired my work on the second edition.

Special thanks go to some of the programs who have been using this book and who have given me excellent input and suggestions to incorporate into this edition:

The Early Discoveries staff of the YMCA of South Hampton Roads, Norfolk, Virginia
The Kamehameha Schools, the Hawaiian Islands
Northern Pioneer Community College, Holbrook, Arizona
SouthCentral Foundation Head Start, Anchorage, Alaska
Sault Tribe Head Start, Sault Ste. Marie, Michigan
Bay Mills Community College, Brimley, Michigan
Eastern Oregon University Head Start, La Grande, Oregon
Navajo Nation Head Start, Chinle, Arizona

Detailed helpful suggestions for the first edition were made by my excellent reviewers, Laura Dittmann and Lillian Sugarman. I now thank Claude Endfield (Northern Pioneer College) and Jan Morehead (New Mexico State University), who provided excellent suggestions for the second edition. Their comments were immeasurably helpful, and have added to the clarity and content of this edition. I also thank my editor, Traci Mueller, for her patience, and thank my personal friend and proofreader, Jean Coonrod, and my excellent copyeditor Lynda Griffiths for their help and support.

Finally, special thanks go to my entire family, especially to my husband, Jon, and to our daughter, Karin Petersen. Karin was my graphic designer/illustrator for both the first and second editions and deserves the credit for all the tables, forms, and illustrations. My very supportive husband helped me with the new diagrams and various computer crises, as well as the illustration concepts in Chapters 7 and 8.

If you have questions or comments on this edition, you can reach me at my website, www.askevelyn.com or by email at petersen13@chartermi.net. You can also write your own review of this edition at www.amazon.com.

1 What Is Curriculum?

Curriculum is not something you teach to children or give to children. It is a living, ongoing process. Curriculum is what is happening in an early childhood program. When children talk about the good foods they shared that day, or the fun they had at the water table, or what they found on a nature walk, or the words they learned in a tribal language, or how much they liked it when Aimee's mom came to dance for them—all these things are evidence of the curriculum at that particular child development center on a particular day.

This thing called curriculum is often hard to define, because "what happens" in every early childhood program will be different and unique to that program. No two curriculum plans will be exactly alike, nor should they be, because each program's curriculum should be developed to suit its own population, location, resources, community, and cultural values.

Even if there were four classrooms in the same geographic and cultural community, and if there were a written general curriculum for all four rooms, each classroom would have a slightly different "take" on the curriculum. This is because the teacher's style and the children and parents are an integral part of each classroom's specific curriculum. Although the overall written plans for the curriculum might be the same, the ways each teacher implements the plans will be slightly different.

Can we still come up with a definition for curriculum if there are so many differences? Yes, we can, and that's because there are far more likenesses than differences in early childhood programs that base curriculum on sound child development principles, accepted standards of quality, and best practices.

Child Development Principles

Principles are generalizations that are so reliable that they are considered in decision making. The entire knowledge base that is the foundation for early childhood practice is too large to discuss in this book, but there are some major child development principles on which early educators agree, and that guide best practices. The following principles are universal; they apply to all children, regardless of race, gender, or country of origin:

- The physical, intellectual, emotional, and social domains of development in children are closely related. (Children are active and holistic learners; development in each domain influences others and is influenced by them.)
- Patterns of growth and development are orderly and sequential. (All children learn to babble before they speak; skills are continually built on skills previously learned.)

- Human development proceeds from simple to complex. (All children learn single words before sentences, walk before they run, and use their fingers before spoons, forks, or other tools.)
- Learning is influenced by the child's social and cultural context. (What is valued in a particular cultural or social environment influences children's learning.)

Best Practices and Accepted Standards in the Field

In spite of the wide diversity of early childhood programs, there is a well-documented consensus in the field as to accepted standards of quality and indicators of best practices. Here is a short summary of these criteria, which are based on the child development principles just listed. Best practices include the following:

- Developmentally appropriate practices that are based on what is known about child development and learning; what is known about the strengths, interests, and needs of each child; and what is known about the social and cultural contexts in which children live
- Ample time for children's choice making and hands-on learning in appropriate settings in which children actively explore, interact, and experiment as they construct their own knowledge (new knowledge is added to the base of knowledge which teachers, families, peers and other adults impart to children)
- Methods that support all areas of growth and development, including self-esteem, competence, healthy physical development, positive social-emotional development, self-discipline, critical thinking and reasoning, and other psychomotor and cognitive skills
- Respect and support of children's parents and families, and a commitment to work in partnership with parents, building positive relationships, and including parents in decision making about their children's care and education

Standards of quality, including these criteria, have been published in the early childhood field for many years. These publications vary from the Head Start Performance Standards to the accreditation criteria of the National Academy of Early Childhood Programs, the Child Development Associate Credential, and the standards of quality for early childhood programs published by State Departments of Education. The criteria or other summaries of these criteria are seen in various formats in many resources in the field, often accompanied by comprehensive discussions and references. References for some of these important publications can be found in the suggested resources at the end of this chapter.

Perhaps the most widely known and quoted statements on these standards can be found in the National Association for the Education of Young Children's (NAEYC) Position Statement of July 1996. Programs that are developing curriculum will find an extensive discussion on child development principles in the statement. In addition, the publication includes guidance on the roles of teachers and parents, guidance for the ongoing assessment of children's development, and guidance in curriculum development and developmentally appropriate practice.

Developmentally Appropriate Practice

The term *developmentally appropriate practice (DAP)* has been so frequently used in the field that one sometimes forget the real meaning of these words. Developmentally appropriate practice is based on two equally important criteria: (1) what teachers know about the ways *all* children develop and learn, and (2) what teachers continually learn day by day about each *individual* child and family. Therefore, DAP is based on *both* age appropriateness and individual appropriateness. Used, overused, challenged, and often misunderstood, DAP is definitely part of the mainstream of educational language, and should be fully understood by all early educators.

The new edition of *Developmentally Appropriate Practice in Early Childhood Programs,* revised edition, edited by Sue Bredekamp and Carol Copple (1997), begins with the NAEYC Position Statement of 1996:

> Developmentally appropriate practices result from the process of professionals making decisions about the well-being and education of children based on at least three important kinds of information:
>
> 1. What is known about child development and learning . . . a knowledge of age related human characteristics that permits general predictions within an age range about what activities, materials, interactions, or experiences will be safe, healthy, interesting, achievable and also challenging to children.
> 2. What is known about the strengths, interests, and needs of each individual child in the group and to be able to adapt for and be responsive to inevitable individual variation.
> 3. Knowledge of the social and cultural contexts in which children live to ensure that learning experiences are meaningful, relevant, and respectful for the participating children and their families.

Further insight can be found in *Reaching Potentials: Appropriate Curriculum and Assessment for Young Children,* volume 1 (1992, pp. 1–26), as editors Sue Bredekamp and Teresa Rosegrant tell us some of the things that DAP is *not.* The editors explain that DAP is not a curriculum with a rigid set of expectations, but a developmental framework and philosophy. Appropriate practices are reflected in the way a curriculum is carried out. Bredekamp and Rosegrant make it clear that DAP supports curriculum ideas that emerge from children, families, and teachers, not just from teachers. They also make it abidingly clear that DAP does *not* mean that teachers abdicate their roles as adult leaders and allow children to run the classroom or be in charge of curriculum!

Goals and objectives that include skill-based experiences are an integral part of appropriate curriculum, and, contrary to misconceptions, many skills are taught both directly and indirectly through hands-on learning in which children learn and construct knowledge in all developmental domains. Curriculum is integrated and meaningful, and is structured by the setting, materials, and the teacher's careful preplanning. Outcomes for children are achieved naturally and gradually as children experience both the planned curriculum and the ways emergent curriculum is integrated with it.

Developmentally appropriate practice supports the use of ongoing goals in a framework of careful, appropriate planning. It supports ample time for learning and discovering through play, but what is initially offered in the learning centers is carefully preplanned by teachers to mesh with curriculum goals. In essence, DAP supports the emerging interests of children and expands on these interests to build on children's knowledge and skills.

The Reggio Emilia movement in Italy and the success of its children's long-term collaborative projects have provided new insights to developmentally appropriate practices about process versus product issues and time issues. Many early educators now feel that in-depth, long-term studies or projects leading to children's representations or "products" can be undertaken by young children if these projects relate to curriculum goals and if the children's interests remain high.

In spite of many individual program differences, you can see that what is actually happening in programs where curriculum is based on sound child development principles and best practices will be much the same. Yes, curriculum is what happens, but in reality, nothing happens without *planning*. As the title of a vintage NAEYC book edited by early childhood specialist Laura Dittmann so wisely states, *Curriculum Is What Happens: Planning Is the Key* (1970). The definition of *curriculum* must include that there will be a *written plan* for what will be happening.

So now we can say that curriculum is a written plan, or a "road map," for what will be happening in a program, and that what will happen will be based on sound child development principles, accepted standards, and best practices in the field. Things that must be included in the written plan are goals, learning experiences, materials, and the roles to be played by adults.

Goals

Road maps show two things: where you want to go and how to get there. The written plan for your curriculum must show these things, too. First, where do you want to go? What are your goals for children's development and learning, and what do you, your staff, and the children's parents want children to achieve? Most written curriculum plans start with a mission statement or a statement of philosophy that includes or is followed by the goals.

As staff and parents write these goals together, be aware that the goals must match what is reasonable and appropriate in terms of child development and learning styles. In some cases, programs will need to spend some time doing parent education about what is reasonable and developmentally appropriate in terms of goals and expected outcomes.

TIP

If parents ask why you do not plan for children to be drilled on numbers and the ABCs, give specific examples of how children are taught literacy and numeracy through hands-on activities with concrete materials, which is the way children learn best. Explain how you train the children's eyes, ears, hands, and minds so that they feel both success and challenge as they gradually master skills. Reassure the parents that the children will easily be able to do numbers and ABCs later, when it's time to do them.

Explain that if you were going to become a qualified parachute jumper three months from now, your trainer would not take you up to 20,000 feet the first day and keep throwing you out of the plane. In the same way, educators do the things with children that the children can do now, and these things will prepare them well for the things they will do later. Precious time in the preschool years are not wasted by having children practice specific things that are expected of them the next year or the year after.

In addition, curriculum planners must be aware that the culture of a program, a community, or a tribal nation may have particular values that might translate into goals for the children. In many American Indian tribal nations, cultural curricula reflecting heritage, customs, and celebrations are developed and used simultaneously or integrated with a "traditional" early childhood curriculum.

Each program's goals may differ, but here are some goals that are commonly shared among many programs. Remember that goals are where you want to go; they are what you want for children.

Sample Goals for Children

To develop positive relationships with adults and peers
To respect the feelings, needs, and rights of others
To work independently and with others as part of the group
To develop a sense of trust and security
To increase self-esteem, feeling both lovable and capable
To increase pride in oneself, both as an individual and as a member of the group
To express thoughts and feelings
To do critical thinking and to identify and solve problems
To use imagination and creative processes to express feelings and ideas
To develop literacy, numeracy, reasoning, and decision-making skills that will
    form a foundation for school success
To develop motor skills and physical health
To develop self-discipline and a sense of responsibility

The Spring 2001 Michigan Association for the Education of Young Children newsletter, *The Beacon*, presented a revision of the 1987 digest called "What Should Young Children Be Learning" by renowned early childhood educator Lillian Katz. In this article (pp. 1, 4–5), Katz emphasizes that children should learn whatever will ultimately enable them to become healthy, competent, productive, and contributing members of their communities. We can see that the preceding list of sample goals matches this emphasis. Katz also discusses *four major categories of learning goals* that all early educators should consider in curriculum development:

1. ***Knowledge:*** Facts, concepts, ideas, vocabulary, stories, and other aspects of children's culture that are acquired from adults, and also acquired through the children's active process of making sense of their own observations.
2. ***Skills:*** Small units of action that occur in relatively short periods of time and that are easily observed. An almost endless number of skills are learned in the early years, among which are physical, verbal, perceptual, memory, counting, estimating, drawing, and other skills. Skills are most often learned by use, and they can be improved with guidance, practice, and encouragement.
3. ***Dispositions:*** Habits or tendencies to respond to certain situations in certain ways. Curiosity, friendliness, bossiness, creativity, and generosity are all examples of dispositions. These dispositions are not learned by formal instruction, but are inborn in children, or acquired by being around people who exhibit them. These dispositions are strengthened by being used and being appreciated.
4. ***Feelings:*** Subjective emotional states. Some feelings are innate and others are learned. Feelings such as competence, confidence, belonging, and security are learned, mostly through the child's interactions with others and from reinforcement.

If you look again at the earlier list of sample goals for children, you can see that they overlap with the four categories of learning goals that Katz listed in her article.

Experiences and Materials

Your goals are where you want to go. Next, your curriculum plan should include how you will get there: What experiences will you provide or offer to children that will help them grow and develop enough to achieve what you want for them? This part of your written plan may be lengthy, so try to look at one goal or one type of goal at a time.

For each major goal, think of the time, space, and materials in your setting that you will use as the foundation for the learning experiences you plan. Ask yourself and your fellow planners what activities children will need to experience in order to meet the goals. As you look at each type of goal and think about how you will achieve it, consider whether your equipment and materials are appropriate and adequate. Will some experiences require you to purchase or create new materials or use what you have in new ways? How will you use computers and technology in the classroom? How will you manage technology time so that it won't diminish other skills or development?

How will you "order" your experiences throughout the year so that children's learning will proceed from simple to complex, and so that their mastery of skills will take place gradually and naturally? How will you ensure that you plan a balance of activities in all learning domains? Can you list the major types of materials that will support your children's learning experiences? When and where will the experiences occur? All these questions should be answered and noted in your written plan for the curriculum.

TIP

Plan ways to collect authentic, performance-based information on children's gradual progress toward specific goals in all learning domains (i.e., children's outcomes). Outcome information is now being expected by most funding sources as an indicator of program quality (see Chapter 8). Performance-based assessment can include observations, video- or audiotapes, and photographs organized in the child's file or portfolio.

Two Major Types of Curriculum

As they create the written curriculum, teachers should also reflect on the fact that as they implement their plan, they will be organizing and using two broad types of curriculum information: *interest based* and *skill based*. When teachers are planning experiences relating to basic or general themes for the weeks or months of the year, they are dealing with *thematic* information based on the children's interests. When new interests emerge from the children, and plans for experiences are changed based on that emerging interest, this is called *emergent* curriculum information. Note that the thematic and emergent experiences are both *interest-based* information.

The other broad type of curriculum information used for planning experiences is *skill-based* information. This type of information will be used to plan experiences that will help children gradually develop or master a variety of developmental skills. Organizing all of these types of curricular content for the purposes of monthly and daily planning will be discussed in Chapters 7 through 9.

Roles of Adults

As you look at the ways you plan to achieve your goals, you will also need to describe the roles that all the adults will play in the implementation of your curriculum. Other adults, in addition to your classroom staff, will support your planned experiences as team teachers, resource persons, visitors, and volunteers.

Don't forget that your teaching team, support staff, supervisor, and children's parents all have roles to play in both planning and implementing your children's learning experiences. They all have roles to play in making your written plan for curriculum happen and keep happening smoothly all year long. Adult roles will involve their work in implementing systems for planning, observation, recording (data collection), communication, record keeping, monitoring, assessment, and individualization. It is wise to describe these roles in your written curriculum plan so that everyone participates and everyone knows who does what and when they do it.

TIP

In all Head Start programs, the written curriculum must include goals, learning experiences, roles of adults, and materials to support curriculum. It must also be consistent with the current Head Start Performance Standards.

Infant-Toddler Curriculum

Although this book is written primarily for teachers of 3- to 5-year-olds, the explosive expansion of programs for 0- to 3-year-olds and the trend toward full day care require that I touch on the kind of curriculum that is appropriate for infants and toddlers. Although the general goals for children's learning are much the same, the curriculum for infants and toddlers should not be a watered-down 3- to 5-year-old curriculum full of adult-planned learning activities that are supposed to happen at particular times and in specific places during the day. Neither should the curriculum be simply dependent on an environment for safe care in which no effort to stimulate learning occurs.

Ron Lally defines and describes an infant-toddler curriculum in his article "Infants Have Their Own Curriculum: A Responsive Approach to Curriculum Planning for Infants and Toddlers," pages 6 and 7, in the March 2000 *Head Start Bulletin,* Issue 67:

> In high quality infant toddler programs, the interests of the child and the belief that each child has a curriculum are what drive practice. It is understood that very young children need to play a significant role in selecting their learning experiences, materials and content. Curriculum plans, therefore, do not focus on games, tasks, or activities, but on how to best create a social, emotional, and intellectual climate (and setting) that supports child initiated and child pursued learning. . . . Responsive curriculum planning focuses on finding strategies to help infant toddler teachers search for, support, and keep alive children's internal motivation to learn, and their spontaneous explorations of people and things of interest and importance to them.

We can see that in infant-toddler programs, the child is the driving force that creates the curriculum. Teachers and home visitors must be keen and intuitive observers, and strive to catch any spontaneous moment, no matter how fleeting, to expand on an infant or toddler's own interests. They must see the environment as a powerful learning setting, and be quick to interpret the child's body language and facial expressions in order to anticipate and adapt actions to meet the momentary interests of the child. They must also understand each child's particular temperament and learning style, and realize that each child is a self-motivated, active learner who learns holistically from each experience.

Relationships with both the child and parents or caregivers are crucially important, because both the home culture and the child's relationships with adults are primary factors for development in all learning domains. Relationships and interactions with others also help form the child's identity and sense of self. A primary goal for teachers and home visitors in infant-toddler programs is to share their observations and what they notice about changes in children's development with the parents. This, in turn, helps parents and caregivers observe, interpret, and respond appropriately to their children, nurturing well-being and growth.

In the "observe and respond" curriculum of infants and toddlers, it is more important for caregivers to prepare themselves and the environment so that infants and toddlers can learn, rather than to figure out what to "teach" them. Most written curriculum plans for infants and toddlers will deal with ways to thoroughly ground the staff in knowledge about child development and the child's family culture. Plans will also include ways to make strong, caring connections with the child's family, ways to develop a safe and interesting place for learning, ways to establish flexible small groups within the large group for care and development, and ways to select materials that are appropriate for the needs and interests of the children served.

Summary

This chapter has given you some insight and answers to the question: What is curriculum? We have discussed the fact that curriculum is what happens for children, and that it should be based on sound child development principles and developmentally appropriate practices. In addition, curriculum planners must consider four types of learning: knowledge, skills, dispositions, and feelings. We talked about the written plan as a road map for curriculum goals, looked at four general categories of learning, and examined a list of sample goals for children. We discussed the learning experiences and materials used in implementing the curriculum, as well as the roles of adults. Also, we talked about interest-based (thematic and emergent) curriculum information and skill-based curriculum information that teachers organize and use in planning experiences for children. The chapter ended with a discussion of what is emphasized in infant-toddler curriculum planning.

A final thought is that curriculum should be fun—fun for the teacher, the children, and their families. And if a teacher makes a curriculum uniquely his or her own, if it's based on the children's interests as well as the principles of child development and best practices, it *will* be fun. You can read more about curriculum in the resources listed at the end of this chapter, which include excellent books about curriculum development in kindergarten, primary grades, infants and toddlers, and preschoolers.

Self-Study Activities

1. Access the Internet and go to the naeyc.org website for NAEYC. Go to "Join NAEYC" and "About NAEYC" to read about this organization and to see the application for membership. Now go to acei.org, the site for the Association for Childhood Education International (ACEI), and read about it and review its application for membership. Which of these organizations would you join and why?

2. On the Internet, go to the Head Start Information and Publications Center at headstartinfo.org. From the homepage, go to "Publications," then "Program Design and Management," then "Revised Performance Standards," then "Child Development and Education," and finally to Part 1304 subpart B, which is the section on early education. Print out these pages. Now go to the "About NAEYC" section of the NAEYC site and click on "Position Statements." Print out the standards for accreditation by the National Association for the Education of Young Children. Compare this printout with the Head Start standards for common elements.

Resources and Suggested Readings

Armington, D. *The Living Classroom: Writing, Reading and Beyond.* Washington, DC: National Association for the Education of Young Children, 1997.

Barbour, Nita, & Seefeldt, Carol. *Developmental Continuity across Preschool and Primary Grades: Implications for Teachers.* New York: Teachers College Press, 1993.

Beaty, Janice. *Preschool Appropriate Practices.* Orlando, FL: Holt, Rinehart and Winston, 1992.

Bergen, Doris; Reid, Rebecca; & Torelli, Louis. *Educating and Caring for Very Young Children.* New York: Teachers College Press, 2001.

Bickart, Toni S.; Jablon, R.; & Dodge, Diane Trister. *Building the Primary Classroom: A Complete Guide to Teaching and Learning.* Washington, DC: Teaching Strategies, 1999.

Bredekamp, Sue, & Copple, Carol, eds. *Developmentally Appropriate Practice in Early Childhood Programs,* rev. ed. Washington, DC: National Association for the Education of Young Children, 1997.

Bredekamp, Sue, & Rosegrant, Teresa, eds. *Reaching Potentials: Appropriate Curriculum and Assessment for Young Children: Vol. 1 and Vol. 2.* Washington, DC: National Association for the Education of Young Children, 1992 and 1995.

Brewer, Jo Ann. *Introduction to Early Childhood Education: Preschool through Primary Grades.* Boston: Allyn and Bacon, 1995.

Cromwell, Ellen S. *Nurturing Readiness in Early Childhood Education: A Whole-Child Curriculum for Ages 2–5.* Boston: Allyn and Bacon, 2000.

Cuffaro, H. K. *Experimenting with the World: John Dewey and the Early Childhood Classroom.* New York: Teachers College Press, 1995.

Dodge, Diane Trister, & Colker, Laura J. *The Creative Curriculum,* 3rd ed. Washington, DC: Teaching Strategies, Inc., 1992.

Dombro, Amy; Colker, Laura; & Dodge, Diane Trister. *The Creative Curriculum for Infants and Toddlers, rev. ed. Spanish and English.* Washington, DC: Teaching Strategies, 1999

Elkind, David. *Images of the Young Child: Collected Essays on Development and Education.* Washington, DC: National Association for the Education of Young Children, 1993.

Fortson, Laura Rogers, & Reiff, Judith. *Early Childhood Curriculum: Open Structures for Integrative Learning.* Boston: Allyn and Bacon, 1995.

Gandini, L., & Edwards, Carol Pope, eds. *Bambini: The Italian Approach to Infant/Toddler Care.* New York: Teachers College Press, 2000.

Goffin, Stacie G. & Stegelin, Dolores A., eds. *Changing Kindergartens: Four Success Stories.* Washington, DC: National Association for the Education of Young Children, 1992.

Head Start Bureau, Administration for Children and Families, Department of Health and Human Services. *Revised Head Start Performance Standards.* Washington, DC: U.S. Department of Health and Human Services, 1996.

Head Start Bureau, Administration for Children and Families, Department of Health and Human Services. *Head Start Bulletin, Issue 67, Curriculum in Head Start.* Washington, DC: Department of Health and Human Services, March 2000.

Head Start Bureau, Administration for Children and Families, U.S. Department of Health and Human Services. *Head Start Bulletin, Issue 69, Early Head Start.* Washington, DC: Department of Health and Human Services, October 2000.

Helm, Judy Harris, & Katz, Lillian. *Young Investigators: The Project Approach in the Early Years.* New York: Teachers College Press, 2001.

Hemmeter, Mary Louise; Maxwell, Kelly L.; Jones, Melinda Ault; & Schuster, John W. *Assessment of Practices in Early Elementary Classrooms.* New York: Teachers College Press, 2001.

Jones, Elizabeth; Evans, K.; & Rencken, K. S. *The Lively Kindergarten: Emergent Curriculum in Action.* Washington, DC: National Association for the Education of Young Children, 2001.

Kieff, Judith, & Casbergue, Renee. *Playful Learning and Teaching: Integrating Play into Preschool and Primary Programs.* Boston: Allyn and Bacon, 2000.

Koralek, Derry; Colker, G; Laura, J.; & Dodge, Diane Trister. *The What, Why, and How of High Quality Early Childhood Education: A Guide for On-Site Supervision.* Washington, DC: National Association for the Education of Young Children, 1993.

Meisels, Samuel. "Fusing Assessment and Intervention: Changing Parents' and Providers' Views of Young Children." *Zero to Three,* 21, 4 (2001): 7–10.

National Academy of Early Childhood Programs. *Accreditation Criteria and Procedures of the National Academy of Early Childhood Programs,* rev. ed. Washington, DC: National Association for the Education of Young Children, 1991.

Phillips, Carol Brunson, ed. *Essentials for Child Development Associates Working with Young Children.* Washington, DC: Council for Early Childhood Professional Recognition, 1991.

Schickedanz, Judith; Pergantis, Mary Lynn; Kanosky, Jan; Blaney, Annmarie; & Ottinger, Joan. *Curriculum in Early Childhood: A Resource Guide for Preschool and Kindergarten Teachers.* Boston: Allyn and Bacon, 1997.

Schweinhart, Lawrence; Barnes, Helen; Weikart, David; Barnett, Steven; & Epstein, Ann. *Significant Benefits: The High Scope Perry Preschool Study through Age 27.* Monograph Number 10. Ypsilanti, MI: High/Scope Press, 1993.

Spodek, Bernard, & Saracho, Olivia. *Right from the Start: Teaching Children Ages Three to Eight.* Boston: Allyn and Bacon, 1994.

Surbeck, Elaine, & Kelley, Michael, eds. *Personalizing Care with Infants, Toddlers and Families.* Wheaton, MD: Association for Childhood Education International, 1990.

Taylor, Barbara J. *A Child Goes Forth,* 8th ed, Englewood Cliffs, NJ: Prentice-Hall, 1994.

Wassermann, Selma. *Serious Players in the Primary Classroom: Empowering Children through Active Learning Experiences,* 2nd ed. New York: Teachers College Press, 2000.

Wolfgang Charles, & Wolfgang, Mary. *School for Young Children: Developmentally Appropriate Practices,* 2nd ed. Boston: Allyn and Bacon, 1999.

Websites

www.acei.org   Association for Childhood Education International

www.headstartinfo.org   Head Start Bureau Publications & Information

www.naeyc.org   National Association for the Education of Young Children

www.nhsa.org   National Head Start Association

2 Curriculum and Child Development

Educators need to remember that curriculum is for children, not adults. It is only when teachers truly understand what the children they work with are like, physically, intellectually, emotionally, and socially, that teachers can effectively plan appropriate goals and experiences. The plan must match children's development, needs, and interests at each step of growth. The challenge is that their interests, needs, and development keep changing week by week as they proceed through the program year. Educators must be attentive to these changes.

British child development authority Penelope Leach (1977) once said, "We spend too much time concentrating on what the child is not doing, instead of noticing and respecting and appreciating what he is doing now." In a live television interview on CNN in January 1997, Leach went on to talk about the importance of letting children grow at their own rates, realizing that children do whatever they have to do when they are ready to do it. She cautioned that when children are "pushed" unnecessarily and ineffectively, it can do more harm than good, and the child's feelings about being pushed are negative, even if the pushing was "successful." Leach went on to say, "The question is, are we with them or ahead of them or behind them? We should be with them, side by side."

These thoughts are echoed by Schweinhart and Weikart (1977) in their research studies on "lasting differences." They found that pushing children before they are ready may not serve their best long-term interests for learning. In their comparison studies, very early instruction in beginning reading skills required so much drill and practice to be successful that it seemed to undermine children's dispositions to become readers. There is not much benefit in a child's ability to read if he or she doesn't enjoy reading.

Being with children, side by side, means being aware that the curriculum activities are planned for the children, not for their parents or for teachers. The curriculum must take into account experiences that give children feelings of both success and challenge, experiences in which they have full interest and involvement. Being with children, side by side, also means that when during the planning, educators should not be the only ones who are aware of "where children are" in terms of child development. The children's parents must also be included in the planning, because they have valuable and ongoing input to share about their children's changing interests, strengths, and needs.

Who Are the Children for Whom Teachers Plan?

No matter how many children a person has taught or birthed, the details of growth and development become blurred in one's memories. When teachers develop curriculum or choose learning experiences, it's wise to check references to the sequences of child development to be sure that age-appropriate activities are included. When busy teachers plan, they don't always take the time to check these references. To resolve this problem, this chapter includes thumbnail sketches of children's development from birth to age 8.

In addition, as a more detailed reference, children's developmental profiles are included in Appendix C of this book. These profiles list the developmental milestones or outcomes that are usually expected physically, intellectually, socially, and emotionally as children grow from birth to age 8. You can refer to these reference guides, or copy, enlarge, and post them in planning centers or parent rooms to help parents and staff know more about what to expect at different ages.

Be highly aware, however, that children move through the developmental milestones in each growth category at different speeds. This is why it is more important to pay attention to the *sequences* of the developmental steps in each area than it is to set up rigid expectations based on particular milestones for all children in a particular age group. For example, Appendix C will list milestones that are characteristics of 3-year-olds, but curriculum planners must consider the ways children's personal and gradual development will impact the weekly and monthly planning of learning experiences that gradually lead children to these milestones or outcomes.

As you examine Appendix C and read the narrative sketches in this chapter, you are reminded that you should not think of developmental milestones as static outcomes or "achievements," but as signposts along a road or path of continuous, gradual human development. All children are following the same path, but each child will reach each of the signposts in his or her own way and at different times. Some children will go through these developmental sequences and pass the signposts at a much faster rate than average, and some will proceed more slowly, but they're still on the same path. Some will go through sequences quickly in one area of development and slowly in others. These deviations are not abnormal; they are simply individual differences that are well worth the teacher's attention. Observing individual differences with focused interest will help teachers make appropriate modifications in curriculum planning and in weekly and monthly lesson planning.

Later in this chapter, we'll look at some examples of ways child development knowledge impacts curriculum planning. But first, let's review what young children are like in the thumbnail sketches that follow. Let's learn more about the *who* that teachers address in their curriculum and the concerns of the parents.

TIP

Development researchers agree that, at each stage of growth, the child has particular goals to accomplish. Sometimes the child's goals, whether conscious or subconscious, mesh well with the parents' goals. Sometimes they don't. This is why occasional conflicts between parents and children are a normal and natural part of the child's growth and of parenting; parents may need reassurance on this point.

What Are Infants Like?

Infancy is one of the most amazing periods of human growth. In just two short years, the child changes from a helpless, dependent, demanding, and noisy little bundle, into a walking, talking individual who perseveres in expressing a personality and will of his or her own.

During infancy and toddlerhood, one of the child's goals is the security of having his or her physical needs met. Infants and toddlers are trying to establish a sense of trust, in spite of the fact that they are totally dependent and helpless. This trust in the surroundings and trust in the caregivers or significant others interacting with the child will be the foundation of self-esteem.

Besides the obvious goal of the parents to adjust to a new person in their lives, parents are concerned about the physical and emotional needs of the infant. Parents of infants and toddlers usually ask questions about the child's health and growth, safety, and the needs for immunizations, foods, rest, stimulation, and security.

As soon as the child begins to respond and interact, parents begin to be able to interpret what the child tells them with facial expressions, body languages, as well as crying and cooing. Parents usually wonder about the baby's alertness and how to stimulate his or her intelligence. The best stimulation is the parents' own attention, voice, facial expression, and body language. Clean, safe baby toys or objects that encourage the infant to explore with all the senses should be part of the environment.

What Are Toddlers Like?

As the infant becomes a curious and constantly exploring mobile infant, and then a toddler, parents discover that there is an even greater need for safety-proofing the home. They want to know more about physical skills and coordination, and about finding toys or activities to keep the child safely occupied and interested in appropriate things to look at and handle. Toddlers are constantly in an "explore and learn" mode, and they're eager to learn with all their senses. This keeps parents and caregivers alert, delighted, and thoroughly challenged.

Parents often wonder why toddlers between the age of 1 and 2 develop fears of strangers or particular adults, or why their children imitate adults and repeat actions that get attention. The reasons lie in the fact that this age group is increasingly conscious of adults and adult reactions. During this time of first steps and first words, the toddler also expresses a wide range of emotions, sometimes has tantrums, and begins to want to do things for himself or herself.

What Are 2-Year-Olds Like?

The 2-year-old poses new kinds of problems. In addition to being extremely curious, mobile, and sensory in experimenting with everything around them, 2-year-olds are beginning to understand being "persons" in their own right—separate from their parents. Their emerging sense of individual identity makes them highly aware of "me" and "mine." They test their parents to see what reaction they will get and how much control they really have. This new assertiveness is normal, healthy, and basically temporary, even though temper tantrums and conflicts at mealtime, during dressing, and at bedtime are common. Being firm, positive, calm, and very diplomatic is the best way to cope with 2-year-olds who are trying hard to establish their identities.

As parents try to be patient, keep their tempers, and stay in control, they often need help with these daily power struggles. They wonder about bottle breaking, security objects, tantrums, and toilet training. They begin to have questions about the child's reactions to themselves and others—children, relatives, and sitters. Parents often ask about choosing safe and appropriate child care; they need to know that it's okay to observe potential child-care centers carefully, and ask many questions.

What Are 3-Year-Olds Like?

Basically, 3-year-olds are more relaxed, more cooperative, and very eager to please adults. They're more verbal and social, and more interested in other children. However, their world still revolves around their home and their own family, where they feel more secure. At age 3, children begin to express their ideas and identities; they practice their language and use their imaginations. They still explore the world with their senses; they pretend, and often have imaginary friends. They like to do things for themselves, and if parents can be patient while 3-year-olds dawdle, they will discover that youngsters of this age really are capable of many things. They can help themselves and help out in small ways at home.

Parents wonder why their loving 3-year-olds may still have tantrums at the store, or why they are so extremely jealous of new babies, other people, and telephones. These behaviors are normal. Children this age do not like changes in routines! They don't like changes at all, unless they are reassured and prepared for them. The security of daily routines and rituals is important to them. Some parents also worry about behavior that is fairly normal for this age, such as thumb sucking, bed-wetting, developing language, and discipline; they become concerned about safety, social behavior, and intellectual development. The most important thing that parents of 3-year-olds need to know is that these children want to feel loved by their parents and/or caregivers and that they like feeling proud of their growing accomplishments.

If parents of 3-year-olds wish to begin to set patterns about using the personal computer, they should occasionally hold children on their laps at the PC and do simple point and click games that are fun ways to show cause and effect. Keep these experiences simple, enjoyable, and short.

What Are 4-Year-Olds Like?

The 3-year-old may have been fairly relaxing for parents to live with, but the 4-year-old probably is not! Children of this age seem to be in a constant state of motion, eager for new experiences of any kind! They're very active and very verbal; this is the age of constant questions—the age of "hands-on" experimenting and learning about the give and take of friendship and cooperative play. They also make messes as they play, and get grouchy when they are overtired. Parents often worry about hyperactivity at this age, sometimes unnecessarily; in fact, 4-year-olds are workaholics about play.

Four-year-olds are insistent on doing everything themselves, are often boastful about what they can do, and often bite off more than they can chew. They love to pretend and role-play, but are still unsure of the difference between reality and fantasy. They're extremely friendly and outgoing with adults, and interested in everything adults do, which often causes parents to worry about their child's safety and about strangers.

If parents are trying to start setting patterns of computer and Internet use, they should always be with the children, using the computer and software together. Typically, 4-year-olds are able to manipulate the mouse and use a variety of software. Children should always use the computer with their parents and be introduced to safe websites on the Internet with their parents. It is important to remember, however, that the attention span of a 4-year-old is short, and there is a great need for active play; keep computer time simple and brief.

Often, parents ask questions about the very normal interest of 4-year-olds in their bodies and their sex; they worry (quite unnecessarily) about boys who play dress-up. They ask questions about kindergarten readiness, about discipline, about helping out at home, and about the new fears that 4-year-olds develop as they learn more about the real world. Pediatricians, extended family, Internet resources, and books can all help ease these fears and provide information.

Children of this age also love name-calling, "naughty" words, silly jokes, and tattling. They frequently test their parents in a battle of wills in public places.

Parents find that 4-year-olds can be embarrassing and exasperating, but they are always exciting and interesting!

What Are 5-Year-Olds Like?

Five-year-olds are more likely to tell you their age before they tell you their names! They're excited about new experiences, such as school, but are also very vulnerable, needing reassurance and support to face these new experiences. Calmer, more confident, and more cooperative than 4-year-olds, they want to be liked by others and they thrive on adult praise.

Although very practical and industrious little people, 5-year-olds also love fun and jokes. They love to learn and they love to laugh, but they hate to be embarrassed or wrong. They are beginning to like rules, especially if the rules are for other people. They still tattle. Generally, however, 5-year-olds have good self-control and can understand and follow through on adult expectations.

Parents will find that children who are age 5 are usually cooperative about rules for using the computer and Internet. They will enjoy simple games and safe children's sites in the company of parents. Most can use pull-down menus, launch programs, create art projects, and do simple research. They will be able to work on their own for short periods if parents are close by and supportive.

It is normal for parents of 5-year-olds to ask questions about their child's learning, how the child can get along better with friends, or their child's school progress. Good communication with teachers and caregivers, as well as common sense, usually resolves these concerns. Parents need to continue to reinforce personal safety and good health habits, and be careful not to overschedule their children.

Some 5-year-old children whine or interrupt, which is attention-getting behavior. What usually works is to give clear expectations about what is appropriate, and to give attention only for the behaviors you want children to repeat. Children of this age can clean up their rooms, but they still need adult help to organize this process.

By the time he or she reaches age 5, the child has developed a sense of trust (or sometimes, mistrust) about the world, as well as a sense of his or her own identity. By the early school years, the child also has developed a drive to express his or her own initiative and a sense of industry and accomplishment. Self-concept is growing, based on feeling both capable and lovable.

What Are 6- to 8-Year-Olds Like?

During the early school years, parents and teachers sometimes believe they don't need to do much listening or praising because the child appears to be so confident and independent, but this age group is actually very vulnerable, and still needs reinforcement, reassurance, hugs, and attention.

The fact that 6- to 8-year-olds still need attention is obvious when you look at many of their behaviors. It's quite normal to hear parents asking questions about why their children act out by interrupting, whining, having school problems, fighting with friends or siblings, telling "tall tales," maintaining continually messy rooms, and being naughty on family trips. Sometimes parents focus on these very normal problems and forget that the need for attention and "quality time" is still very important during these formative years. Children this age not only need clear, firm guidelines for their behavior at home and at school but they also need adult attention, praise, and support. Adults also need to help children learn that privileges always go hand in hand with responsibilities.

Teachers can often help parents become aware of the complex growing that children do in the school-age years as they soak up an enormous amount of information and begin to use it to develop very individual personalities. Great physical changes begin to occur. Children begin these years as egocentric beings and move toward preadolescence, gradually becoming able to do abstract thinking and conceptualizing. They develop rapidly in all areas—mentally, physically, socially, and emotionally.

These are often the years in which both parents join the work force, expand their social lives, and develop interests or hobbies they had put aside when children were younger. It is vital to remain highly aware of the 6- to 8-year-olds' needs for input and guidance during these years. Listening and talking with this age group, knowing who their friends are, and noticing potential "small" problems is highly important in the prevention of bigger problems in later years.

Children at this age also need and want to be team members, or members of "the group" both at school and in the family. They are capable of cooperative help at home and school, and capable of expressing ideas, feelings, and input that can be very valuable during family or school discussions. They love table or board games, and although they develop many life skills through playing them, the greatest benefit is the sense of belonging and "connectedness" that children feel when they play games with their parents. Enjoying family games together regularly helps cement parent-child relationships.

This age group is increasingly interested and competent in using the computer and Internet, and parents and teachers should consider restricting access only to sites they have visited and feel are appropriate. Children can now search for information from many websites, comparing the quality of sites and software. Parents or teachers can also make use of prescreened "safe" sites, child-friendly browsers, and child-safe search engines. Some parents may wish to investigate setting up a "kid's desktop."

Six- to eight-year-olds can fully understand the need for rules for use of the computer and Internet, and can both follow the rules and help develop consequences for forgetting or breaking a rule. Parents should continue to work with children or be nearby whenever they use the computer and Internet at home. Patterns parents have put in place for computer use should remain consistent. The computer should be set up in the den or family room, where it is accessible and used by the whole family, not isolated in a separate room. Adults need to talk about the sites the children visit, and help them do critical thinking by discussing why some sites are better or more credible than others. Adults should also help children discover why more than one source of information is needed when doing research. These children are capable of comparing and evaluating websites if adults provide the criteria.

Children need positive experiences with sites that are easy to navigate, and their time at the computer should be limited. Fresh air and active play are still very important to physical development, and this age group needs many other interests besides the computer. They need hobbies, sports, friends, and group activities, such as Scouts and 4H. They need a good balance of varied daily activities, but they must not be overscheduled or overloaded.

Children at any age are miraculous and fascinating to observe; they are lovable, interesting, and challenging. The things adults do as teachers, parents, and caregivers and the ways adults interact with children from infancy to age 8 have a great impact on the kinds of people they will become!

Now let's look at some examples of the ways knowledge of child development can affect early childhood curriculum planning.

Planning for Children's Health and Well-Being

Health

There are many ways that one's knowledge of child development impacts curriculum development and lesson planning in the areas of children's health and well-being. Setting curriculum goals in health, nutrition, and safety are part of best practices in all quality programs. Both the goals and the ways they are implemented are influenced by child development knowledge. For example, early childhood teachers know that young children don't come into their classrooms with strong skills in health and hygiene. They know that children put things in their mouths, let their noses run, forget to wash their hands, take off their coats at the first sign of spring, and forget to cover coughs and sneezes.

This is why teachers make health education a vital part of the curriculum. They understand that if they don't teach children the importance of cleanliness, good hygiene, and good health habits by planning ongoing and relevant learning experiences, children will probably pick up and pass on germs, get sick, and miss school. Most important, teachers who understand how children learn know that when young children are taught to practice good health habits at an early age, they are likely to become lifelong skills, which is a valuable and unwritten long-range goal.

Two ways to teach children health skills are by doing appropriate adult modeling and by praising children for using good health habits. Basic child development knowledge tells us that this works; we know that young children copy adult modeling and repeat behaviors for which they are praised. Another effective method for teaching health and hygiene is through regularly planned health education activities and demonstrations of good hygiene. These should be seen regularly in the teacher's lesson plans.

--*-*

Early childhood teachers know that most young children don't understand cause-and-effect connections about eating healthful foods instead of junk foods, or brushing their teeth after meals. This is why teachers must put focused experiences in nutrition and dental education into their curriculum and lesson plans, and also invite dentists and dental hygienists to visit classrooms or attend parent meetings.

Since teachers or caregivers of young children usually provide meals and/or snacks, it is also important for them to include children in the preparation of nutritious foods. These experiences will encourage children to eat the foods, and simultaneously provide ongoing opportunities to teach them about the nutritional values of foods. During food experiences, children will also practice skills in sanitary food handling, estimating, pouring, mixing, measuring, counting, and cause and effect. Children will reap lifelong benefits from this kind of curriculum planning.

One often overlooked learning experience that should be part of health and nutrition goals and experiences is the weighing and measuring of children. Children love to see proof of how they have grown heavier or taller, and they have an initial understanding of the relationship of their growth to eating healthful foods. Checking heights and weights is a great monthly health activity to do in the classroom, and it's easy to do during free-choice time. This learning experience will boost children's self-esteem and will also help children understand more about measurement and measuring tools. A further benefit in tracking children's heights and weights is that it can prompt teachers to investigate unusual growth spurts or lags.

Some programs arrange for vision and hearing screenings to take place on site, where children are likely to feel more secure about the procedures. This screening is especially important in the light of child development knowledge that affirms how much children learn from their senses and how language acquisition is impacted by hearing.

Health and nutrition are not only important to the early childhood curriculum in terms of physical and health outcomes for children but they are also important for children's families. Early childhood teachers cannot make long-term positive differences in children's health without the support and partnership of parents. Written curriculum should also include ways to share information with parents or caregivers whenever possible—on home visits, in newsletters, at parent meetings, and whenever spontaneous opportunities arise. Parents, like teachers, care about children's health and know that healthy children are better able to learn.

Many other topics relating to children's health and well-being can be part of the curriculum and can be developed jointly with parent input and shared with families. These might include workshops on natural or cultural alternatives to medication or treatment, the prevention of childhood stress, children's contagious diseases, the importance of immunizations, and the values of fresh air and exercise. Tips on hand washing and sanitizing, appropriate health procedures for diapering babies, information on colicky babies, information on sudden infant death syndrome (SIDS), and child abuse prevention are all possible alternatives. The choice of topics will be up to the parents and staff who set the goals for curriculum and suggest the experiences that would be of most benefit to each program's children and families. Working with parents and planning experiences regarding anything that affects children's health and well-being is an important part of the early childhood teacher's job.

Safety

Safety is another aspect of lesson planning that is affected by what is known about basic child development. Young children know very little about danger or its cause-and-effect relationships. They don't know that certain behavior (not looking before crossing a street, playing with matches, or drinking water from an open pond) can put them in danger. Young children move quickly and impulsively; they can be distracted from seeing a potential hazard because they are busy playing. Children rarely know how to handle themselves in an emergency. Without adult guidance, they might not know what to do or whom to go to for help if they were being abused or molested.

It is because early childhood teachers know that young children come to them with so little knowledge of personal safety that teachers plan learning activities relating to safety throughout the year. Safety activities are planned and entered into lesson plans in a variety of ways:

- Large- or small-group discussions with children to develop safety rules for the group
- Whole-group practice of fire and tornado drills with discussion afterwards, including "stop, drop, roll" dramatic play
- Pedestrian safety practiced on outdoor walks
- Bus safety drills on the bus, which are also acted out in the classroom in dramatic play with props
- Practice in seat belt safety in dramatic play with props
- Camping safety and fire prevention with dramatic play props
- Water safety with dramatic play and props about boats, fishing, and swimming at the beach
- Home safety and hygiene practiced with props in the housekeeping area
- The use of special programs or materials to teach about appropriate touch and abuse prevention

Teachers often plan learning experiences to introduce and explain the safe use of new materials or equipment. They also reinforce safety through incidental learning experiences throughout the day as children work and play indoors and outside. When teachers understand the developmental need for children to learn personal safety, they maintain a good staff/child ratio for safe supervision both indoors and outside, and are constantly alert to teaching opportunities relating to safety.

Planning for Other Curriculum Goals

A knowledge of children's development also affects the way that teachers plan to meet their curriculum goals through specific learning experiences and carry out these plans. Young children have not yet developed abstract thinking skills; they learn through concrete experiences. These facts are of the utmost importance when teachers are planning themes and thematic unit activities, and great differences can be seen between the lesson plans of teachers who understand and consider child development in their planning and those who do not.

Thematic Planning

Let's examine two hypothetical examples in which teachers want children to learn more about frogs. One teacher disregards basic child development knowledge about the ways 3- to 5-year-olds learn. The other bases her plans on what she knows about child development.

The early childhood teacher who disregards child development knowledge about children's thinking processes might decide to have young children sit for 30 or 40 minutes in a large-group circle time while she explains the life cycle of a frog with charts and pictures. (We can easily imagine what children will be doing after they lose interest in 10 or 15 minutes!)

The early childhood teacher who understands basic child development might stimulate an interest in frogs by bringing frogs into the classroom in an aquarium and showing them to children in a large group. Then she would explain safe ways in which children could observe and talk about the frogs during free-choice or activity time. Children would be delighted as they looked at the frogs up close and personal in small groups in the science area.

Additionally, the children might take a walk to a pond and find tadpoles to put in the science area. This would encourage future observations and dictation about the changes children would see in the tadpoles over several weeks time. The teacher might even plan to play some instrumental "frog-jumping" music during large-group music time so children could practice creative movement and jumping skills as they represent frogs.

Basic Planning

Knowing developmental sequences is also important in making the dialogues of teachers with children more meaningful as children work and play with familiar materials during the classroom day. For example, children learn to construct with blocks over time, in a sequence of small events or stages. As infants or toddlers, children handle (and probably taste) the blocks. Next, they repeatedly put them into containers and take them out. Then they carry the blocks about, or lay them flat on the floor, or stack a few. Later, they will discover how to make a bridge with three blocks, and set blocks in a pattern to enclose a space. Still later, by the time they are age 4 or 5, they will build taller, more complex structures, build with repeated patterns, and eventually name their buildings and plan ways to build them together.

An understanding of the sequence of block play in child development is important as teachers arrange for the use of blocks in free-choice time. As children play, teachers can encourage and expand children's constructing and thinking skills by helping them notice bridges, shapes, sizes, and repetitive patterns. Knowing the sequences of development in children's use of blocks helps teachers ask appropriate questions of children who are at different skill levels.

Knowing what comes *next* in the developmental sequence also enables teachers to use dialogues to support children's problem-solving skills as they reach each level of accomplishment. In this way, teachers *scaffold* learning experiences, helping children move forward and upward, as they keep mastering new skills. Here are some examples of scaffolding.

A teacher might provide soft, stuffed, fabric blocks for mobile infants, and praise their further exploration of these. Also, a teacher may praise a 3-year-old for a flat "road" she built all by herself with blocks, and talk about where the road might be going, possibly encouraging construction at the end of the road. Perhaps a teacher might ask questions of a 4-year-old to motivate a discussion about shapes, or about comparing heights, counting blocks, or seeing repeated patterns. A teacher might also praise a group of older 4-year-olds for their block construction, take a photo of it, and mount the picture on a poster. This could lead to children's dictation about their building and how they built the structure, which could be printed and posted in the block area. In other words, when teachers know the steps of developmental sequences in skill-based activities, they can make their planning and their interactions with children richer and more productive in terms of enjoyable learning, provocative collaboration, and children's outcomes.

Understanding child development also affects other areas of planning. Knowing that infants need sensory stimulation may prompt a caregiver to provide rattles, mobiles, or wind chimes in the setting. Understanding the differences in motor skill development in a mixed-age group will help the teacher plan the variety of physical experiences that should take place indoors and outside with 3- to 5-year-olds. Knowing that 3-year-olds have a strong need for familiar routines and security and a distrust of change will affect curriculum planning about field trips early in the program year. Knowing that 3-year-olds dawdle and dress slowly, especially if they try to talk at the same time, will mean that the teacher needs to allow more time in the schedule for the children to dress for outdoors or going home.

Physical Objectives

When early childhood teachers understand the developmental need for children to engage in active play in order to develop physical strength and large-muscle skills, teachers include in their lesson plans specific ways to practice these skills, both indoors and outdoors.

Children learn many valuable things from the outdoor environment, and teachers who understand the health benefits of fresh air and activity always include outdoor activities in their curriculum and lesson plans. This may mean that children will take a walk around the block (practicing safety skills at the same time), walk on a nature trail, practice using skis and snowshoes, or use outdoor equipment in an outdoor play area. A variety of equipment or activity options must be provided for children with diverse skills and interests. Adults also need to model their value of fresh air and exercise with active participation in outdoor experiences. Children should go out everyday, even if time must be short on cold winter days.

When teachers understand the developmental need for children to use their large muscles every day, lesson plans will also reflect active play indoors, during free-choice or children's activity time. Some activities might be walking on a balance beam, tossing a pillow filled with crumpled newspaper, or using tumbling mats. If there is enough space in the setting, children might practice a variety of skills in a planned obstacle course. No matter how small the classroom space, the lesson plan should reflect the teacher's plans for indoor large-muscle activity of some kind. This kind of planning will lead to increased strength and skills that will demonstrate developmental outcomes in physical growth.

Creative Arts

A variety of creative art media and materials is also important in developing children's manipulative and fine-motor skills. In the creative art area, when teachers provide open-ended art media—such as crayons, markers, paper, glue or paste, painting materials, playdoughs or clays, and various collage materials—3- to 5-year-olds will not become frustrated with activities or materials that do not match their skill levels. Children can use open-ended materials like these according to their own skill levels and they will be totally delighted with their own creations. With adult reinforcement, children will keep using open-ended materials and keep becoming more and more skillful, achieving expected outcomes in eye-hand coordination in natural, gradual ways.

Curriculum planners and teachers who understand child development know that the *process* of using open-ended materials is far more important than the products children create. In the art area, the focus should be on the processes that occur when the teacher offers a variety of open-ended art media to match individual interests, allowing children to imagine, plan, experiment, evaluate, use divergent thinking, and problem-solve as they create their own art.

Unfortunately, at times teachers become so excited about something "cute" that can be created as a product in the art area that they may forget basic child development knowledge and the varied skill levels of 3- to 5-year-olds. For example, a teacher who wants all the children to cut out a predrawn turkey, or even a facsimile of a turkey made by tracing around the child's hand, forgets that although some 4- and 5-year-olds might have no problem creating this "product," most 3-year-olds and some young 4-year-olds would be very frustrated in trying to create it. If such turkeys are really important to the children, varied options and materials for creating them should be available to match all skill levels and allow for individual creativity.

Teachers should probably keep in mind that children may be cutting out turkeys, making identical Christmas trees, and fashioning daffodils with nut cups over and over again for years in elementary school. Why do it when they are 3- and 4-years-old? With such products, the focus is on small-motor skills and following directions. In the early childhood center, there are many other opportunities for children to learn small-motor skills and how to follow directions.

There will always be certain times of the year when teachers encourage children to create something "special" for a holiday or a gift. However, teachers should always remember that differences in the skill development of 3- to 5-year-olds must still be considered. No gift—whether it is a scribble drawing, a card, or collage, or a piece of driftwood decorated with moss and pebbles the children have collected—should be made with all the children sitting together at tables, following step-by-step instructions. The skill levels of children in most early childhood settings vary too widely for this to be effective or enjoyable.

It is easier for teachers and more age appropriate for children if teachers plan for the activity to occur for several days as one of the regular choices in the art media area during free-choice time. After several days, with the encouragement of adults, all the children would have had time to complete the creation at their own skill level and pace. A separate "art project" time scheduled for all children in daily lesson plans usually indicates that the teacher prefers product over process in the use of art media. This is not appropriate. The art area and its experiences should be one of the options children can always choose during daily child activity time.

Sensory Materials

Young children, from birth onward, learn both through their active interactions with materials in the learning environment and through all their senses. Planning that takes this basic knowledge of child development into consideration will always show sensory learning taking place. Daily lesson plans should contain entries such as listening to sounds or matching sounds; planned tasting of healthful foods, and the use of tactile materials such as fabrics, collage materials, sand, water, and playdough or other clays made by the teacher and children.

Some of these experiences might take place and be seen in the lesson plan in large-group time, such as listening to sounds; some might take place in small-group time, such as the planned tasting of nutritious foods. Many of these sensory experiences, along with the cognitive skills of observing, telling, pouring, estimating, counting, sorting, and seeing cause and effect can take place during free-choice time.

Summary

In this chapter we have been talking about how important it is to understand child development and growth. Teachers cannot teach young children successfully if they don't know how children grow and learn. We have looked at general characteristics of children from birth to age 8, and we know where to find specific developmental profiles for these ages in Appendix C. We have discussed ways child development relates to curriculum planning for children's health, well-being, and safety, and have seen examples of ways that the knowledge of child development affects curriculum, lesson planning, and dialogues for many learning activities.

All this boils down to the fact that if the curriculum and learning experiences for young children are to be effective, they must be based on sound principles of child development and a constant sensitivity to the many patterns of children's learning as they grow from birth to age 8. In Chapter 3, we will look at another aspect of curriculum, and find out more about *where* the curriculum takes place.

Self-Study Activities

1. Plan a way in which you can observe varied ages of children in public. You may decide to go to a mall, to a family fast-food restaurant, or to pediatrician's office waiting room. (If so, identify yourself and your reasons for being there, and obtain permission from the doctor or receptionist.) Take notes on the physical appearance, behaviors, and skills you observe being performed by various children. See if this information helps you estimate the ages of the children you are observing. Then, if possible, check to see how close you were to being correct.

2. Arrange to visit a child-care center (but not one in which you are already involved and know the children) and engage in the same process. Check with the child-care provider or teacher to see if your determination of ages is correct. You may also wish to make notes, for your own personal use only, on whether planning in the center matched skill levels of the children.

Resources and Suggested Readings

Albrecht, Kay, & Miller, Linda. *Innovations: Infant and Toddler Development.* Beltsville, MD: Gryphon House, 2001.

Ames, Louise Bates; Ilg, Frances; & Haber, Carol. *Your One Year Old: The Fun-Loving, Fussy 12- to 24-Month-Old.* New York: Dell, 1995.

Ames, Louise Bates; Ilg, Frances; & Haber, Carol. *Your Two Year Old: Terrible or Tender.* New York: Dell, 1976, 1980.

Ames, Louise Bates; Ilg, Frances; & Haber, Carol. *Your Three Year Old: Friend or Enemy.* New York: Dell, 1985.

Ames, Louise Bates, & Ilg, Frances. *Your Four Year Old: Wild and Wonderful.* New York: Dell, 1976, 1980, 1994.

Ames, Louise Bates. *Your Five Year Old: Sunny and Serene.* New York: Dell. (Temporarily out of print; can be ordered used online at amazon.com.)

Ames, Louise Bates, & Ilg, Frances. *Your Six Year Old: Loving and Defiant.* New York: Dell, 1981.

Ames, Louise Bates; Haber, Carol; & Ilg, Frances. *Your Seven Year Old: Life in a Minor Key.* New York: Dell, 1987.

Ames, Louise Bates; Haber, Carol; & Ilg, Frances. *Your Eight Year Old: Lively and Outgoing.* New York: Dell, 1990.

Berk, Laura E. *Infants and Children: Prenatal through Early Childhood.* Boston: Allyn and Bacon, 1994.

Brazleton, T. Berry, & Cramer, Bertrand. *Earliest Relationship: Parents, Infants, and the Drama of Early Attachment.* Reading, MA: Perseus, 1991.

Brazleton, T. Berry. *Touchpoints: Your Child's Emotional and Behavioral Development.* Reading, MA: Perseus, 1994.

Brazleton, T. Berry, & Greenspan, Stanley. *The Irreducible Needs of Children: What Every Child Must Have to Grow, Learn and Flourish.* Reading, MA: Perseus, 2001.

Brazleton, T. Berry, & Sparrow, Joshua. *Touchpoints: Three to Six. Your Child's Emotional and Behavioral Development.* Reading, MA: Perseus, 2001.

Bredekamp, Sue, ed. *Developmentally Appropriate 1976, reprinted 1994. Practice in Early Childhood Programs Serving Children from Birth through Age 8,* expanded ed. Washington, DC: National Association for the Education of Young Children, 1992.

Dodge, Diane Trister, and Colker, Laura. *The Creative Curriculum for Early Childhood,* 3rd ed. Washington, DC: Teaching Strategies, 1988, 1992.

DeVries Rheta, & Kohlberg, Lawrence. *Constructivist Early Education: Overview and Comparison with Other Programs.* Washington, DC: National Association for the Education of Young Children, 1987.

Elkind, David. *A Sympathetic Understanding of the Child: Birth to Sixteen,* 3rd ed. Boston: Allyn and Bacon, 1994.

Engstrom, Georgianna, ed. *The Significance of the Young Child's Motor Development.* Washington, DC: National Association for the Education of Young Children, 1971; 8th printing, 1994.

Katz, Lillian; Evangelou, Demetra; & Hartman, Jeanette. *The Case for Mixed-Age Grouping in Early Education.* Washington, DC: National Association for the Education of Young Children, 1990.

Kendrick, Abby; Kaufman, Roxanne; & Messenger, Katherine. *Healthy Young Children: A Manual for Programs,* revised ed. Washington, DC: National Association for the Education of Young Children, 1994.

Leach, Penelope. *Your Baby and Child: From Birth to Age Five.* New York: Alfred A. Knopf, 1997.

McAfee, Oralie, & Leong, Deborah. *Assessing and Guiding Young Children's Development and Learning.* Boston: Allyn and Bacon, 1994.

Miller, Karen. *Ages and Stages: Birth through Eight Years, revised.* West Palm Beach: Telshare Publishers, 2001.

Petersen, Evelyn, & Petersen, Karin. *Sams Teach Yourself e-Parenting Today.* Indianapolis, IN: Macmillan, 2000. (Available on amazon.com.)

Phillips, Carol B., ed. *Essentials for Child Development Associates Working with Young Children.* Washington, DC: Council for Early Childhood Professional Recognition, 1991.

Schweinhart, Lawrence, & Weikart, D. P. *Lasting Differences: The High/Scope Preschool Curriculum Comparison Study through Age 23, Monograph 12.* Ypsilanti, MI: High/Scope Press, 1997.

Surbeck, Elaine, & Kelly, Michael, eds. *Personalizing Care with Infants, Toddlers and Families.* Wheaton, MD: Association for Childhood Education International, 1991.

Smith, Richard M., ed. "Your Child Birth to Three." *Newsweek,* Fall/Winter 2000 Special Issue; entire issue.

Websites
www.aap.org   American Academy of Pediatrics

www.zerotothree.org   National Center for Infants, Toddlers and Families

www.brazelton-institute.com   Brazleton Institute

www.touchpoints.org   Brazelton's Touchpoints Center

www.babycenter.com   Baby Center

www.tnpc.com   The National Parenting Center

www.earlychildhood.com   Early Childhood. Com

www.iamyourchild.org   I Am Your Child

www.kidshealth.org   Kids Health

www.safekids.org   Safe Kids

3 The Setting

Where Curriculum Happens

The setting or learning environment is *where* curriculum happens for young children. Where it happens not only includes the classroom but also the way it's arranged, the learning centers, the equipment, the materials, all others in the environment, and the ways adults present learning opportunities to children.

There is much diversity in the types of classrooms where early childhood teachers and caregivers work. They need to make the most of what they have, which means they often have to do some creative improvising and problem solving. But in the end, what's really important is not how beautiful your setting is or how new your materials are. What's important is getting the space and all the elements of the setting to work *for* you, supporting and reinforcing what you offer children as you implement your curriculum.

From infancy on, children are in an "eager to learn" mode. Young children do not learn in pieces or compartments; they learn holistically with their bodies, senses, minds, and feelings in lively interaction with whatever surrounds them. What surrounds them, including their social interactions with adults and peers in the setting, influences their knowledge, skills, dispositions, and feelings. For example, in centers where children use large-muscle equipment every day, children will probably value active learning and have stronger motor skills than children who have no access to large-muscle equipment. When early childhood programs never expose children to the traditions, art, foods, music, and books of other cultures, children are likely to have little interest in cultures other than their own. When adults support children with descriptive praise, genuine affection, and appropriate limits, and when they encourage choice making, self-help, and independence, children become capable and feel both competent and lovable. Children learn where they live.

In this chapter we are going to find out ways that leaders of the past influenced the use of the early childhood setting. Then, after some important general remarks about settings, we'll look at the elements of each learning center in an early childhood program. The chapter ends with other considerations about early childhood settings, and provides three floor plans, one of which is for an infant-toddler center.

Advocates of the Learning Environment

The theories of child psychologist Jean Piaget, inventive educator Maria Montessori, self-made theorist and researcher Lev Vygotsky, and the Reggio Emilia movement have all impacted the belief of twentieth-century early childhood educators that children are always learning from the physical and social environments in which they find themselves. This impact continues to unfold and develop as one takes the teachings of these authorities and makes them one's own, using them in personalized ways, in one's programs.

Piaget emphasized that children learn through active multisensory and physical exploration, beginning in infancy. Montessori stressed the importance of a prepared learning environment, including the careful selection and introduction of self-correcting materials that children at all skill levels can use successfully in the setting. It is easy to observe young children assimilating new information through manipulative, concrete, and sensory experiences, and integrating new information with other information they already have. One can see that, with experience, children become more adept at "plugging in" new information—a process that Piaget called *accommodation,* and that Montessori felt was supported by the unique self-correcting materials she designed. Early educators call Piaget's approach a *cognitive developmental* or a *constructivist approach,* because when children take new knowledge and use it in their own unique ways to act on or change the environment, they are "constructing" their own knowledge.

The theories of Lev Vygotsky, who believed that the teaching/learning process was all this and much more, gave early educators insights on new ways to use the setting, the learning centers in it, and the staff. Vygotsky stressed the active role of children in learning discovery centers and in dialogue with their teachers and other children, using not only materials and props but also engaging in collaborative and reciprocal discussions to reach their goals and set new ones. Vygotsky believed that no limits should be placed on the diversity of thematic experiences through which children could learn; he felt that children were competent, when supported by responsible and facilitative adults, to work cooperatively in their own ways to accomplish group and individual goals. In this approach, projects that emerge from the children's interests are continually expanded through the collaborative dialogues of children and adults. The exciting trend to use the investigative *project approach* with preschoolers and in the primary grades was born of Vygotsky's theories.

Scaffolding, the changing quality of support given by adults to children as they practice and gradually master various skills that are an integral part of their projects, describes the facilitative strategies used in the Vygotsky's approach. It is also used by early educators who understand that scaffolding is a natural strategy in providing children opportunities for both success and challenge, and that it's a logical way for adults to help children learn. It is also an integral part of the systems for skill-based planning, which will be shared in Chapter 8 of this book.

In the early 1970s, the Reggio Emilia movement started as a child development program for a small town in northern Italy; today, that movement is world famous. Reggio Emilia captured the core of Vygotsky's theory and took it to new heights of collaboration in which children, parents, teachers, and the entire community are intensely involved. Early educators from all over the world go to Italy to see the Reggio Emilia approach in action, taking away new insights about child-centered and emergent curriculum, and "where" it happens.

Vygotsky and Reggio Emilia followers respect and do not discount Piaget and Montessori theories, but they believe intellectual discovery is not only a developmental process, but a largely social process. They see children as competent social beings who are motivated by and learn, not only from hands-on experiences in the environment but also from social collaboration in which teachers, parents, and other adults play alert, facilitative, and provocative roles.

In today's programs for young children—influenced by Piaget, Montessori, Vygotsky, and Reggio Emilia—the setting or "where" of curriculum continues to play a primary role. In best practices, the setting is rich in hands-on, developmentally appropriate experiences, cultural experiences, and active social interactions. Teachers, parents, and staff, who are important parts of that setting, are active observers and facilitators, offering children materials and experiences that reinforce pride in their cultural heritages and that also match their changing skill levels. They support children with dialogue that stimulates motivation and problem solving, and provide children ample time to explore, communicate, and collaborate as they develop their goals in the learning centers. They also use a scaffolding approach to encourage children to stretch and reach as they gradually attain outcomes and master new skills.

Learning Centers: General Remarks

Definition

Learning centers are spaces within the early childhood setting where materials or equipment are gathered and arranged in order to promote hands-on learning and specific skills, such as large- and small-motor skills, language and literacy skills, creative thinking skills, and math and science problem-solving skills. Learning centers can be identified as separate from an adjacent area by the kinds of learning materials found within them, by the placement of their furniture or equipment, and by the low, open shelves that are often used to define their space.

Size

Learning centers do not all need to be large. Some materials need much more space than others. The reading area and writing centers that teachers arrange may be very small and cozy, but the large-muscle and blocks areas will need ample space. In centers with very limited space, such as "temporary" portables, which all too often become permanent, teachers must prioritize, improvise, and rotate materials in order to provide adequate spaces for learning centers. The floor plan examples found at the end of this chapter, as well as in the books listed in the Resources, will assist teachers in arranging learning centers effectively in whatever space is available to them.

Traffic Flow

Safety is one of the major considerations in the arrangement of learning centers in the setting. Learning centers must be arranged so that exits to the room are unobstructed and so that a safe traffic flow is inherent in the room plan. Learning centers should be placed strategically so that there are no long, straight areas, which, like hallways, invite children to run indoors. For safety and confidentiality, learning centers and the materials in them should be arranged so that they are separated from the teacher's materials, resources, and files.

Noise Level

Another factor in planning the arrangement of learning centers is noise level. It is generally recommended that active, noisy learning centers not be placed next to quiet learning areas, such as the writing center, reading center, and science/math center. However, the dramatic play of the housekeeping area is often encouraged to overflow to the large-muscle area. There is no problem with this, as both housekeeping and active play areas are often filled with the good noises of children's language and learning.

One common problem concerning noise level is the placement and setup of the woodworking center. Woodworking areas offer excellent and varied opportunities for problem solving and skill development. Some teachers provide a stout log or stump and short roofing nails with hammers; others provide a workbench, vise, and tools. One advantage of arranging the woodworking center in an uncarpeted area is easy cleanup of scraps and sawdust. The disadvantage is the noise level that escalates when the area is uncarpeted.

TIP

A happy solution to the noise problem in the woodworking center is to place a commercial foam-backed carpet remnant under the workbench itself, and to cover the surface of the workbench completely with another carpet remnant of the same type, using carpet glue. Workbenches are not built to be "furniture," and their surfaces are not intended to remain smooth and unscarred. The addition of carpet on the surface and under the workbench almost completely absorbs the sound and dramatically reduces the noise level, which reduces stress in both adults and children

Accessibility

Another consideration in arrangement of learning centers is accessibility. Learning centers and the equipment in them should be accessible to all children, including those with temporary or permanent disabilities. This must be carefully considered if teachers plan to build a loft for literacy, dramatic play, or other activities. Whatever is available in the loft should be duplicated elsewhere in the center so that all materials are always accessible to every child. Learning center equipment should be flexible in purpose and construction so that it can be modified when necessary.

Collaborative Play Spaces

Another important aspect of the arrangement of learning centers is that they be supportive of cooperative work and responsible, enjoyable play. Teachers can promote positive social interactions and cooperative work by designing learning center spaces that are suitable for small groups of various sizes, because it is in small groups that children best learn to cooperate. In small groups, children discover, exchange new ideas, act on goals, and design collaborative ways to carry out their plans.

Some centers can be very small, such as a quiet spot where a child or two might rest on big pillows. Other areas, such as the computer center or the writing center, could serve two or three children at a time. The reading center might serve three or four children, depending on the space available, whereas the housekeeping area might serve as many as four or five. The sand table used might be built for four or for six children to use cooperatively, and the block area should have plenty of space for six to build together.

The point here is that learning centers should encourage cooperative play for a wide variety of group sizes and, especially in centers for 3- to 5-year-olds, should include some space for individuals to work and play alone, as well as near or with other children.

Play Slots

Another important element of the arrangement of the setting is the number of work and play slots or spaces it offers. If you were to count up the number of spaces available in every single learning center of your classroom—including the spaces at the tables for art and table toys, and the spaces for observing at the fish aquarium or science table—you could conceptualize these spaces as your total of work/play slots. There should be at least twice as many or up to two and a half times as many work/play slots as children in a rich and effective learning setting. An ample number of play slots in the setting prevents overcrowding in any of the learning centers and provides enough interest and variety to prevent the problem of children wandering aimlessly or distracting other children during free-choice time.

To keep children busy, happy, and learning with the materials in the setting, the teacher must make sure that many and varied interest areas are available in free-choice time. The more work/play slots, the more learning. As a bonus, there will also be far fewer problems in classroom management.

Materials

Equipment and materials in the learning centers should be in ample supply so that children will have duplicate items to use or share easily. Storage of extra materials should be easily accessed. For example, art materials and supplies should be accessible and in the learning center where they will be used.

Materials that will be stored and rotated into classrooms at different times must be organized so that all children can share these items on an equitable basis. Many materials and pieces of equipment in early childhood settings are rotated to promote new interest or to meet the needs of new skill levels; the challenge of finding adequate storage is often considerable. Creative solutions can often be found through staff brainstorming to develop collaborative systems for joint usage.

Materials within the learning centers themselves should be accessible, on low, open shelves. Children are not likely to enter or work in learning areas in which they see no materials ready to use. It is helpful if the shelves for materials are labeled with pictures and/or words so that children can be responsible in both finding and putting things away easily. This kind of labeling on shelves and storage units, often called *perceptual labeling,* adds to a print-rich setting and provides practice in perception and memory skills.

Equipment and materials in the learning centers should meet the developmental skill level needs of the children served. Because children may be of many different ages and skill levels, and because their skills change as they grow, a wide variety of developmentally appropriate materials encompassing all skill levels will be needed.

Equipment and materials in learning centers should be flexible and easily adapted for special needs or purposes, as when efforts are made to include all children in all activities and learning centers. Flexible materials can be easily modified and used in more than one way, which is also very cost effective.

Physical Definitions of Space

For children to see the opportunities and plan careful choices of different learning centers in the classroom, the teacher must define the space of each learning area, and make the space inviting and attractive to children.

Learning centers can be defined with the use of different types of floor coverings and area rugs, but it's best to define them with walls created with low, open shelves. It is important that these dividers are low so that the adult's view of the children and what they are doing in each area is not impaired. Unobstructed vision of all the areas of the setting is a management factor as well as a safety factor.

To further define learning center space, most teachers label the learning centers with simple signs or posters noting the names of the areas. These signs should be printed clearly in large letters in the kind of lettering the children will be expected to use in kindergarten.

The signs might indicate "Reading Area," "Woodworking," "Blocks," or "Construction." The sign for the creative media and paint learning center should imply in its choice of wording that open-ended art media are used. Signs that state that the area is for "Art Projects" are inappropriate because they imply that the art *project* (a product) is more important than the creative *process*. A better choice is simply "Art Media" or "Creative Art Area."

It is also helpful to staff, parents, and visitors when posters are placed in each learning center, explaining the purposes of the areas in terms of the children's learning. For example, in the art area, a poster might say, "Here is a place I learn to use my imagination, to express my ideas and feelings, and to learn eye-hand coordination and fine-motor skills. I learn to be responsible for materials and cleaning up, and I learn to feel pride and self-confidence."

If teachers depend partially on floor coverings to define some learning centers, and if teachers have input concerning floor coverings, they should consider uncarpeted areas for food service, painting, sand, and water. It is also important to try to use flat carpeting in the block areas, which will add to the structural stability of block constructions and will also cut down on the noise level.

Teachers should be aware that most 3-year-olds and many 4-year-olds will prefer to use puzzles and table toys on the floor, and carpeted floor space for such use should be available. It is important to use solid colors in such carpeted areas so that children's figure-ground skills will not be impaired (the ability to focus on one thing while seeing, but not being distracted by the background). It is extremely frustrating for a child to look for a particular puzzle piece on a patterned carpet.

Learning Centers in Infant-Toddler Programs, Kindergartens, and Primary Classrooms

Since they are not the emphasis of this book, comments on these settings will be limited to major points; you are urged to do personal observations and further research. Top priorities in infant-toddler centers are health, safety, and comfort. Adult roles were described briefly in Chapter 1. There should be quiet areas for cribs and for diapering and feeding infants, as well as appropriate equipment for their exercise and their observations and interactions with other infants and toddlers. Mobile infants need spaces in which they can creep, crawl, pull themselves up, and climb safely. Interesting things to explore or see will motivate mobility in both infants and toddlers. For example, a two-step platform, with wide treads covered in thick carpet, could be placed next to a window where children could see their outdoor area (perhaps bird-feeders). Toddlers also need spaces where they can either be alone or interacting in small groups, exploring sensory and art media at their own pace, eating together, using manipulatives, listening or moving to music, and enjoying picture books.

Teachers of infants and toddlers should provide materials that are continually clean and sanitized. These materials might include colorful, lightweight, sturdy table blocks, stacking rings, nesting toys, large bristle blocks, large beads, cloth books, picture books, very simple puzzles, and gadget boards to manipulate.

Safe mirrors, mobiles, and wind chimes also enhance the setting. A floor plan example for an infant-toddler center is included at the end of this chapter.

In kindergartens or primary classrooms, the teacher's desk and files and the children's desks or tables will take up some space. However, this equipment is quite movable. Teachers can arrange children's tables or desks to match the types of activities and projects in which children are engaged. Most of the time, they are arranged in small clusters in which children are working together on various projects. There is usually a special, carpeted floor space for gathering all children for discussions or adult-led activities.

In primary classrooms, depending on the size and shape of rooms, learning spaces are set up for computers, math, science, and literacy activities, as well as spaces for whatever projects the children are working on. Children might also use various art media or woodworking to represent objects or concepts, bring out a puppet theater, or use a listening center to hear or create music and stories relating to study projects. What is changed or added will largely depend on the changing goals of children's investigative projects.

Kindergarten settings will usually look much like classrooms for 3- to 5-year-olds, although learning centers may be more limited, more materials may be rotated, and, as in primary rooms, gyms and playgrounds will replace large-muscle areas. Children will usually have learning centers for books/literacy, blocks, manipulatives, science materials, art materials (including clays), a sand and water table, and a variety of concrete math materials, as well as computers. Again, the spaces will be rotated and changed, depending on the projects in which children are engaged.

Basic Learning Centers in the Setting

The use of learning centers to provide appropriate hands-on learning is the heart of the early childhood curriculum, so it is important for us to review the learning centers that should be available for all 3- to 5-year-olds that promote quality programming. Programs in which classroom settings have restricted space should still strive to include all of the following learning centers, even if some will be small or if some equipment and space must be rotated.

Science and Math Discovery Learning

Science and math materials don't have to stay in a "corner"; in fact, it's far better for children when these materials are seen in many areas. Groupings of discovery and problem-solving materials can be placed in small interest centers in various places in the setting, keeping in mind that they should be fresh, interesting, and reflective of children's thematic and emerging interests.

In these areas should be groupings of plants, small animals (such as fish, toads, guinea pigs, or snails), items collected from nature, and pictures and books related to current thematic or emergent interests. (In some programs or cultures, having animals in the classroom is restricted or not allowed.) Also, some centers might display items from the outdoors (such as wild flowers, sage, berries, and herbs) that are important in the particular culture of the program.

Tubbing, sorting, graphing, and counting materials of all kinds, and tools with which children can observe, weigh, and measure should be available. Posters with the children's dictation about their observations, and postings about the results of their experiments should also be seen.

In fact and in actual practice, science- and math-focused discovery materials are teaching and learning opportunities that cannot be relegated to any one space. Math and science learning will continually occur in all of the areas of the classroom—in the sand and water center, the sensory center, the table toys area, the art area, the computer area, the housekeeping area, the "cooking" area, and in other active play areas, including the outdoors. (Chapter 11 will provide more information on math and science experiences.)

Sensory Learning

The sensory learning center would include a table or bins of sensory materials that are rotated for children's exploration, as well as the sand table, the water table, and clays or playdough. Usually playdough is offered in the art area. Sometimes the sand and water tables are separate pieces of equipment, and sometimes the sand or water is rotated within one table. It is always recommended that sand, water, and playdough or clay be available daily, and that other sensory materials be provided additionally in small tubs if at all possible.

Sometimes space dictates that the sand or water must be placed in a defined space or learning center. In that case, rotated sensory materials might be placed in the small-muscle area on a table, or even in the art area. One solution would be to use dishtubs for water and other sensory materials and to define a space for the sand table, and use it only for sand. It is wise to divide the sand in the table with a smooth, tightly fitted piece of wood, so that both wet and dry sand can be available to children every day. (Some children prefer to experiment by pouring and filling, and some by digging and molding.)

If the sand table is used only for sand, water can and should still be available daily. Water play can be provided in easy-to-fill plastic tubs that could be conveniently moved or set up (with big towels underneath) on a table in the small-muscle area, in the housekeeping area (to bathe dolls), or on the floor in another area. This method is not only helpful in adding to the number of work/play slots but it also helps draw children into learning centers they may be avoiding, or to areas in which they do not frequently engage.

Housekeeping and Dramatic Play

The housekeeping and dramatic play center contains play furniture, play foods, dishes, telephones, discarded computer keyboards, tote bags, briefcases, dress-up clothes for both boys and girls, a full-length mirror, and play appliances. It need not be placed in a corner of the classroom. It often works better for teachers to define this dramatic play space in the middle of the room or in the middle of the space at one side of the classroom, leaving openings between the play furniture for "doors" through which children can enter or leave. Housekeeping play furniture is low, and if it is also sturdy, it lends itself well as dividers to define this space.

The housekeeping area should also be changed at times to allow for other types of play to occur there. For example, this space makes an excellent "store," "hospital," "vet clinic," or "beauty parlor." Dramatic play provides an excellent medium for enhancing language, literacy, and children's collaboration, which are all early childhood priorities.

Teachers should also set up the dramatic play area regularly with props stored in "prop boxes" in other learning centers such as the active play area, where large hollow blocks or boxes can be used to create the set for dramatic play scenarios such as stores, hospitals, offices, spaceships, trains, camping sites, and so on. Prop boxes can also be used to help children reenact and retell books and stories heard in the classroom, and many props can be taken outdoors for dramatic play.

Most dramatic play props can easily be scrounged or collected by parents, and most parents truly enjoy this type of involvement. Prop boxes should be sturdy and labeled without stereotyping (e.g., "Post Office," not "Mailman"), and they should be stored in ways that promote rotation and frequent use.

Large-Muscle Area

The large-muscle center is often the same space used by the teacher during large-group circle times, music and movement activities, and story time. Multiple use of this space is not a problem, since the active play/large-muscle area will be used by children during free-choice time, not during teacher-directed times.

It is helpful to have clean, flat carpeting in this area for warmth, because children will be sitting on the floor some of the time. The carpet also will help control the noise level during free-choice time when children use this learning center and its equipment for climbing, obstacle courses, tumbling mats, and big blocks. Low storage units will help define this space. If flat carpeting is not available for this area, teachers often use area rugs effectively, or at least provide carpet remnant squares on which children may sit.

Ample space is ideal for this area, but teachers who have little space will find that they easily can rotate active play equipment such as climbers, balance beams, and tumbling mats on various days. Active play and equipment should be available indoors on a daily basis. Some teachers have additional rooms in their buildings where active play equipment, including wheel toys, is kept, and children either use the additional room together as a whole group, or are rotated in small groups to this space for 15 to 20 minutes of guided active play during free-choice time.

Blocks Area

Table blocks of many types are used daily in the small-muscle or table toys area, but separate areas should be defined for the use of both large hollow blocks and unit blocks. Because of their physical nature, it is fairly easy to store the large hollow blocks by stacking them in a low "wall" against the one of the walls of the large-muscle/active play area. Programs using a separate room for this learning center will find that these large hollow blocks, when used as part of an obstacle course or when used with props, can be just as effectively used in another room as in one's own classroom.

If I were told that I could have only one piece of equipment or set of materials in my setting, unit blocks would be my choice. The daily and appropriate use of unit blocks teaches cooperation and social skills, creativity and dramatic play; spatial relationships; perceptual skills; and math, science, and language skills. They are the most versatile and open-ended of the nonconsumable materials in the early childhood setting, and well worth the investment of their price. (See *1,2,3 Blocks* by Petersen [1998].)

Unit blocks and space in which to construct with them must be ample and should be defined not only to create the learning center but to protect the children's work. The center should not be placed where traffic flow will interfere with construction. *The Block Book* (Hirsch, 1984) suggests that the unit block area encompass at least one-fourth to one-third of the room's floor space, with proper storage on shelves that are perceptually labeled for each type of block. Hirsch (1984) and Petersen (1998) give readers information on all the curriculum areas that can be taught through blocks, as well as suggestions on storage, accessories, management, and guidance.

Small-Muscle Area

The small-muscle learning center is defined for the use of table toys, manipulatives, and materials such as bristle blocks and puzzles, often used by children (especially 3-year-olds) on the floor. The tables and the low open shelves where these materials are stored make it easy to define this area, which is often carpeted. It is important to provide a wide variety and ample supplies of materials that match the developmental skill levels of children, especially in a mixed-age group. Materials should support both success and challenge for children. To motivate interest in this area, some materials should be out on the tables when free-choice or activity time begins.

Food Experiences Area

Classrooms with space large enough to supply children's foods or snack preparation areas are rare, but those lucky centers that have space to include this center place a child-sized table and chairs near the storage and sink/water supply. In most centers, a table is simply reserved for use in the small-muscle area on days when children will make playdough or silly putty, help prepare snacks, make "dips," or taste foods such as fruits and vegetables.

Teachers of quality programs will want children to be involved regularly in foods and "cooking" experiences. Food learning experiences, even if a defined learning center is not available are vital to good curriculum planning. Children learn social skills; literacy, math, science, and problem-solving skills; and nutrition concepts when the setting includes space, time, and materials for foods experiences.

Creative Process: Art Media Area

The learning center for creative processes with art media will include space for at least two tables and one or two easels, as well as for accessible storage of art media materials of all kinds. Clay or playdough and paint, either at the table or at the easel, should be available daily. Other table space will provide opportunities for many types of collage, fingerpaint, construction with recycled materials, drawing, cutting, and other experiences.

Equipment such as easels should be used in the manner for which it was intended. Easels were designed to be used regularly with thick, bright paints and big brushes. They were not intended to be used primarily for paper and crayons or colored chalk.

Experiences in the art area, as we discussed in Chapter 2, should be process oriented and open ended, and materials should be stored accessibly in the area. "Art carts," three-shelf rolling storage units, are perfect for bringing art materials into the area when storage or shelves in the area are inadequate. The carts are also useful in removing materials and paintbrushes to utility sinks when free-choice time ends.

Many art experiences require children to help clean up themselves and the tables, so a water supply nearby is helpful. Rebus pictures instructing children about how to help clean up in the art area, as well as a supply of sponges and toweling and a small bucket of soapy water, are very helpful in enhancing literacy and self-help skills. Children love cleaning tables and chairs, especially when small, all-purpose brushes are provided, and this task helps them learn that privileges come with responsibilities.

Music and Movement

The music and movement learning area usually doubles with the large-muscle/active play area, and includes records and record player, tapes and tape player, musical instruments, and accessories for movement, such as paper pom-poms, scarves, ribbons, and streamers. Music and creative movement will usually take place during teacher-directed times, but children should also be encouraged to use some of the musical instruments, tapes, and accessories for spontaneous play with rhythms and music during free-choice time.

Reviewers of program quality will usually check to see that music and movement materials are appropriate, accessible, and frequently used, and that they include instrumental music without words and multicultural music as well as traditional music.

Literacy and Library Areas

Sometimes the perfect small space for an inviting "library" or reading center may be adjacent to a writing center, but this is not necessary. What is most important is that the reading area be quiet, attractive, and comfortable. Books and picture books should be age appropriate, accessible, free of bias, include multicultural subject matter, and properly stored so that children can see their choices. Books should be rotated and should reflect children's current interests.

Literacy and invented writing or dictation experiences, like math and science experiences, cannot be relegated to just one learning center. Sometimes small writing centers are adjacent to or within reading areas, but they can also be found in art areas, in blocks area, in computer areas, and even within science and math centers. Children will need materials such as old greeting cards, paper, note pads, envelopes, big pencils, crayons, and markers. Storage of these materials in simple baskets on shelves is effective and takes little space.

Reviewers of program quality will look for defined spaces and materials that enhance literacy, including experience stories and children's dictation posted at children's eye level. Literacy is a teaching and learning web that actually takes place everywhere in an early childhood setting, and even extends to the child's neighborhood, library and home.

Computer Area

Computers are not considered developmentally appropriate in most settings for children under age 3 who don't have the motor coordination to use the mouse. Most classrooms for 3- to 5-year-olds, kindergartens, and primary grades have one or more computers and a printer.

Computers should be placed in a quiet area with good light and with ergonomically correct heights for monitors and chairs. A bulletin board display area should be placed so that children can display and share their work and build collaborative projects with peers. The children's posted comments or summaries also expand literacy.

Many teachers who are not familiar with computers might say, "I have these computers; now what do I do?" The most important factor in making teachers comfortable in this situation is the chance to use the computer and some software on their own, either at home or in the staff room, before introducing it to children. When it is introduced, teachers will probably find some children who will prove to be excellent mentors.

Developmentally appropriate software, suitable to the ages being served, is a crucial factor in making the computer beneficial to children's learning. Software that is primarily "drill" will not help children experience interest, curiosity, surprise, enjoyment, or social collaboration. It is critical that software be open ended and exploratory in nature. When it is, children can control the programs, make decisions, and experiment and problem solve (often in cooperation with peers) to see and manipulate concrete representations of people, animals, and objects. With appropriate software, children can imagine and express feelings and ideas in print or illustration, do project research and critical thinking, and discover empowering concepts.

More information on the potential benefits of computer technology will be shared in Chapter 11, but a particular reference with information on developmentally appropriate software is so important that it should be mentioned here as well as in references at the end of this chapter. The book *Young Children and Technology: A World of Discovery* (Haugland and Wright, 1997) contains excellent information, comprehensive references and appendices, and two definitive chapters about selecting and evaluating developmentally appropriate software with the thoroughly tested and highly approved Haugland/Shade Developmental Scale. Criteria of the scale includes age appropriateness, child control, clear instructions, expanding complexity, independence, nonviolence, process orientation, real-world models, and antibias considerations.

Construction and Woodworking

The construction and woodworking center that takes little space if it consists of a log set securely on a carpet remnant to be used with hammer and short roofing nails, brought out at the time of use. Even when a workbench is available, this center takes up little space if creative storage can be developed. A box under the bench could hold wood and styrofoam. Safety goggles and tools could be stored on the wall.

Workbenches should be used for the purpose for which they are intended. They should not be used as countertops or storage units, buffet tables to serve snacks, or places to dry easel paintings.

One reason workbenches are underused is their noise level on an uncarpeted floor. Solutions to this problem were given earlier in this chapter. Woodworking is a fine activity in which children develop language, creativity, problem-solving skills, eye-hand coordination, and social skills.

Outdoor Area

The outdoor learning area is just as important as indoor learning centers. Children should have fresh air and outdoor exercise daily, unless weather conditions are prohibitive to their health and safety. The outdoor area is important not only for the development of children's physical skills and fitness but also for its opportunities to observe and discuss changes in the outside environment, nature, and ways to care for the environment.

In addition to the permanent, well-anchored, and safe equipment recommended for early childhood settings, quality programs provide areas for digging or for gardens, climbers that encourage dramatic play, space for homemade instruments and wind chimes, space for resting under a tree or rolling on the grass, space for riding wheel toys and using hoops and jump ropes, space for using balls and parachutes, and sometimes even space for animals. Outdoor areas should be fenced and away from hazards. Outdoor space for inclusion of these items is sometimes hard to come by, so programs often become very creative in partnering with parents and/or community programs to develop outdoor areas, incorporating adult-made equipment and recycled materials.

Many indoor learning center materials and pieces of equipment can be taken outdoors for children's use. Children love using easels outside, as well as colored chalk, buckets of water and big paint brushes, dramatic play props, and musical instruments and tapes. Some urban programs must take all their equipment outside and back inside daily, but children happily help with this job. Some programs have no outdoor area because no space is available for them to develop one. In these programs, teachers are encouraged to consider walking to a nearby park, taking walks in the neighborhood, or partnering with a nearby school for play sapce.

Children in rural areas often have wonderful opportunities for observing nature on outdoor walks, but urban programs have much to offer in learning opportunities for children on their walks, too. In addition to the good exercise of walking, children often become familiar with stores or homes in their neighborhoods, greet older people on their porches, watch workers fix the street, and chat with traffic police officers. Children in urban programs can still observe the changes in sky, weather, and plants, and will have daily opportunities to practice traffic and pedestrian safety.

Field Trips and Visitors

Extensions of the setting or environment are also important to children's learning. A nature walk, a trip to the grocery store, a trip to the fire station, and other field trips extend children's knowledge. Visitors coming into the center to share talents, skills, and knowledge also extend the learning environment. At the beginning of the year, in programs for 3- to 5-year-olds, trips outside the center should be kept simple and to a minimum. Visitors, parents, or elders who come into the center and share songs, stories, and knowledge can take the place of many field trips early in the year.

Other Considerations in the Setting

We can see that teachers need clearly defined learning spaces, storage, equipment, materials, and staff in order to implement curriculum. Here are some other basic elements that should be in place in the setting in order to make planning more effective:

1. *Orderliness:* When children see that materials in the setting are orderly, attractive, accessible, and well organized, it is easier for them to make thoughtful choices and be more responsible in taking care of their environment. Clutter is distracting to both children and adults; accessibility and orderliness facilitate learning and responsible cleanup.

2. *Children as Helpers:* Children should be encouraged, on a daily basis, to be involved in the setup and care of the setting and learning environment. Teachers use helpers in various ways; in some programs, four or five helpers are rotated on a daily or weekly basis, giving every child the opportunity over time to help. Occasionally, programs arrange to have every child do one small job every day. Visual cues are used to remind children of their jobs. One of the best visual cues is actual photographs of the helper jobs, with space underneath for the name of the current helper.

3. *Displays and Decoration:* The most important wall coverings in early childhood settings are displays of children's own work and open-ended art; this should predominate over adult-made or purchased items. Children can even be encouraged, whenever possible, to help post their own artwork on walls or in appropriate spaces of their own choosing. Items from the heritage and culture of the children in programs should also be an integral part of the decoration and display in various areas. Photographs of children and/or their families and homes should also be posted in a special space at children's eye level.

   Teachers should avoid purchasing cartoon or caricature-type wall decorations that present numbers, letters, and health information in vibrant colors that are overpowering and distracting to children. A far better alternative is to have children and/or their parents create relevant health and safety education postings. Letters and numbers are best displayed as they are introduced, not all at once, and alphabet illustrations can also be created by talented parents or creative children.

4. *Personal Space:* There should be individualized space for each child in the group, and these spaces should be personalized. One of the best ways to individualize children's personal spaces is to label them with names and photographs. This is a great self-esteem builder. In extremely small centers with no cubbies or personal tubs, personal space can still be successfully created with personalized shopping or tote bags set on the floor or hung on hooks.

5. *Safety and Health:* Settings for young children should be safe, and aspects of the health, sanitation, and safety of the environment should be regularly checked by professionals—for example, proper heating and ventilation systems; fire exit plans; water and sewage systems; safe, clean equipment; child-sized furniture, toilets, and sinks; separate storage (inaccessible to children) for cleaning supplies and other hazardous substances; and safe entrances and exits.

6. *Required Postings:* All required documents, licenses, emergency procedures, emergency telephone numbers, and fire exit plans (in both print and picture/diagram form) should be clearly posted, and emergency or first-aid

materials should be easy to find. Emergency procedures in sequenced, step-by-step picture posters are very helpful to children.

7. *Parent Information:* A parent bulletin board or information area should be part of every early childhood setting, and information there should be clear, attractive, and up to date. Free information relevant to families' interests should be provided.

8. *Social-Emotional Climate:* Some aspects of the early childhood setting are important but less tangible, such as the nurturing and positive attitude of adults, and their appropriate interactions with children, both in teaching and in guidance situations. Adults who model positive social interactions and praise children descriptively for following suit will find that children copy and learn positive social behaviors very quickly.

Positive social-emotional climate indicators are a relaxed atmosphere where children are enjoying the setting and where there is an overall sound of children and adults in dialogue. Adult voices should not predominate, and staff should treat parents and children with attention and respect, verbally and nonverbally. Language, interactions, and materials should be free of stereotyping, should include multicultural materials, and should reflect antibias attitudes that build pride and self-esteem.

Summary

In this chapter we have discussed the importance of the environment and its materials for children's hands-on learning, and talked about some of the early childhood leaders of the twentieth century who have influenced our thinking about how children learn from the environment.

We have described the learning centers that should be a part of every early childhood setting, and discussed the fact that teachers in the setting need to use methods and materials that match the changing skill levels of children. Teachers facilitate learning in the environment with ample work/play slots and time to use them. They use positive modeling and interactions, with open questions that scaffold children's thinking and problem solving. Hopefully the three examples of floor plans for early childhood settings which are presented at the end of this chapter, will be helpful; you should examine them before continuing to Chapter 4.

Let's close with a self-assessment checklist for the early childhood setting:

1. Children have personal, identified space.
2. Children's art and work are posted at their eye level and predominate over purchased items.
3. Photos of children and their families are posted at children's eye level.
4. The setting encourages safe, self-directed movement and choice making.
5. Materials and equipment are safe and clean; the setting is free of hazards.

6. There is a clearly defined and attractive parent information area that promotes two-way communication with the program.
7. All required documents and emergency plans are clearly posted.
8. If group rules are posted, they have been jointly developed with children and are stated positively.
9. Learning centers include literacy, the arts, motor, sensory, science, and math experiences and are easily defined. The names and purposes of the areas are posted, and there are areas for active and quiet activities.
10. There are ample supplies and a variety of developmentally appropriate materials and equipment.

Self-Study Activities

1. Study the floor plan examples at the end of this chapter (Figures 3.1, 3.2, and 3.3). Reread sections of the chapter concerning learning center and room arrangement that present solutions to your particular challenges or problems in the setting. Using the floor plan examples and information in the chapter as a guide, draw a floor plan of your center, with any modifications you want to try out.

2. Draw a floor plan for your *own* "dream center" or "ideal classroom" without looking at the list of basic learning centers to be included in the setting. Check the list when you are done with your floor plan to see if you have included all learning centers. Modify as needed.

3. Examine catalogs containing materials for the early childhood setting. Which sections of these catalogs are most relevant to the children with whom you work? Make a list of materials and equipment needed by your group.

Resources and Suggested Readings

Baker, Katherine R. *Let's Play Outdoors*. Washington, DC: National Association for the Education of Young Children, 1966, 1994.

Barbour, Nita, & Seefeldt, Carol. *Developmental Continuity across Preschool and Primary Grades: Implications for Teachers*. Wheaton, MD: Association for Childhood Education International, 1993.

Berk, Laura E. "Vygotsky's Theory: The Importance of Make-Believe Play." *Young Children,* 50, 1 (1994): 30–39.

Berk, Laura E., & Winsler, Adam. *Scaffolding Children's Learning: Vygotsky and Early Childhood Education*. Washington, DC: National Association for the Education of Young Children, 1995.

Brewer, Jo Ann. *Introduction to Early Childhood Education: Preschool through Primary Grades*. Boston: Allyn and Bacon, 1995, pp. 38–59.

Bronson, M. B. *The Right Stuff for Children Birth to 8: Selecting Play Materials to Support Development*. Washington, DC: National Association for the Education of Young Children, 1995.

Casey, M. Beth, & Lippman, Marjory. "Learning to Plan through Play." *Young Children,* 46, 4 (1991): 52–61.

Dodge, Diane Trister, & Colker, Laura J. *The Creative Curriculum*, 3rd ed. Spanish & English. Washington, DC: Teaching Strategies, 1992.

Dombro, Amy; Colker, Laura; & Dodge, Diane Trister. *Creative Curriculum for Infants & Toddlers,* rev. ed. Washington, DC: Teaching Strategies, 1999.

Edwards, Carol; Gandini, L.; & Forman, G. *The Hundred Languages of Children: The Reggio Approach, Advanced Reflections,* 2nd ed. Stamford CT: Ablex, 1998.

Elkind, David. *Images of the Young Child.* Washington, DC: National Association for the Education of Young Children, pp. 13–29.

Forman, George E., & Kuschner, David S. *Piaget for Teaching Children: The Child's Construction of Knowledge.* Washington, DC: National Association for the Education of Young Children, 1983.

Gandini, L. "Fundamentals of the Reggio Emilia Approach to Early Childhood Education." *Young Children,* 49 (1994): 4–8.

Haugland, Susan W., & Wright, June L. *Young Children and Technology: A World of Discovery.* Boston: Allyn and Bacon, 1997.

Henniger, Michael L. "Planning for Outdoor Play." *Young Children,* 49, 4 (1994): 10–15.

Hill, D. M. *Mud, Sand, and Water.* Washington, DC: National Association for the Education of Young Children, 1977.

Hirsch, Elisabeth. *The Block Book,* rev. ed. Washington, DC: National Association for the Education of Young Children, 1984.

Isbell, Rebecca, & Exelby, Betty. *Early Learning Environments That Work.* Beltsville, MD: Gryphon House, 2001.

Kritchevsky, Sybil, & Prescott, Elizabeth, with Walling, Lee. *Planning Environments for Young Children: Physical Space,* rev. ed. Washington, DC: National Association for the Education of Young Children, 1977.

McCracken, Janet Brown. *Playgrounds Safe and Sound.* Washington, DC: National Association for the Education of Young Children, 1990.

Miller, Karen. *The Outside Play and Learning Book.* Beltsville, MD: Gryphon House, 1989.

Montessori, Maria. *The Secret of Childhood.* New York: Ballentine Books, 1992. (Original copyright Fides Publishers, 1966.)

NAEYC Information Service. *Facility Design for Early Childhood Programs Resource Guide,* rev. ed. Washington, DC: National Association for the Education of Young Children, 1991.

Petersen, Evelyn. *1,2,3 Blocks: Block Activities for Young Children.* Grand Rapids, MI: Totline Imprint/McGraw-Hill Children's Publishing, 1998.

Petersen, Evelyn, & Petersen, Karin. *Teach Yourself e-Parenting Today: Using the Internet and Computers.* Indianapolis, IN: Macmillan, 2000.

Skeen, P., Garner, A.P., & Cartwright, S. *Woodworking for Young Children.* Washington, DC: National Association for the Education of Young Children, 1984.

Spodek, Bernard, & Saracho, Olivia. *Right from the Start: Teaching Children Ages Three to Eight.* Boston: Allyn and Bacon, 1994, pp. 42–46, 73–76.

Vergeront, Jeanne. *Places and Spaces for Preschool and Primary: Indoors.* Washington, DC: National Association for the Education of Young Children, 1987.

Website

www.iste.org   International Society for Technology in Education

Additional Resources

An excellent selection of videotapes on the infant-toddler setting and the development of infants and toddlers can be obtained from the National Association for the Education of Young Children, Publications/Resource Sales, 1509 16th St., NW, Washington, DC 20036-1426. Call 800-424-2460, ext. 2001, or www.naeyc.org. For information, email resource_sales@naeyc.org.

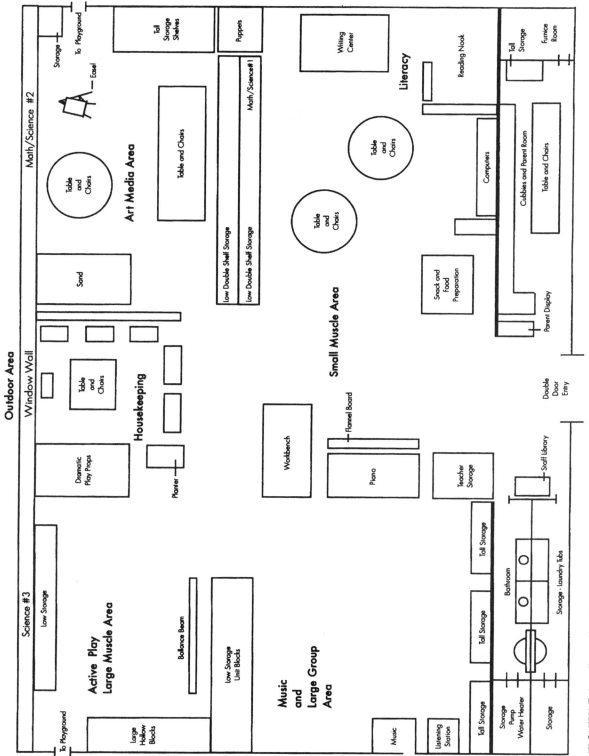

FIGURE 3.1 Floor Plan 1

47

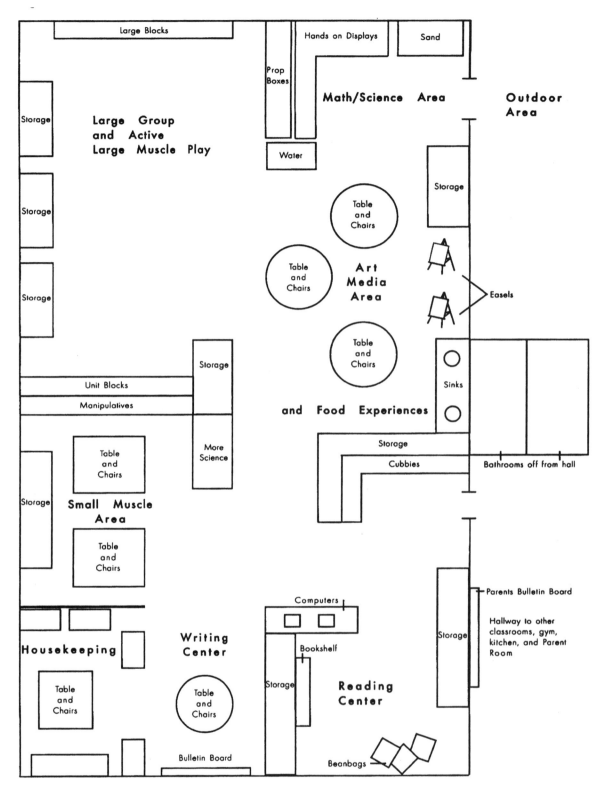

Large Blocks

Hands on Displays

Sand

Prop Boxes

Math/Science Area

Outdoor Area

Storage

Large Group and Active Large Muscle Play

Storage

Storage

Water

Storage

Table and Chairs

Table and Chairs

Art Media Area

Easels

Storage

Unit Blocks

Manipulatives

Table and Chairs

More Science

Table and Chairs

Sinks

and Food Experiences

Storage

Storage

Small Muscle Area

Storage

Cubbies

Bathrooms off from hall

Table and Chairs

Computers

Parents Bulletin Board

Housekeeping

Writing Center

Bookshelf

Storage

Hallway to other classrooms, gym, kitchen, and Parent Room

Table and Chairs

Storage

Table and Chairs

Table and Chairs

Reading Center

Bulletin Board

Beanbags

FIGURE 3.2 Floor Plan 2

48

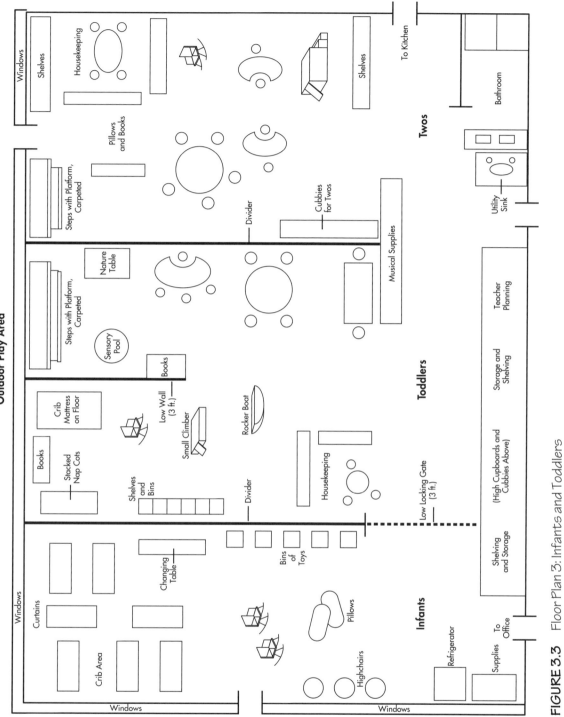

Outdoor Play Area

Windows

Shelves

Housekeeping

Pillows and Books

Steps with Platform, Carpeted

Divider

Cubbies for Twos

Shelves

To Kitchen

Twos

Nature Table

Steps with Platform, Carpeted

Sensory Pool

Musical Supplies

Books

Crib Mattress on Floor

Low Wall (3 ft.)

Small Climber

Rocker Boat

Books

Stacked Nap Cots

Shelves and Bins

Divider

Housekeeping

Low Locking Gate (3 ft.)

Toddlers

Bins of Toys

Changing Table

Curtains

Crib Area

Pillows

Highchairs

Refrigerator

Supplies

To Office

Infants

Shelving and Storage

(High Cupboards and Cubbies Above)

Storage and Shelving

Teacher Planning

Utility Sink

Bathroom

Windows

Windows

Windows

FIGURE 3.3 *Floor Plan 3: Infants and Toddlers*

49

4 The Schedule

When Curriculum Happens

This chapter presents some very practical information about what daily schedules are like in the real world of early childhood programs. Schedules are often a challenge to teachers due to circumstances beyond their control, such as bus schedules, preset meal service, or outdoor play times. Appropriate schedules can be designed, however, with compromises and creative problem solving. We are going to discuss the major elements of the schedule and why daily schedules are important for adults and children. We'll look at the ways schedules provide guidelines for and documentation of teacher practices, and we'll discuss some of the specific challenges of designing daily schedules. The emphasis in this chapter will be to provide examples and practical assistance to teachers in developing daily schedules that are appropriate for 3- to 5-year-olds.

Schedules as Guidelines

The daily schedule of an early childhood program establishes *when* curriculum happens for children. The schedule is one of the ways that the teacher's curriculum ideas are set down on paper, and it shows the teacher's plan for the regular events of a program day and when those events should occur, starting from the time children arrive until they leave. Time frames for activities and routines are given, including meals.

In reality, the times for activities on the schedule may not exactly match to the minute what actually happens. This is because early childhood teachers continually adjust to children's needs and interests, their energy levels, spontaneous teaching opportunities, and small, unforeseen crises, such as late buses or meal service. However, the times on the schedule are a helpful guideline for staff and other adults who visit or observe, telling them when to expect each curriculum activity to occur throughout the day. Schedules also show the sequence and flow of the day's curriculum activities from beginning to end.

Teachers often post the schedule before children actually begin attending the program. When they find that parts of the schedule are not working well, they keep refining the schedule until it does work. This is exactly what should happen, but it's also very important to revise the posted schedule so that it matches what's really happening and when it happens. Maintaining a consistent and predictable schedule gives children a sense of trust in the learning environment. When the events of the classroom occur in the same order each day, children feel more secure. Children ages 3 to 5 (especially age 3) need a predictable routine.

When the schedule of the day and sequence of events is also posted at children's eye level and in picture form, it is an important way for children to begin to understand temporal concepts, or time as it relates to them. A series of picture posters on the wall that show the order of the day, particularly in the first months of the program year, is far more meaningful to children than a calendar. What will happen and when it will happen *each day* is what's important to 3- and 4-year-olds. These children do not yet fully understand the concepts of yesterday, tomorrow, weeks and months, or numerals placed on a grid that represent days. Keeping this in mind, not only can teachers make drawings of the major events in the daily routine and post them but they can also duplicate the series of daily events for children's use on a flannel board. With the flannel board, children can practice their concept of time (the flow of events) by putting the representations of the day's events in sequence.

Daily schedules state *when* curriculum happens, but they don't spell out how it happens or tell about the activities taking place. Lesson plans give much more detail about what happens and how it happens. However, the teacher's schedule is actually a good foundation for constructing appropriate daily lesson plans based on curriculum and sound child development principles.

Schedules as Documentation

Schedules are also important as written documentation that monitors of program quality need to see and evaluate in terms of best practices. They often provide a good entrée to questions or discussions about ways the curriculum, as summarized on the schedule, is meeting developmental needs. This can be done because daily schedules provide important insights about the teacher's curriculum and priorities, even when the children and teaching staff are not in the room. For example, the schedule shows (or prompts questions) about the following indicators of the teacher's practices:

- It shows how often and for how long children sit in a circle or whole-group activity led by adults.
- It tells if and when small-group, adult-directed activities occur.
- It shows how long children are engaged in uninterrupted, child-initiated, free-choice learning time and project collaboration.
- It tells whether there is an appropriate balance between adult-directed time and child-initiated time.
- It states how much time is designated for routines, as compared to children's other learning experiences.
- It provides information about when the teacher does specific individualized teaching.
- It tells whether children have outdoor play or a similar alternative.

- It tells whether children have a specific time for planning and evaluating the day's experiences.
- It shows whether children are sitting for long periods, because two or more quiet, sit-down activities are scheduled back to back.

Critiques of Daily Schedules

Let's try an exercise in which you critique an actual schedule. This hypothetical schedule is for a program in a warm climate where children have a five- hour day, starting at 9:00 A.M. and ending at 2:00 P.M., and over an hour bus ride to and from school.

TRY THIS NOW

Get a pencil and several sheets of paper. Look at the following schedule. First, look at the time frame entries on the left, and find out how many hours or minutes are delegated to adult-directed time and to child-initiated time. Think about the balance of these time frames. Then find out how many hours or minutes are designated for routines, including outdoor play, meals, hygiene, and other routines. Use one sheet of paper to figure this out, and then use each of the bullets in the preceding list to ask yourself questions about this schedule, taking notes.

9:00	Arrival; greetings; use of table toys; prepare for breakfast.
9:15–10:00	Breakfast
10:00–10:15	Tooth brushing and health check
10:15–10:45	Large-group music and movement
10:45–11:00	Outdoor activities
11:00–11:45	Small-group activities
11:45–12:00	Wash hands and set tables
12:00–1:00	Lunch
1:00–1:15	Brush teeth
1:15–1:45	Nap
1:45–2:00	Prepare to dismiss

Were you surprised to find out how many hours of the 5 available for children's learning experiences are used in routines? (about 3½) Only one 15-minute time for an adult-led activity is seen. No story time is listed. You may have had trouble guessing when child-initiated time occurs, because it is labeled as "small-group activities." (Later in this chapter we will talk more about how the words *small group* are used in our field.)

What is known about child development and from observations of children show that children do not need over an hour to wash hands, eat breakfast, and brush their teeth. Also, when children are not busy engaging in and learning from appropriate activities, they usually become bored and restless and have behavior problems. The most disturbing thing about this schedule is the possibility that time that could be spent in enjoyable, constructive learning is being spent in unnecessarily long routines and waiting in lines.

TRY THIS NOW

Now take another sheet of paper to rewrite and improve this schedule so that we see other adult-led activities, ample child-initiated time, and more appropriate time frames for routines. Think about transitions to move children smoothly from one activity to the next. Schedule events so that they flow from active to quiet to active to quiet throughout the day.

Here is a possible rewrite for the schedule, showing over 1 hour for child-initiated activities, about 1 hour for adult-directed activities, a half-hour for outdoor time, and about 2½ hours of routines:

9:00–9:15	Short circle for greetings and exercise to music
9:15–9:45	Breakfast and health routines
9:45–10:00	Circle time for sharing and planning work/play time
10:00–11:15	Child-initiated time, projects, and individualized teaching
11:15–11:30	Recall and small-group time to practice skills
11:30–12:00	Outdoor time and transition to lunch
12:00–1:00	Lunch
1:00–1:15	Story time circle
1:15–1:50	Flex time (3-year-olds may nap or participate; 4- and 5-year-olds may do journals, cultural activities or projects)

TRY THIS NOW

Now take another sheet of paper and write out your own daily schedule, making improvements as necessary. Next, study and reflect on the schedules that follow. Look for the amount of adult-directed and child-initiated times in the schedule, look for the balance of these in the schedule, look for individualized teaching time, and look at the flow of the activities throughout the day.

Example 1: Half-Day Schedule, Three Hours, No Meals

8:45–9:00	Arrival and conversation
9:00–9:10	Circle; plans for activity time
9:10–10:30	Child activity time/free choice, including open snack, individualizing, and children's projects
10:30–10:45	Cleanup and small-group time
10:45–10:55	Music and exercise
10:55–11:10	Story time and evaluating our day
11:10–11:30	Outdoor time
11:30–11:45	Goodbyes and plans for tomorrow

Example 2: Half-Day Schedule, Four Hours (Meals Served)

8:30–9:00	Arrival/open breakfast/conversation; read independently
9:00–9:15	Singing; planning for activity time
9:15–10:30	Child activity time/free choice, individualized teaching, projects
10:30–10:45	Recall—evaluate our activities
10:45–11:00	Music and movement
11:00–11:10	Small-group skill practice
11:10–11:30	Stretch and story
11:30–12:10	Lunch, conversation, toothbrushing, planning
12:10–12:30	Outdoors
12:30	Dismissal

Example 3: Half-Day Schedule, Four Hours (Meals Served and 15-Minute Staggered Bus Arrival)

8:30	Bus A arrives. Greeting in circle; planning for activity time. Children start simple breakfast, read or start independently when finished
8:45	Bus B arrives. Greeting in circle. Children eat breakfast; teachers converse with Bus B children at breakfast about plans for activity time
9:00	Short circle; sing and start transition
9:05–10:30	Child activity time/free choice and individualized teaching
10:30–10:45	Cleanup and small-group time
10:45–11:00	Music and movement
11:00–11:30	Outdoor time or activities in gym
11:30–11:45	Story time and fingerplays
11:45–12:15	Lunch and conversation about our day; brush teeth
12:15–12:30	Transition to rug
12:30	Bus A leaves; Bus B children read independently
12:45	Bus B leaves

Example 4: Half-Day Schedule, Four and One-Half Hours (Meals Served and 30-Minute Staggered Bus Arrival)

8:00–8:30	Bus A arrives. Do story and journals
8:30	Bus B arrives. Join Bus A children preparing to eat
8:30–9:00	Breakfast and routines; discuss plans for free choice at meal
9:00–10:30	Free choice and projects; individualized teaching
10:30–10:45	Cleanup and have small-group time
10:45–11:15	Outdoor time (or alternative)
11:15–11:30	Music; Bus A children transition to lunch at 11:20
11:30–12:00	Bus B children join others for lunch

| 12:00 | Bus A children leave |
| 12:00–12:30 | Bus B children do journals and have story |

Full Day Schedules

Full-day schedules will probably follow any of these four examples rather closely in the mornings. In the afternoons, children, especially 3-year-olds, may rest. Other children will work on special projects or journals, enjoy visitors or cultural activities, do storytelling, read, and have another outdoor time. Snacks are often served before dismissal in preschool programs.

Older children will appreciate the extra time in the afternoons for collaborative projects, using the computer and tape recorder, planning or acting in dramatizations, creating representations to support their projects, and having extra one-on-one individualized time with teachers.

Challenges in Scheduling

Time Management

Daily scheduling often presents tough challenges to the early childhood teacher. Various factors can affect the schedule of the day, such as the number of hours, bus transportation, and meal service. One can easily see the challenges that arise in the schedule when two buses arrive with children at different times, as in Examples 3 and 4.

When time is short and a healthful snack or meal must be provided, teachers can save time for other important things in the schedule if they offer an "open breakfast" or an "open snack" instead of having all the children and adults sit down at the same time to eat.

Example 1 shows the daily schedule of a parent cooperative center. Prior to the development of the schedule shown, some parents wanted a sit-down snack time to practice manners, but providing this took up 15 minutes of the daily schedule. Other parents and teachers wanted to add a small-group time in which children would practice skill-focused activities, but did not want to take this time away from outdoor time or from free-choice time, in which ongoing assessment and individualized teaching took place. After much discussion, parents agreed that having all children end the program year with the mastery of appropriate skills was more important than having a sit-down snack.

This small change in schedule proved to be a real boon. Children still had time to practice good manners, passing, serving, and cleaning up. They were also able to become very independent in these activities. Best of all, the daily schedule was adjusted to include small-group time, which parents and children loved. This anecdote points out that good teachers must be continually innovative in squeezing out the time they need from every opportunity. They often use meal times for planning and for conversation, they talk about health and hygiene during meals and health routines, and they do their individualized teaching during free-choice time or in other opportune moments during the day.

Small-Group Time

Small-group time may or may not be part of the teacher's daily schedule. However, to avoid confusion and make sure the choice of this event is an option for anyone who wishes to schedule it, it is important to define clearly what *small group* means. The reason this term is often confusing to students and to early childhood teachers is that *small group* can describe three different situations.

First, many small groups occur naturally and spontaneously during free-choice or child-initiated time. These groups, which the children form themselves, consist of small numbers of children and usually keep changing throughout free-choice time. The way learning centers are set up encourages small-group collaboration. In these groups, children will choose with whom they will play, where they will play, and how long they will play.

Next, there is the small group that is formed during individualized teaching, when a teacher chooses one, two, or occasionally three children to sit and do a skill activity for about five minutes. Even when the teacher works with one child, it is still "a small group." During the activity, the adult will scaffold the experience with comments and questions that gently and gradually move children toward eventual skill mastery or expected outcomes. In this situation, the teacher is selecting children in order to help them practice specific skills based on their needs as found in ongoing assessment (see Chapter 6). Each child in the classroom will have this kind of one-on-one small-group experience regularly, at least once every three to four weeks. This planned individualization happens each day. Sometimes opportunities arise for teachers to do additional spontaneous individualizing, after which the activity should be noted on the lesson plan and/or in records.

The last type of small-group situation is the one that pertains to daily schedules. In this kind of small group, which is an adult-directed event that is actually in the daily schedule, all children and adults participate. Each staff member (including volunteers and sometimes bus drivers and cooks) takes a small group of children to a separate area of the room, such as housekeeping, manipulatives, a book corner, or the circle time rug. In these groups, all children play a game or do an activity designed to practice a motor, memory, perceptual, language, or problem-solving skill for about 8 to 10 minutes. Because different skills are practiced each day, all children benefit by getting practice in every skill area over time. Usually the same game or activity is done in all the groups on a given day.

In some cases, where the schedule is very tight, teachers may want to schedule a small-group time, but have no time to do it. In these cases, some teachers find it workable to set up one or two small tables for practice in specific skills during free-choice time. In these cases, an adult(s) works with a small group of children for five to eight minutes. When these children return to their choices of other learning areas, other children join the adult for their turns. In this case, the "small group" is not a separate scheduled time but occurs within free-choice time. What will be done is planned, and adults encourage skill building, but it is a group activity for the general practice of various skills that supplements the skills children are learning during free-choice time. In other words, it is *not* considered individualized teaching unless it is one-on-one time in which the skills being scaffolded with individuals are based on each child's specific needs as found in ongoing assessment.

TIP

Many programs require teachers to demonstrate ways their planned learning experiences match or lead to expected children's outcomes. There are many opportunities to help children toward outcomes in various learning domains during free-choice time and small-group time. When teachers are working with individual children on specific needs found through their assessments, however, the one-on-one experiences may or may not always relate to specific outcomes.

Examples of Small-Group Activities in Five Learning Domains

Motor
Draw a picture with markers or crayons (also problem solving).
String beads, pasta, or cereal.
Tear paper and make a collage with the pieces.
Snip the edge (fringe) of a quarter piece of construction paper.
Build structures with a small number of small blocks (also problem solving).
Work with playdough; use hands only.
Tie one simple knot with shoelaces or tie a shoe.

Perception
Play with simple puzzles or learn how to do a puzzle.
Sort and group twigs, seeds, leaves, or stones by color or size (also problem solving).
Smell and taste small pieces of several fruits and discuss (also language).
Close eyes and identify sounds and sound direction (also memory).
Match pairs of identical sounds using filled film containers.
Match types of bottle caps from a mix of these.
Guess what is in a bag by touch only (also memory).
Take off shoes, mix up, and sort into pairs.

Memory
Tell friends' names in this group.
Sing a familiar song or do a fingerplay (also language).
Tell about classroom rules, or tell about fire drills (also language).
Copy a clapped rhythm.

Remember and rebuild (copy) a simple block structure (3–5 blocks) after it has been knocked down.

Tell what 2–3 items have been removed from a group (see, hide, see).

Follow 2–3 simple directions while remaining seated.

Language

Take turns talking about self, family, pets, etc. (also memory).

Tell stories about photos or talk about photos or magazine pictures.

Play with playdough and describe the activity; adult lists all the words child says on a large piece of paper that can be posted later (also motor).

Draw a picture and tell about it; adult prints words child says on the paper (also motor and literacy).

Child tells what he or she had for breakfast or what he or she did last night (also memory).

Child tells what he or she thinks when adult asks, "What would happen if . . . " (also memory and problem solving).

Problem Solving

Count the people in the group.

Count the noses in the group.

Count the ears in the group.

Blow bubbles in one-half inch of water in small individual cups set on paper towels. Discuss what happens.

Play a game of identifying own potato in a group of 6 of them after studying it.

Guess, then test, what objects float or sink in a small margarine tub of water.

Make own playdough or silly putty, following a picture recipe (also literacy).

Make a dip for vegetables, following a picture recipe (also literacy).

Graph a cereal/nut snack on a paper place mat, then eat the snack.

Using buttons, pebbles, or other items, guess and then see how many it takes to fill a small cup.

Sort some items taken from an adult's purse (or pocket) in different ways.

Put items in order, smallest to largest.

Balance

Balance in the schedule means the balance between teacher-directed and child-initiated time. This has to do with the duration of time spent by children sitting and listening attentively to an adult or engaging in conversation or activities led by an adult, as compared to the time spent by children in choosing and concentrating on self-selected activities.

Basic child development knowledge supports the need for young children to learn factual content, thinking skills, and concentration skills through active play and hands-on concrete experiences. Basic child development knowledge also shows that young children have difficulty sitting and focusing attention on an adult for long periods, and that sitting still for short-group, large-group, or teacher-directed times should last only about 10 to 15 minutes. Although these are well-known facts, parents (and some teachers) often want children to practice learning to sit and "concentrate" for much longer periods. This presents a dilemma to early childhood teachers who are doing their best to meet children's developmental needs. Sometimes teachers need to explain their rationale for balance between adult-directed and child-initiated time to parents or other adults in terms of children's needs.

To be successful in this endeavor, the first thing teachers might do is clarify to others their need for ample time during the day to do observation, assessment, and individualized teaching. The free-choice period is the most practical time during the day for teachers to accomplish these tasks. Parents and supervisors will be able to see from the daily schedule and from observation that the teacher is free to address individual needs more easily during free-choice time.

Teachers will also need to clarify for parents the specific ways in which children learn the skills of concentration and attentiveness through other activities. Concerned parents (or adults having difficulty with this issue) should be invited to observe children during free-choice time to see the intensity with which children concentrate as they are engaged in meaningful learning experiences. Teachers should explain that as children move through the year, these concentration and attention span skills keep improving.

Next, the teacher should focus on the actual skill about which parents or others are concerned—the skill of listening to an adult. Reach agreement that it is not the *time* duration of the listening that is important, but the *skill itself.* Children are actually practicing the skill of attentive listening to adults at many times during the day. The best way for young children to practice this skill is during *several short large-group times* and *a small-group time* totaling 30 to 45 minutes, instead of practicing it by sitting for 30 to 45 minutes at a stretch.

Observe a group of 3- to 5-year-olds who have been asked to sit still for 30 minutes and listen to an adult. You will find them "losing it" after about 10 minutes. They will be wiggling, lying on the floor, touching the children next to them, and paying little or no attention to the adult. In other words, children would actually be practicing *poor* concentration and attention span habits instead of good ones. Add up the minutes in the schedule examples presented earlier, and notice that there is an approximately equal balance of time between teacher-directed and child-initiated activities.

Flow

Young children's learning experiences are most effective when they flow in an alternating active-to-quiet-to-active pattern throughout the program day. Incorporated into this flow of active and quiet times is the flow of indoor and outdoor activity.

An appropriate flow of activities is easily achieved by teachers because usually the order of events in the daily schedule is up to them. Care must be taken not to schedule two sit-down quiet periods back to back. Whenever this seems impossible to avoid, teachers can add a minute or two of exercise, or bending and stretching with or without music, in between two quiet, sit-down activities. See examples 1, 3, and 5 of the daily schedule. Outdoor time, like free-choice time, is considered an active time when children make choices among options offered by adults.

Children need time and freedom to experience fresh air and exercise outdoors with a variety of age-appropriate equipment, or with the elements of the natural environment itself (snow, grass, sand or earth, small hills, curbs, and sidewalks). It is not necessary or appropriate to structure all outdoor activities. After an active outdoor time, children need a quiet transition or an activity like story time.

Summary

In this chapter, we've discussed posted daily schedules and their benefits for adults and for children. We also learned that many insights about the teacher's curriculum can be found by studying the daily schedule. After examining and critiquing several schedules in terms of sound child development principles, you were asked to create appropriate daily schedules of your own. We also covered some of the challenges of scheduling, such as time management, flow, small-group time, and the balance between adult-directed and child-initiated time. In Chapter 5 we will look at another aspect of curriculum—the "how" of curriculum, which is seen in lesson plans.

Self-Study Activities

1. Create a schedule for a four-hour program in a very cold climate. Plan for meal service, but not staggered bus arrival. What things will you need to do to make sure there's enough time for children to put on and take off winter clothing?

2. Now adjust the same schedule for a program in a hot climate. What kinds of things will you do with the extra time you have? What kinds of learning experiences will occur in that time?

Resources and Suggested Readings

Due to the special nature of this chapter, very few reading resources are suggested. However, you are encouraged to spend time visiting and observing in at least one preschool, kindergarten, or primary classroom to see what kinds of schedules are posted and how well they work.

Christie, M. Beth, & Lippman, Marjory. "How Much Time Is Needed for Play." *Young Children,* 47, 3 (1992): 28–32.

Elkind, David. "Work Is Hardly Child's Play." *Images of the Young Child: Collected Essays on Development and Education.* Washington, DC: National Association for the Education of Young Children, 1993, pp. 21–29.

Barbour, Nita, & Seefeldt, Carol. *Developmental Continuity across Preschool and Primary Grades: Implications for Teachers.* Wheaton, MD: Association for Childhood Education International, 1993.

5 Lesson Plans

How Curriculum Happens

This chapter is about the *how* of curriculum. Lesson plans show *how* the curriculum is actually carried out on a given day or week. Like daily schedules, lesson plans are important tools for the early childhood teacher. In this chapter we will learn about the purposes of lesson plans and the kinds of comprehensive information they should include. We'll begin by looking at the purposes of lesson plans as implementation tools, blueprints for action, and written documentation. Then we'll address the issue of how much detail should be included in lesson plans, and learn the seven steps for effective lesson planning. The chapter will conclude with five examples of lesson plan forms used by programs in the field.

Lesson Plans as Tools for Planning

One of the main purposes of the lesson plan is to help the teacher consistently implement his or her long-range, monthly, and daily goals and objectives. For example, an experience like being weighed and measured may have objectives for both self-esteem and for learning about measuring tools. These objectives would relate to long-range goals for self-esteem and numeracy. Daily self-help activities might have short-range objectives in hygiene or learning how to care for one's teeth, but these relate to the long-range goal of life skills of good personal health practices. As teachers look at long-range and monthly curriculum goals, they use the daily lesson plans to consistently establish objectives as learning experiences that will gradually make the curriculum goals attainable.

In addition to being an implementation tool, a lesson plan is a blueprint or plan of action. Incorporated into this blueprint are reminders of all the curriculum elements that should be included every day, such as the use of creative media, blocks, sensory materials, literacy, math and science experiences, props, and active play equipment. Sometimes the blueprint even includes a daily schedule so that staff can see at a glance the consecutive order of the day's events. The plan may also include staff responsibilities, or who is to do what and when to do it.

In this way, the lesson plan blueprint also serves as a summarizing tool, providing a summary of all the teacher-directed and child-initiated experiences that will take place in the learning centers of a particular setting on a particular day or week and when they will happen. Adult-directed experiences will take place during large-group time, in small-group time, and with individuals during free-choice or child-initiated time, or even outdoors. Within the setting and time frames described in the lesson plan, children will engage in many types of learning activities that teachers plan, offer, encourage, or facilitate.

Remember that the teacher is always working with two broad types of curriculum information: interest based and skill based. These can be easily identified in the lesson plan by looking for experiences that are thematic or emergent, and experiences that primarily focus on skill practice, even if they relate to themes or emergent projects.

Most of what is seen in the lesson plan are planned learning experiences, but spontaneous learning excursions might also take place in the setting during a particular day or week. These on-the-spot teaching/learning experiences are sometimes called *teachable moments*. They may even be noted by the teacher in the lesson plan after the fact as "possible emerging interests." When children's interests in a topic discovered spontaneously continue to emerge, a whole new set of teaching and learning experiences can become part of the curriculum and future lesson plans. In this way, children's emergent curriculum ideas are added to the teacher's interest-based information, and may become the beginning of a new theme or collaborative project.

Lesson Plans as Documentation

Additionally, the lesson plan is an instrument that provides written evidence of developmentally appropriate practices that are being implemented, evidence of what actually occurs during each classroom day, and evidence of the relationship of daily planning to the written curriculum plan. In this way, written plans help to document compliance with the criteria or standards of the program or its funding sources. Lesson plans are also an immeasurable help in the monitoring and supervision of the program. Every good program has a system for monitoring and maintaining quality practices, just as they have systems for planning, communication, training, and parent input and involvement.

Problems arise when teachers do not know what the supervisor or monitor wants to see in the lesson plan because expectations have not been clarified, or when no training has been given to staff in what elements should be included in the plan. Problems also arise when a program has many sites or classrooms in which each teacher is using a different lesson plan format, making it very difficult for the monitoring of best practices. It is necessary for both teaching and administrative staff to brainstorm, discuss, and develop the kind of lesson plan format that includes all the elements that should be seen in a comprehensive daily or weekly lesson plan. The entire teaching and monitoring staff should come to agreement on one format that is acceptable to everyone.

Elements of a Comprehensive Lesson Plan

What should be included in a good lesson plan? This list of questions is indicative of those most often asked by supervisors who are looking for evidence of sound child development principles and best practices:

1. Are adult-led activities used for large-group times as well as small-group times? How many are there and what is their duration? Is the duration age appropriate?
2. Are there clearly seen activities or experiences in which the teacher works with individuals? Over the individualization cycle of three to four weeks, will all children's names be seen in the lesson plans?
3. Is there ample child-initiated or free-choice time, in at *least* equal balance to the total time for adult-directed times? Are all centers open each day, providing enough play slots and choices for constructive play and learning?
4. What actually happens in the learning centers? What is offered that is special or indicative of changes, themes, or emergent curriculum (e.g., "Play with materials" tells nothing about what happens in the block area)?
5. Are there times for daily physical large-motor activities, both indoors and outside?
6. Can the teacher's thematic activities be seen and inferred from lesson plan entries?
7. Can the children's emergent interests be seen or inferred from lesson plan entries?
8. Do the lesson plan entries show that children are engaged in experiences where they are practicing developmentally appropriate skills based on the long-range goals in the curriculum plan?
9. Do the lesson plan entries show that children are engaged in hands-on, concrete experiences in discovery problem solving with sensory or math and science materials?
10. Are the children engaged in a variety of language and literacy experiences as seen in the lesson plan entries?
11. Does the lesson plan show that regularly scheduled health, nutrition, and safety education experiences are taking place?
12. Do the lesson plan entries show that the children are engaging in other experiences that reflect program priorities, if any, such as cultural, antibias, or environmental activities?

A supervisor or qualified observer/reviewer of best practices could not use the lesson plan alone as evidence or to make assumptions about what happens in a teacher's classroom. One would need to look back over many lesson plans to determine if what is seen in the plans is consistent. Children's files would need to be checked to see if their specific needs, as found in assessment, are being met. Interviews would also be done with the teachers, other staff, and parents. As a written instrument, however, the lesson plan is an important indicator of the quality of early childhood teaching that is being done by the teacher. This gives teachers excellent motivation to do good lesson planning that documents the quality of their work.

Quality Lesson Plans Incorporate Detail

Great differences are found in the ways teachers write up their activities on lesson plans. The quality of content, as is seen or not seen in the details given about an activity, is sometimes an issue. The range of detail in written lesson plans is diverse and encompasses a very broad spectrum. At one end are plans that offer no detail at all, and at the other are plans in which the detail is mind boggling.

Too Much Detail

Some lesson plans spell out every activity in terms of behavioral outcomes—for example, "The children will each walk with alternating steps on the balance beam, then they will jump with both feet onto a carpet square. Then they will balance on one (dominant) foot for five seconds, then they will climb up and down three steps. Next they climb to the climber and slide down the slide; last they will crawl through a cloth tunnel. They may begin the obstacle course sequence again, on the balance beam." This much detail not only is unnecessary but it is a recipe for teacher burnout!

Instead of this overload of detail, the teacher could simply have stated, in the space on the lesson plan for "Large-Muscle Activities," what would happen in that area. "Obstacle course" might not tell quite enough, but "Obstacle course—climber, slide, beam, carpet squares, steps, tunnel" would give a clear picture of what large-muscle activities would be practiced that day.

Another example of overdoing detail would be: "Easel. Large newsprint; both sides. Large brushes. Four jars tempera, both sides, in white, yellow, red, and blue." Since the usual daily procedure is to use several kinds of tempera, both sides of the easel, and large brushes, it is not necessary to detail these points. (Teachers would note changes such as the use of special paper or small brushes.) The lesson plan would provide adequate detail if it stated, "Easel; experiment with pastels" or "Easel; white and primary; mix pastels."

Too Little Detail

On the other hand, one should always add detail that is necessary. The teacher should not put "Book" or "Read story" on the lesson plan in the area for literacy or story time. He or she should list the name of the story or book, perhaps adding, "with puppet" or "children will retell." In the space on the lesson plan for music and movement, the teacher would not write "Dance," but would be expected to write what kind of music, rhythm, or chants would be used. In the space on the lesson plan for sensory activities, the teacher would be expected to detail what kind of experiences would occur, such as "Pour/fill colored rice" or "Make and use silly putty."

One area of lesson plans that often gets short-changed on detail is the child-initiated experiences in the various learning centers. As we saw in the list of elements that should be included in the lesson plan, listing the learning centers without telling anything about what happens in each one is not appropriate. Here are some examples:

What is entered in the "Blocks" space on the lesson plan should answer the questions: "What kind of blocks?" "What accessories?" "What literacy or math experience will be integrated?" In the "Writing Center" space on the lesson plan, "Invented writing" is not adequate. What kinds of materials will be offered for children's use in engaging in this activity—old greeting cards of all kinds and large pencils? In the space on the plan for "Math," one cannot merely say "Tubbing." Rather, the plan should state what objects will be sorted and into what categories. One needs to specify if comparisons such as "more and less" will be made. In the space for "Science," the lesson plan should state what new things might be introduced to the children and placed in a science area. What changes in plants, animals, or other science materials should be observed? Will children's comments be dictated? Will results of experiments be noted and posted?

Often, improved attention to quality and detail in lesson plans correlates with improved teacher competence. But sometimes supervisors find that teachers who do a competent and enthusiastic job in action while they are being observed with young children may have lesson plans that are vague and general. These may be teachers who rationalize that vague lesson planning helps them be more spontaneous.

However, when one looks at the lesson plans of such teachers, the plans may provide no clear documentation proving that the teacher does good work consistently. These might be plans that have no long- and short-range goals for children, either individually or as a group; thematic units and their objectives may be unclear. They may be plans that give no detail about the daily materials or planned activities.

Assistance in Lesson Planning

To provide assistance in lesson planning, two things could be done. First, training could be given to teachers in what elements should be seen in their lesson plans, and what kind of detail is expected. Teachers should agree on the format to be used. The time taken for training would be well worth the effort, both to teachers and to administrative staff. Making lesson plans comprehensive by adding necessary elements and detail will show supervisors the *how* of the teacher's curriculum, and document activities promoting knowledge, physical skills, literacy, math/science discovery, problem solving, social skills, collaboration, and self-esteem.

The second way to help teachers write consistently clear lesson plans has to do with the lesson plan form itself. Formats should include certain headings and spaces to remind teachers of activities that must occur. If spaces and headings are provided on the lesson plan format for "Theme," "Main Skill Objective," "Large Muscle," "Fine Motor," "Sensory," "Literacy," and so forth, it saves teachers time, energy, and paperwork, ensures that necessary entries will be made, and allows teachers to use their time and energy to fill in the details with activity content. Examples of helpful and practical formats for lesson plans are included at the end of this chapter.

Documenting Individualized Teaching

Earlier in this chapter, we discussed the need for teachers to indicate the time on the daily schedule that individualized teaching occurs. However, the daily schedule does not give enough detail to provide evidence of individualized teaching. It is important for teachers to document their individualized teaching in the lesson plan itself. Brief entries can provide written evidence of what skill or skills are practiced, and when and with whom the teacher has one-on-one interactions. Space for this kind of entry should be provided in the lesson plan format, as it is in all the lesson plan examples at the end of this chapter.

It is necessary to place the initials of the child or children with whom the teacher is working in the lesson plan, and briefly state what the experience is. These details indicate that the teacher is using information that has been discovered about each child's needs through screening and observation and is meeting children's needs in actual practice.

The use of initials is not a breach of confidentiality; the teacher cares about and will spend one-on-one time with every child in the classroom. All the children's initials will be seen in the lesson plans over approximately a three- to four-week period; no discrimination is taking place. Chapter 6 will provide information and details about systems for individualizing and documentation.

Seven Steps in Effective Lesson Planning

When you have jobs or chores to do regularly, it saves time when you think first about what has to be done, and then accomplish the task, step by step until it's completed. It also seems that when you do the steps of a task the same way each time, you become faster and faster at getting the job done. This is because you have a system for doing the job, and doing things systematically is more efficient. The same strategy, having a step-by-step system and doing it the same way each time, also works well with lesson planning.

First, you think about what has to be done. This means you might check your program's monthly calendar to see if anything will affect your lesson plans for the day or week. It's also a good idea to think about the age and development of the children with whom you work, and how they are growing and changing. Think about your program's mission to serve these children. Getting in touch with the program's mission and philosophy will give you a positive mindset for the lesson planning task. Also, think about any input you may have received from the children's parents. Is there any way that this input could be incorporated into your weekly lesson plans?

Next, after the five or so minutes you have spent in reflection, do your lesson planning by following these seven steps, one at a time:

1. ***Choose and enter basic daily activities*** for the entire week of child-initiated time on the form, adding details as needed (changes or additions to blocks, paint, playdough, dramatic play props, sand or water, etc.).
2. ***Review individual needs and enter a planned experience*** for one or two children each day.
3. ***Choose skill-based activities*** from each of the five major domains in Appendix A of this book, choosing from an appropriate time block. Use whatever you like from the time blocks columns, or use your own ideas for domain activities. Enter these activities on the lesson plan in any of the large-group, small-group, or free-choice time spaces, wherever they fit best. Note that in each column of the five categories in Appendix A, sequenced activity ideas are divided into three sections: large group, free choice, and small group.
4. ***Choose and enter thematic or emergent activities.*** These will probably affect your large-group circle/sharing time and your story and music time. Consider thematic and emergent activity entries for other spaces on the lesson plan, too, such as in free-choice time.
5. ***Choose and enter health, nutrition, or safety activities.***
6. ***Consider children with disabilities or challenges.*** Will your plans for the week work well for all of them, or will modifications be in order? Note these as needed.
7. ***Gather special materials*** you might need to implement the plan, and **smile.**

Lesson Plan Examples

All of the lesson plan forms included at the end of this chapter (Figures 5.1 through 5.5) were used in actual programs. You may copy, modify, and use them. The examples present formats that incorporate all the elements that should be a part of a lesson plan, even though each format has a different "look." In two of the lesson plan examples, the daily schedule is incorporated on the form. In one, the day's schedule on the left margin runs concurrently with the activities of the day, limiting the writing space available, but making it easy for the staff to follow each part of the daily plan as it occurs. Three plans are designed for four-day weeks, and one is for a five-day week. Adjustments could be made in any of these forms to suit any schedule.

All of the forms shown include a space to note that health, nutrition, and safety activities all occur regularly. Spaces on all the forms are clearly designated for literacy, discovery learning, and math/science or problem-solving experiences. In three forms, there is a space for emerging interests of children and/or changes to the environment due to children's changing interests. In two plans, there are spaces for ecology and environment, and in some of the forms, there are spaces for culture, showing the priorities of these programs.

A space to encourage parent input or comments is included on three lesson plan forms. Many programs require that parents give input to the curriculum. Parents who visit the classroom or volunteer may have good comments that are forgotten when they leave for home, unless they are encouraged to give input. Even if parent comments are brief, teachers will have documented that they provided the opportunity for parent input without creating a new form or more paperwork

Summary

In this chapter we discussed daily lesson plans and some of the challenges that the lesson plan, as a curriculum tool, presents to the teacher and program. Examples were provided to help the teacher make appropriate choices about the content of lesson plans, and make improvements in the clarity and detail of written plans. Attention has also been given to the lesson plan as a written instrument that helps to document planned curriculum experiences, individualized instruction, and what actually happens with children during the program day. Lesson plan form examples are provided at the end of this chapter (Figures 5.1 through 5.5). In Chapter 6, we will learn more about individualizing and outcomes.

Self-Study Activity

1. Choose two of the lesson plans provided at the end of this chapter. Copy, enlarge, and print them, and then write two lesson plans for two imaginary days occurring at different times of the program year. Compare the way each of the lesson plan formats worked for you; make notes of modifications or changes you would make in the forms. If you are a teacher, consider changes on your own lesson plan that might improve it.

Resources and Suggested Readings

Because of the special nature of this chapter, no specific books are suggested. However, it is suggested that you might examine early childhood resource books or college texts to reread any information that may have been presented about lesson planning.

		Monday	Tuesday	Wednesday	Thursday
Week of _____	Individualizing				
Center _____	Circle				
Teacher _____ Notes	Story				
Schedule	Small-Group Activity				
8:45 Arrival	Music				
9:00 Breakfast					
9:30 Circle	Notes		Gross and Fine Motor		Foods, Health, Safety
9:45 Free Choice					
11:00 Small Group					
11:10 Outdoors					
11:30 Circle/Music					
11:45 Story					
12:00 Snack/Meal					
12:30 Circle and Dismissal					
DAILY USE: Blocks, Paint, Sensory, Dramatic Play, Active Play		Open-Ended Art/Sensory Media		Pretend Play/Musical Play	
Horizontal Theme _____ Thematic/Unit _____ Skill Focus _____ Vocabulary _____		Discovery/Problem Solving Math & Science		Literacy/Writing Center—Computer	
Emerging Interests			Ecology		Self-Esteem

FIGURE 5.1 *Lesson Plan Example 1*

Teacher _____
Week of _____ .

	MONDAY		TUESDAY		WEDNESDAY		THURSDAY		WEEK LONG
	NOTES		NOTES		NOTES		NOTES		THEMES
8:30 Arrival/Open Breakfast and Circle									Health/Nutrition | Safety
9:00 Planning									
9:15–10:30 Free Choice									
Literacy–Sensory									
Dramatic Play									Anti Bias/Inclusion
Art Media/Fine Motor									Outdoors/Trips | Ecology
Large Motor									
Individualizing									Discovery/Problem Solving
10:30 Recall									
10:40 Large Group Music/Movement									
11:00 Small Group									
11:10 Large Group Stretch and Story									
11:30 Lunch 12:00 Outdoors 12:30 Dismissal									Parent Comments (Sig. and Date) Continued on reverse

FIGURE 5.2 Lesson Plan Example 2

Teacher:	Date:	Theme:	Objectives:		Daily Schedule
Shape:	Color:	Numbers:	Letters:	(Parent Comments & Signature)	

	Monday	Tuesday	Wednesday	Thursday	
Arrival/Breakfast/Routines/Hygiene					
Music/Movement Large Motor					Emerging Interests
Transition:					
Small Group					
Transition:					
Circle/Sharing & Planning					
Transition:					
Work Time Free Choice for the week	Creative Process	Sensory	Motor	Dramatic Play	
	Manipulatives	Computer	Books/Writing Center	Blocks	Special Math and Science / Special Literacy
Individualization					
Discussion and Story					
Hygiene/Lunch Routines					
Cultural activities and Projects					
Health/Safety/ Nutrition/Mental Health/Self esteem					Visitors and Trips

FIGURE 5.3   Lesson Plan Example 3

71

Theme Focus					
Skills Focus					
Teacher/Center		Week of:			

Health/Nutrition/Safety	Housekeeping/Dramatics	Sand/Water	Art		Notes/Visitors/Trips
		Woodworking			
Emerging Interests	Blocks	Literacy	Puzzles/Manipulatives		Science/Math (Problem Solving)
	Ecology/Environment		Gross Motor		

	Mon.	Tues.	Wed.	Thurs.	Fri.
Circle					
Story					
Music					
Individualizing					

FIGURE 5.4 Lesson Plan Example 4

LESSON PLANS Teacher _____ Class _____ Week Beginning _____ 20 ___ Theme _____

Large Group/Circle	Small Group	Ind. Teach	Free Play for the week	Outdoors	Safety, Health, Nutrition	Culture	Visitors/Field Trips & Notes
Sharing: Music/Movement: Story:			Art, Media & Sensory:				
Sharing: Music/Movement: Story:			Science/Math:				
Sharing: Music/Movement: Story:			House Keeping Dramatic Play:				
Sharing: Music/Movement: Story:			Blocks and Motor:				
Daily Schedule	Goal - Objectives Skill Emphasis		Language/ Literacy:	Emerging Interests			

FIGURE 5.5 Lesson Plan Example 5

73

6 Individualizing

The Why of Curriculum

Why does a teacher write a curriculum in the first place? Why does anyone do so much careful planning of experiences to match goals and objectives, simultaneously focusing on the diverse and changing development of the children? The *why* of curriculum has to do with the *outcomes.*

Why? Because teachers want their curricula to help children grow and develop to the best of their potential in every way possible, and in all learning domains. Teachers want this for children because it will give them a strong foundation of self-esteem, well-being, self-discipline, social/collaborative skills, and a sense of responsibility. Teachers want children to have physical and intellectual skills, creative thinking and problem-solving skills, numeracy skills, literacy skills, and a love of reading. Yes, all that and more—teachers also want children to have curiosity, an eagerness to learn, and a zest for life that will predispose their success in the years ahead. Early childhood educators believe that if they can help children attain these outcomes to the best of their abilities, the world will be a better place.

These outcomes cannot be attained successfully unless curriculum planning is continually checked and reevaluated to be sure it is appropriate to the development, interests, strengths, and needs of the group as well as the individual children in that group. The way to check curriculum planning is through ongoing assessment. *Ongoing assessment* leads to information with which to do appropriate planning; planning leads to individualizing and scaffolding children's experiences, and that, in turn, leads to the outcomes teachers want for children. Outcomes provide information with which educators can do better planning. Now let's learn more about the different steps that take us along the path to outcomes.

Assessment

Simply put, *assessment* is a way to find out things—to gather information so that one can make the right decisions about one's planning. Early childhood educators perform *ongoing* assessment, which means information is gathered, organized, and evaluated, and used in planning curriculum learning experiences throughout the year. The goal is to gather information from as many sources as possible in order to do the best ongoing planning. The information gathered also provides information about the child's progress, which is shared with parents and helps the teacher do collaborative curriculum planning.

A variety of information is gathered by using initial developmental screening instruments, using developmental assessment instruments, and doing ongoing observation. Observations are recorded in many ways. Teachers use various types of written observations, and collect examples of the children's work in individual portfolios. Sometimes teachers also use regularly taped conversations with children or periodic videotapes of what children are doing in different domain areas. Some teachers take photos of children as they perform tasks.

Ongoing observation does not mean just teacher observations, but the ongoing observations of everyone involved in helping each child develop successfully, including support staff, parents, and other caregivers. Teachers periodically exchange information they have gathered with information that parents have gathered. In this way, educators continually share children's progress with parents, get their input, and do collaborative planning. In this chapter we'll be looking at the components of assessment, planning, and individualizing in more depth.

Developmental Screening Tools

At the beginning of the year, many early childhood programs (and all Head Start programs) do vision and hearing screening and health assessments on all children. Most quality programs for children, even infant-toddler center programs, also use an initial developmental screening instrument to get a "snapshot" of each child's current developmental level as it relates to specific functional language, motor, and self-help skills. Developmental screening instruments may also check vision, hearing, and perceptual skills. Many programs use the newest edition of the Denver Developmental Screening, called the Denver II, for this purpose. Some programs use the DIAL Plus or other instruments for initial screening. The developmental screening instruments used should be standardized, as culturally relevant to the children as possible, and done as early as possible in the program year so that results can be addressed and shared with parents.

Initial developmental screening tools do not provide comprehensive information on many different skill areas, but they do identify children who might possibly have learning disabilities or developmental lags. With parent support and agreement, these children would be referred for further diagnostic testing and evaluation by specialists.

IEPs and IFSPs

If problems are found, efforts are made to find ongoing help for the child and family. If physical problems were affecting the child's ability to learn, or if other learning deficits or disabilities were found, an individual education plan (IEP) is developed for the child by the specialists who did the testing and evaluation, in collaboration with the parents, teachers, and other pertinent staff persons. In programs serving infants and toddlers, this individualized plan may also be called the individual family service plan, or IFSP.

Teachers are expected to use IEPs or IFSPs to develop ways to individualize their daily teaching with those children who have been assessed as having special needs or disabilities. The IEPs or IFSPs are kept in the children's file folders with their diagnostic information but should be referred to when the teacher is doing lesson planning.

The strategies developed on the IEP or IFSP are useful in meeting the daily needs of children with disabilities or deficits only if they find their way into daily planning. This information must be easy to access.

The practice of using screening instruments to find special needs in children and to develop education plans to meet those needs has also led to the practice of using both screening instruments and ongoing observation to do better, more comprehensive planning for *all* children in the group or classroom.

In the early childhood programs of today that demonstrate developmentally appropriate practices, every child has an individual education plan. This plan is jointly developed with parents or caregivers, and is regularly reviewed and modified as children grow and develop, achieve planned goals, and move toward new goals. Using parent input, screening information, and staff observations, teachers create a simple education plan for every child (whether the child has a disability or not). They list individual needs and goals on that plan, and keep it in the child's record folder.

Developmental Assessment Tools

Developmental assessment tools are used in programs for 3- to 5-year olds and other early childhood programs to assess a child's skills in a number of different areas and to provide more detailed developmental information to help teachers in their planning. This kind of information can tell teachers the child's skill levels in particular learning domains or growth areas. As mentioned in the discussion of sequencing in Chapter 2, developmental assessment information tells teachers and parents the "signposts" the child is currently passing as he or she is moving toward particular developmental milestones or outcomes.

In early childhood programs, the staff uses authentic performance-based assessment strategies (various types of observation and work sampling) to find out what they need to know about children, not standardized tests. Authentic assessment shows what the child can do or apply. In performance assessment, the child demonstrates learning or understanding while performing an activity. In addition to providing information on specific outcomes, performance-based assessments are meaningful to the child, relate to the real world, and can sometimes inform the teacher about the child's learning style.

There are three main purposes for using performance-based assessment in early childhood programs: Assessment provides information that (1) helps evaluate children's progress, (2) helps the teacher plan more appropriate curriculum, and (3) improves program quality. That's what assessment is—whether or not it identifies particular outcomes.

Parents and staff can readily understand the meaning of authentic, performance-based assessment; it is simply a logical way of finding out what they want to know about young children. It is important to know about the child's progress along a continuum of human development in different learning domains; often, the child's progress is explained as a series of steps that are easily observed as the child moves toward attainable goals.

Outcomes

In today's programs, early educators need to be able to explain children's progress in terms of *outcomes*. What are outcomes are and how are they used? There is an increasing push and a corresponding trend in early childhood programs to assess, analyze, and report children's progress to administrators, policymakers, and funding sources. This means that the information gathered from the ongoing assessment of young children will not only be used by staff and parents to improve planning and help children progress in reaching individual goals but it will also be used as indicators of program quality.

The data on the progress of groups of children (which is seen as an indicator of program quality) will be given to funding sources and administrators who may or may not be well-versed in child development. This is why the information must be given to them in terms that are readily understood. They can understand "outcomes" because, from their perspective, the child's learning process is often seen as input and output data (teaching goes in; learning comes out) instead of a developmental continuum.

Regardless of the ways receivers of outcome information perceive children's progress, teachers need to understand outcomes in terms of their own perspectives as early educators and the perspectives of the parents of the children. Outcome data not only indicate quality but also provide opportunities to help teachers *improve* program quality.

Now you know what outcomes can do, but what *is* an outcome? Let's look at it this way: We know the child progresses in a sequence of steps along the path of development in each learning domain, reaching various small signposts and large milestones along the way. Authentic performance-based assessment can show where the child is as he or she proceeds along that particular path of development. It tells where the child has been and where the child is going next in a particular domain area. An *outcome* in a domain area is simply an indicator of the developmental signpost or milestone the child is passing. Outcomes are also the natural and gradual result of developmentally appropriate planning.

When specific outcomes are used to collect information, such as indicators that are clear to anyone and commonly understood, teachers can communicate children's progress to others who are concerned about program quality, even if they don't want to know more about child development or curriculum. When a program lists a commonly understood indicator ("Can name and write 10 letters of the alphabet") in a learning domain as an *outcome,* it does not mean that the child is all finished with development and progress in that domain. The child will continue to develop, become literate, read and write, and enjoy literature. An outcome is not the "end" or final result, but simply one particular place along the path of development in a particular learning domain.

To summarize, when one uses *outcomes* to show progress to administrators and funding sources, one is simply choosing to *highlight particular signposts* or milestones as indicators along the path of development in each learning domain. When information is collected on certain outcomes, the progress of groups of children is shown and these data can indicate or inform program quality.

Many excellent standardized developmental assessment tools can help teachers collect developmental assessment information, such as the Battelle Developmental Inventory, the Work Sampling System, the Hawaii Early Learning Profile, and the High/Scope Preschool Child Observation Record (COR). Another tool, the Creative Curriculum Developmental Continuum Assessment (2001), provides an accompanying option, CD-PORT, a software program to help early childhood programs create reports that show progress on groups of children. The Work Sampling System is comprised of ongoing observations, progress reports, and developmental checklists. There is also a Work Sampling System for Head Start, published in 2001. The publishers of the Work Sampling System have done extensive field trials of their assessment tool for infants and toddlers, "The Ounce of Prevention Scale." This assessment tool becomes available in early 2003.

All of these developmental assessment tools use authentic, performance-based methods. They all contain various strategies for collecting and recording information about children's progress in learning domains, such as personal and social/emotional development, language and literacy, mathematical thinking, scientific thinking, the arts or creativity (divergent thinking), and physical and motor development. In most of these assessment tools, the domains being assessed overlap with the eight domains listed in the Head Start Outcomes Framework: Language Development, Literacy, Mathematics, Science, Creative Arts, Social/Emotional Development, Physical Health and Development, and Approaches to Learning. It must be made clear that the Head Start Outcomes *are not* a developmental assessment tool. The Outcomes Framework simply lists the learning domains to be assessed, the elements that define these learning domains, and some indicators of development in each learning domain that could be used as guidance by teachers to gather information on children's progress.

Regardless of the methods teachers might use to collect information, in each learning domain of the Outcomes Framework, several domain elements are listed that help the teacher to observe and evaluate what the child is doing; indicators are also provided as further guidance. For example, in the Head Start Outcomes Framework domain of "Approaches to Learning," the three domain elements are "initiative and curiosity," "engagement and persistence," and "reasoning and problem solving." Some of these elements are dispositions related to feelings, not skills, but they can still be "taught" with modeling, encouragement, and reinforcement; they are certainly behaviors that can be observed. The indicators that are provided aid teachers in observing the three elements in that domain.

In other domain areas, the domain elements are specific skills, and the indicator guidance for teachers reflects this. For example, in the "Literacy" domain in the Head Start Outcomes Framework, one domain element is "alphabet knowledge." The four indicators are as follows:

1. Shows progress in associating names of letters with their shapes and sounds
2. Increases in ability to notice beginning letters of familiar words
3. Identifies at least 10 letters of the alphabet, especially those in his or her own name
4. Knows that letters of the alphabet are a special category of visual graphics that can be individually named (it is believed that children can understand this, even if they cannot express it in these particular words)

Head Start programs have always done ongoing assessment in all learning domains in order do better planning and to share children's progress with parents; doing assessment is not new to them. They are now required, however, to use the Head Start Outcomes Framework as a guide, along with their chosen methods of assessment, to collect specific outcomes information three times a year and use it in planning.

Using outcomes in the process of ongoing assessment will be a new challenge to many early childhood teachers. If outcomes are seen in the correct developmental perspective, and *not* seen as the components of a "test," outcomes can help teachers accomplish their purposes to collect information on children's progress and improve the quality of learning for children.

Considerations in Choosing Screening Instruments

Here are some questions that programs and decision makers should consider when they choose standardized assessment tools:

1. ***Will the results of screening benefit children?*** Will the screening information, along with other information, help teachers do a better and more individualized job of planning for children? Will it help teachers find children who may need additional services?
2. ***Do these tools or instruments meet needs?*** Do they meet the needs of the children? Do they meet the needs, capacities, and values of the staff? Will the staff be able to use this new information to enhance good teaching?

3. *Are the tools or instruments credible?* Are they standardized and valid in terms of the development of the children being served?
4. *What information is wanted?* What does the teacher want this screening or observation tool to do? Does it contain everything the teacher needs? Does it address all areas of development?
5. *Is it supportive of children?* Can this instrument be easily administered in appropriate, supportive ways for children? Can it be implemented as an enjoyable classroom experience for all the children, even the youngest? Is it free of bias?
6. *Will it help teachers communicate children's needs and progress to parents?* Will it show parents their children's strengths and capabilities, as well as current areas of need? Will it help teachers continue their work with parents as a team in an effort to help each child reach his or her full potential?

Observation

Definition

Observation is more than casual looking at children. It means gathering information about children and the program with an open mind. Observation is the basis of much of what we do in working with children. . . . Observation can:
- Provide parents, caregivers, and teachers with increased sensitivity to how children behave, think, and learn.
- Make us aware of the unique qualities of each child.
- Permit us to reflect on and compare what we see to what we have studied about growth and development.
- Help us to understand individual behavior problems and the part that adults and materials in the setting may play in these problems.
- Help us to plan activities based on children's special interests, skills and strengths.
- Provide information we can use in reporting on a child's growth and progress to parents. (Garlick, 1980)

As an early childhood professional, you will be expected to do ongoing observation of all the children who are engaged in learning in your classroom. This is not a problem; if you love teaching young children, you will find that observing them as they grow and learn is a fascinating part of your job.

Purpose

The purpose of observation, which is part of the assessment, is to gather information on individual children so that lesson planning and teacher interactions are as individualized as possible. Observing with this purpose in mind does not only mean the teacher watches children and writes what she or he sees. Teachers need to know why they want to observe, be very attentive while they observe, record objectively, keep information organized, and then reflect and think about what they have learned (evaluate) so they can use it in their planning.

Methods of Observation

In *Reaching Potentials,* Bredekamp and Rosegrant (1990) define and outline four basic methods of observing and recording children's behavior:

1. Narratives
   a. Diary descriptions
   b. Anecdotal records
   c. Running records
   d. Specimen descriptions
   e. Logs or journals
2. Time samplings
3. Event samplings
4. Modified child study techniques
   a. Checklists
   b. Rating scales
   c. Shadow study (in-depth case study)

Five of the most common methods of observation used by early childhood teachers are **anecdotal notes** (a narrative method), **running records** (a narrative method), **checklists** (a modified child study technique), **logs or journals** (a narrative method), and **time samplings.** In today's programs, videotaping (with parent permission) is increasingly being used to provide documented observations that can be reviewed by staff and discussed with parents.

Anecdotal notes are descriptive narratives, recorded after the behavior occurs, which are used to detail specific information. An example of an anecdotal note might be "9/20: Today J. D. poured his own milk without spilling for the first time. He watched the other children and copied their technique of holding the pitcher with two hands and asking a neighbor to hold his cup. He smiled broadly at this accomplishment." *Running records* are recorded while the behavior is occurring to document what children are doing in a certain situation. Running records, like anecdotal notes, are commonly used in most early childhood classrooms. Running records can be narratives written for a duration of five minutes, but they may also be used when the child is having a more in-depth observation of up to an hour or more. *Checklists* are lists on which the adult checks for specific behaviors, and can be done during the behavior or after it occurs. *Time sampling* is the observation of what happens in a given time period while the behavior is occurring, and is coded with tallies or symbols to determine the frequency of specific behaviors. A *log or journal* is a recording of brief details about each child in the group, usually made after the behavior occurs, usually describing the child's status or progress (Bredekamp & Rosegrant, 1992). All five of these methods can give the teacher or adult observer information to use in lesson planning and conferencing with parents or staff.

Some of the most useful information about children cannot be gathered in the classroom. This information is about behavior that occurs during the rest of the child's daily life. It can be gathered from parents—an excellent source of knowledge about their children, which should not be overlooked. The information teachers gather from parents is done in casual conversations, in planned interviews and conferencing, on home visits, or through parent information checklists and questionnaires.

How Do Teachers Observe?

Teachers can usually do their written observations as they "float" to various learning areas during free-choice or child activity time, stopping occasionally to interact or work with children individually or in small groups. The responsibility for supervision in various learning centers can be delegated among support staff and/or volunteers. As other staff and volunteers remain more stationary (perhaps taking additional notes in the learning centers), at least one teacher is free to move about the room to collect observation information with anecdotal notes and/or other forms, depending on the methods or systems chosen.

Sometimes it's not *what* a person does but *how* she or he does it. The most important aspect of observation is the effectiveness of the teacher in focusing on what is being observed. This may seem at first to go without saying, but many people watch without really seeing and listen without really hearing.

Inherent in the meaning of the word *observe* is a sense of calm, quiet detachment. One is not really observing children when one is constantly talking to them or employing a barrage of questions. A person must be quiet to really watch and listen, allowing the children's words and actions tell the observer the things he or she wants to note.

The dictionary includes the phrases "paying strict attention" and "keenly watchful" in defining the word *observant.* It includes in the definition of *observation* the phrase "the power of fixing the mind upon something." Good observing involves a fascination with what is being observed, much as new parents exhibit in observing their firstborn infant, or as a person exhibits while snorkeling on a reef for the first time.

If one is willing to focus on children, observe them without preconceptions, and be open to what one's inner eyes and ears reveal, then the children themselves, with their actions, voices, faces, and body language, will tell the observer what he or she needs to know and what one needs to describe in writing. The ability to observe objectively with unconditional regard and profound interest is possible for all teachers who are fascinated with what children do and how they do it.

An observer must be not only focused and interested but also completely open to whatever may transpire. Teachers should strive to be the kind of observers of children who are able to get inside children's heads and ride *silently* on the wheels that are going around. Teachers need to try not to put the words they want to hear into the mouths of children they are observing.

Here is a story that provides a humorous illustration of the preceding paragraph. In my assessment of a teacher candidate for the Child Development Associate competency-based credential a few years ago, I observed in her classroom during free-choice time. She was eager to demonstrate her use of open and extended questions, and was moving among various learning centers, interacting with children and asking questions.

She stopped near me where a little girl was intensely observing and playing with a yellow rubber duck in a dishpan of water. The teacher's plans indicated that the children had had recent science experiences with things that float and sink. The child we were observing had rummaged a knitted doll's hat from the housekeeping area, and had put the hat on the duck. This caused the duck to flop over instead of floating upright. When the child observed this, she took off the hat (which was a little big for the duck and covered his eyes) and replaced it a few times, but the duck continued to flop over, remaining only half afloat unless she held on to it.

The teacher's eyes sparkled as she asked the child, "Why do you think the duck is not floating very well?" One could almost physically hear the teacher's expectation of the child's unsaid words. She thought the child would say something about the hat making the duck too heavy to float the right way, or upright.

Well, the little girl put her hands on her hips and said emphatically to the teacher, "He is falling down because he can't see where he's going." This delightful answer, which both of us enjoyed immensely, was not the answer the teacher expected, but it was an excellent answer, indicating good thinking on the part of the child. This incident serves as a reminder that adults learn the most about children and their thought processes when they observe with open minds.

Record Keeping

One of the problems some teachers have in writing up observations is a lack of skill in writing objectively. Unfortunately, inservice training on how to write objective notes is a simple but important piece of teacher training that is frequently omitted by programs.

Teachers should describe in writing *exactly* what they see and hear, and should not use subjective generalizations in their notes. For example, it is inappropriate to say, "2/24: M was crabby and fussy." Instead, the note should describe exactly what the child said or did: "2/24: Today M cried and came to me for assistance at three different times during one hour of free choice. These incidents occurred after M confronted and struggled with other children over the use of the climber, the sand toys, and a puzzle."

If the teacher's anecdotal observation includes a possible reason for the child's behavior, it should be stated as a possible reason, not a fact, unless the reason is truly based in fact: "2/24: During the daily casual health check at arrival time, M looked very tired; red eyes. After calling the parent, I learned that M got very little sleep last night; M is not running a fever, but lack of sleep may be the reason for this behavior." The words in the observation notes should paint a brief but objective and detailed picture of a real, living child in a real-life situation.

Observation notes that are dated, that describe objectively, and that can be clearly read when retrieved are useful in planning and teaching. Subjective, undated, and unreadable notes are not helpful.

Here are some helpful hints for objective writing/recording of observations.

1. Record only the facts.
2. Try to record every detail; omit nothing.
3. Use action words (verbs) whenever possible.
4. Observe without interrupting action or conversation.
5. Record only what you see and hear.
6. Use words that describe; don't judge.
7. Record your facts in the exact order they occur.
8. "Red flag" words are subjective; avoid them. These are words that try to describe things that *cannot* be described objectively, like feelings, intelligence, reasons for doing things, and self-concept. Here are examples of red flag words:
   a. "Feelings" words: *sad, happy, crabby, lazy, laid back, cooperative, angry, kind*
   b. "Intelligence" words: *smart, bright, mediocre, overwhelmed, bewildered*
   c. "Reasons" words: *provoked, helpful, forced to, motivated, out-of-control*
   d. "Self-concept" words: *weak, strong, secure, insecure, self-esteem, pretty*

These hints were taken from the Head Start Training Guide "Observing and Recording: Tools for Decision Making," which is available online at www.headstartinfo.org, Head Start Publications. The "Observing and Recording" training guide also presents many excellent samples of child observation forms, such as summaries, running records, checklists, and anecdotal notes, all of which are in the public domain.

Early childhood program administrators and supervisors often contract with special education or mental health professionals who are required to supply periodic notes on the progress of children with special needs. These professionals should not be exempt from the requirements listed above to provide clear, objective, dated, signed, and readable observation notes that are shared with teachers.

All sorts of forms for collecting observation information are used by early childhood teachers, and teachers are continually trying out or designing new ones. The most important thing to know about whatever form you are using is, Does it work for *you?* The types of forms you use and their formats must be usable and efficient; they must work *for* you, not against you. In determining the effectiveness of your forms, you should be able to answer "yes" to the following questions:

1. Does this form help me collect the information I specifically want?
2. Does this form give me relevant information I can really put to use in planning and teaching?

3. Is it necessary to keep this form in a secure place? If so, do I have a safe place to keep it, so that a breach of confidentiality will not be an issue?
4. Do I have a system in place for easy retrieval of this information so that I can use it regularly in my planning, teaching, and my work with parents?

An Original Observation Form

An effective observation form helps staff to accomplish goals in a practical way. Sometimes teachers must take the initiative to create their own observation forms, especially if the form is to serve several purposes at once. The original observation form example seen in Figure 6.1 was designed to gather information on children in a cooperative preschool in which I was the teacher/director. The preschool served 24 5-year-olds with a staff of one qualified early childhood teacher and three assisting parents who took turns as staff, rotating day by day in a monthly cycle. Figure 6.1 combined some of the elements of a checklist with four other methods: running record, anecdotal notes, time sampling, and log.

The two main purposes of the form were to find out what activities children were engaged in during free-choice time, and to discover what skills were being practiced each day at "game" time or small-group time. Parents also wanted to know more about the ways children interacted with each other and the materials, and wanted me to have more opportunity to do individualized teaching, assessments, and running record observations in free-choice time.

In small-group time, the parents and I took notes on each child in our groups as we did the planned activity (same for all) for about 10 minutes. Short anecdotal notes were taken when possible. The notes were transferred to the child's weekly observation form, one form for each child, after school, during our after-school staff meeting. This information told us what activity took place each day in small group, and what skills were practiced during these activities. For example, if the children did a drawing with dictation, the skills practiced were fine motor and literacy.

During free-choice time, while I used a developmental assessment tool or did individualizing and running records, the three parent staff persons in three areas of the room used steno pads to record which children came into each learning area and what they played with. If time permitted, the parents also noted for how long and with whom children played. All the notes from all areas were transferred to the weekly observation form after school by placing the letter of the week next to all the materials or equipment the child used that day. By the end of the week, one could see exactly on what days children used various areas and equipment; this also told us what areas were being used or avoided by particular children.

The form was easy to use and collected objective information quickly. Using it as part of a system, combined with the enthusiasm of parents about their tasks, helped us to accomplish all our purposes. The weekly forms (30 by year's end) were put into the children's portfolios with other examples of their work and

Name _____ Week of _____

GAMES/SMALL GROUP

Mon. _____
Tues. _____
Wed. _____
Thurs. _____
Fri. _____

SKILLS PRACTICED

	M	T	W	T	F
Motor					
Perceptual					
Memory					
Literacy					
Problem Solving					

SMALL MUSCLE AREA

___ Peg boards   ___ Flannelboards   ___ Sorting games
___ Puzzles   ___ Parquetry   ___ Sewing/lacing
___ Legos   ___ Water play   ___ Shapes
___ Colorforms   ___ Bristle blocks   ___ Memory games
___ Playtiles   ___ Stringing   ___ Lotto

ART AREA

___ Playdo or clay   ___ Fingerpaint   ___ Paper and glue
___ Sand/texture table   ___ (Recycled) Junk   ___ with scissors
___ Easel painting   ___ Construction   ___ Other tempera painting
___ Crayons or markers   ___ Collage (any)   ___ Paper with scissors

LARGE MUSCLE AREA

___ Obstacle course   ___ Using nuts and bolts   ___ Rocking boat/steps
___ Tumbling mat   ___ Using pipes and joints   ___ Big hollow blocks
___ Balance beam   ___ Climber   ___ Unit blocks
___ Play with props   ___ Trucks   ___ Throwing and catching
___ Fishing with magnets   ___ Creative movement   ___ Using measuring devices

DRAMATIC PLAY

___ Housekeeping
___ Dollhouse
___ With other props
___ With puppets/dolls, etc.

BOOKS

___ Alone
___ With other children
___ With adult
___ Writing center

WOODWORKING

___ Hammer and nails
___ Screwdrivers and screws
___ Saws
___ Drill

SCIENCE/MATH

___ Animals   ___ Scales   ___ Magnifying glass
___ Battery   ___ Plants   ___ Measuring
___ Count/sets/graphs   ___ Magnets   ___ Cooking

Teacher Comments:
_____
_____
_____
_____

FIGURE 6.1 *Weekly Observation Form*

examined with great delight at monthly parent meetings, motivating a 90 percent attendance.

The greatest benefit of the form (Figure 6.1) was to the parents themselves. When they observed, even though they took brief and objective notes, they kept becoming better observers. They learned more about their own children, about other children, and about how intensely children work and learn through play experiences. At least five of these parents, as a result of their experiences, decided to go back to college to pursue early childhood endorsements or degrees, and some became directors of other preschools.

One parent (whose child is now 30 years old) said to me recently, "The experience of being a team teacher and observer helped me to see my child in an entirely different way than I saw her at home. That made a very positive impact on the kind of parenting I did over the following years." This original observation form and this story point out how important it is for teachers and parents to work in partnership, and it demonstrates that parents can and should be involved in the observation, recording, and planning process whenever possible.

If you believe this system would be too difficult to implement in programs with less than a 1 to 5 adult-child ratio, you might consider modifying the system. The form could be used only one or two days a week, or to observe only a few particular children each week.

Evaluating and Organizing Information for Appropriate Planning

We can see that early education teachers can gather a great variety of information from the children's parents, screening, developmental assessment tools, and ongoing observation. But gathering it will not lead to children's outcomes. Teachers must be able to compile and organize the information so they can *use* it to plan experiences that will lead children to *outcomes*.

Before they can use the information for planning, teachers must evaluate the information, which means looking at it carefully and reflecting on what it tells them about children. Then, teachers will need to organize the information and create a *system* for using it effectively in planning and in action.

We already know that most early education teachers write simple individual education plans (IEPs) or individual learning plans for each child, based on the information they've compiled. This form should be flexible so that it will reflect goals, developmental changes, and strategies. It should allow space for changes in evaluation (current development status) and changes in practices (experiences planned) that will match what is happening as children grow, develop, and reach new milestones.

A hard copy of the IEP documenting teachers' and parents' signatures is kept in a secure file. Because the information on these forms tells teachers the children's changing skill levels and needs, the information needs to be stored where it is easily accessible when teachers do daily and weekly planning. Some teachers simply date each IEP and write new ones each month or as needed. Others use new space on the same forms and add the dates as changes occur. Some teachers put the IEP information on the computer in an electronic file folder for each child, making changes as the year proceeds, but keep the hard copies locked in a file. Another possibility is to put the actual IEP into the child's record folder, in a locked file cabinet. Other teachers, for quicker retrieval, designate one folder for storing all the IEPs in the file cabinet. Some teachers use the IEPs to make an index file, and store the actual IEPs. These teachers use index cards to note each child's individual needs and the ways the teacher plans to meet theses needs. When the planned learning experiences actually occur, they are dated, and new cards are made for each child as needed.

In the past, when teachers did individualizing for only a few children with special needs, these various systems worked fairly well. There are several disadvantages, however, to any of these systems today, when teachers are expected to access children's information for lesson planning that includes individualized experiences, based on assessment, leading to outcomes for *every* child. To get to those outcomes for every child, a better system is needed.

Individualizing for Every Child

We already know, from Chapter 5, that individualized learning experiences should take place each day and be documented on the lesson plan, and that over a period of three to four weeks, the lesson plans would indicate that every child had one-on-one time for individualized attention of some kind. At that point, the individualization cycle would begin again, and this would continue all year.

In addition to the lesson plans, however, teachers need a system that *documents that the individualized experiences planned and implemented were based on actual needs for every child, as found in assessment.* The lesson plans would not document this. One would need to go to the IEP, the index file, or the computer files, and find that every entry in the lesson plans was based on the child's needs as seen in the IEP, which is based on observation and assessment. In fact, in using the preceding systems, when teachers make plans for individualizing (unless the teachers have photographic memories), they would need to go to the IEP, the index file, the computer file, or even the child's record folder before being able to choose appropriate individualized experiences to put into the lesson plans.

Additionally, after a month or so of school, the teacher needs a system that will show which days each child has had one-on-one attention or an individualized learning experience. Finding this out is further complicated by the fact that some children have one need and some have many needs. The system for individualizing, in planning and actual practice, must be fair and equitable to every child.

An Individualization to Outcomes System

I believe a different system for planning and action is needed—one that is practical and one in which the teachers can immediately access a summary of the needs of every child, as based on assessment, and know who they have worked with and who they have not. When this kind of system for planning is used, appropriate action in the form of individualized, scaffolded experiences to suit each child will take place, leading gradually to expected outcomes.

Summary Sheets: Using a System for Individualizing and Documentation

The Summary Sheet system works well for many programs that began using it when it was published in the first edition of this book. It is a simple and logical system. First, teachers should make a summary of the current needs of all the children in the group, on one piece of plain or lined paper. They can do this in a joint session by looking at or remembering information from parents, screening, assessment tools, and their personal observations.

Even though children's needs will undoubtedly change, a summary of children's needs at any starting point will provide teachers with what they need to get started. Teachers will be able to use the summary for at least one cycle or one month. At that point, teachers can either use the same Summary Sheet and mark it with a different color of ink, or make a new summary.

Many changes can occur in a month. Children who appeared withdrawn and didn't talk the first week of school may be chattering to friends by the third week. New children enter the program; others move away or leave the program. This is another reason to use a simple system and a simple summary sheet form. Let's practice by doing a Summary Sheet right now. Find a pencil, some paper, and one blank lesson plan form.

TRY THIS NOW

Most programs, most screening tools, and most observations focus on six to eight areas or learning domains. These are the categories about which teachers gather information on each child and make plans for individualized experiences that will lead children naturally and gradually to expected outcomes. You can choose the six most commonly addressed areas (Large Motor, Fine Motor, Language/Literacy, Cognitive/Problem Solving, Self, and Social) or create your summary based on your assessment framework. If you use the Work Sampling System for Head Start or the Head Start Outcomes Framework, you will have eight categories. For the purposes of this practice session, I will use six.

List the categories on the paper, leaving ample space under each heading for children's names. Now list the children's names under the categories where each child has specific needs, as were actually found in ongoing assessment. Do this activity with a classmate or another teacher, checking IEPs if necessary.

Ask each other, "Which children have problems in large-motor skills?" Put those names under "Large Motor." Do the same for each category. Use the child's first name and the first initial of the last name. Continue until all the children in your group are listed. Some will be listed only once, and some may be listed in several categories. All your children will have at least one area of need, because the outcomes you are reaching for are so varied. Do not list children in categories where assessment has not proven a need.

Put your lesson plan form next to the Summary Sheet. Think about what kind of activity or experience you want to use for individualizing next Monday, making up a date—for example, 9/13. Suppose you chose the category Fine Motor. Think of an activity that would help scaffold children's skills in that area. It might be stringing beads. Write "String beads" in the appropriate space on the lesson plan. Now choose one or two children with whom you will work on Monday, and put their initials next to "String beads." Next, on the *Summary Sheet*, put the date 9/13 next to the names of those two children, because that's the day you plan to do the individualizing. You might be wondering what to do if other children also want to string beads with you. It is fine to allow others to join you at a table, but your entire focus for 5 to 7 minutes, your interactions, and the dialogue you use as encouragement (scaffolding) will be on the two children with whom you're working.

Now think about what you want to do on Tuesday, 9/14, in some other category. Perhaps you choose Self, and you plan to give a particular child extra praise and attention concerning progress in self-help skills. On the lesson plan, enter "Praise self-help/dress; undress" and put the child's initials next to the activity. On the Summary Sheet, put the date 9/14 next to the child's name.

On Wednesday, 9/15, you may want to practice large-motor balance beam skills with two particular children. Put "Balance beam" on the lesson plan and put the children's initials next to that. On the Summary Sheet, put 9/15 next to those two names. Again, other children may actually use the balance beam during the free-choice time when you are working with your two children, but your focus for 5 to 7 minutes will be on them, and what you do to help them (scaffold the experience) will be individualized for them.

Perhaps the next day in the category of Social, you would ask two children to "partner" on certain activities, or be "helpers" for a special job. You would proceed in the same way, writing the activity and initials "(M. I. partner J. S.; sort new blocks)" and then put the date 9/16 on the Summary Sheet.

Continue this method for the entire week's lesson plans. The Summary Sheet will tell you which children have been worked with and which have not. If you continue this method with the next few weeks' lesson plans, always noting dates on the Summary Sheet, eventually all the names under each of the categories will have dates next to them. At that point, you can start again with a different color for dates, or make a new Summary Sheet, saving old ones for documentation.

Have you noticed that some children will have more turns within an individualizing cycle than others? This is not "equal" but it's perfectly fair and equitable. Teachers must always base individualizing on actual needs found in assessment, and some children will need more attention than others due to multiple needs. If Jane's only need is to learn to share, and she gets one-on-one individualization and scaffolding based on that need, she is also being treated fairly within every individualization cycle.

When teachers use the Summary Sheet system in actual day-to-day practice, no child is left out. Everyone gets individualized and scaffolded experiences based on personal needs and expected outcomes, and the individualization leading to outcomes is well documented. If you are a teacher using Head Start Outcomes Framework, remember that *your individualized teaching must match the needs of each child as found in your assessment.* A child's needs might not always be specific Head Start Outcomes, but many one-on-one activities will *lead* to Head Start Outcomes.

TIP

One more important point about Summary Sheets and lesson plans needs to be made. If individualizing occurs spontaneously with a particular child, and if what happened was an important experience that helped to meet one of the child's needs, as found in assessment, the teacher should, after the fact, note (and date) the individualizing that occurred on both the lesson plan and on the Summary Sheet.

In closing this section, you should realize that individualizing doesn't mean *only* planned teacher-child interactions or scaffolded learning experiences. What teachers do to individualize will depend on the needs of the group and of particular children in that group. The ways teachers arrange the classroom individualizes that room for that particular group of children. It might be arranged so that children with disabilities can easily access all learning centers; special equipment might even be set up for those children. It might be arranged and decorated to build pride in the culture and heritage of the children.

Volunteers to work at the computer center with particular children might be a part of the teacher's individualizing plans. The teacher may individualize by inviting a particular child under stress to start each day by playing with playdough, clay, or water, which will help release tension and anxiety. When a new baby arrives in a family, most teachers will give individualized attention or extra hugs and smiles to the child who might feel temporarily left out. When a teacher helps a shy child enter a peer group at play, that is also individualizing.

Offering several types of art media in the art area is one way to individualize. Some children enjoy fingerpainting, and some would rather use crayons and markers. Some like to paint on the easel, and some would rather paint on paper spread on a table. Some children exhibit creativity in the dramatic play and blocks areas, and avoid the art area. Offering many play slots or play spaces in many learning centers is another way to individualize to meet the varied interests and different learning styles of children.

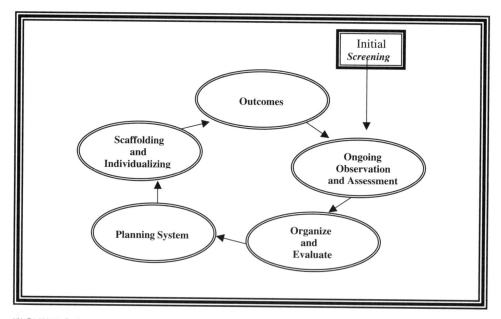

FIGURE 6.2 Individualization Flowchart

The bottom line, however, is this: If the curriculum includes goals to have each child reach certain expected outcomes in as many as eight specific learning domains, a practical and efficient system for individualized teaching that will make that happen in a fair and equitable manner for every child is *absolutely necessary.*

In Figure 6.2, look at the sequence of events in the individualization process only as it relates to the child and to the early childhood teacher. Note that when teachers and programs have resultant information about outcomes, the next step will always be to analyze the outcomes information so that improvements can be made in both teacher planning and program quality.

Summary

This chapter has defined and described assessment, screening, and various observation methods. Guidelines have been presented to help the teacher choose screening, assessment, and observation tools, as well as forms used in record-keeping. We have discussed the role of the teacher as an observer, recorder, and manager of information, and stressed the importance of open attitudes and objectivity in both observing and recording.

The importance of the teacher's use of assessment methods and systems to do a better and more consistently documented job of individualized teaching have been emphasized. Screening and observation information can only help the teacher to meet individual needs when it can be accessed and used effectively in individualizing that leads to positive outcomes for every child.

A Summary Sheet system was shared as an example of a practical method to help teachers plan and document individualized teaching for every child based on assessment. The chapter itself was designed to show the flow of the "assessment-to-outcomes" process—screening, ongoing assessment and observation, evaluation and planning, and individualizing. Another emphasis in this chapter has been observation and the importance of involving parents as partners in the assessment and planning process. Teachers sometimes need to design their own systems and forms for gathering and using information. An example of such a form and its specific uses was shared, along with the impact this experience had on parent observers. In Chapter 7, we will explore ways to organize curriculum information for effective use.

Self-Study Activities

1. If you are an early childhood student or teacher, you are often required to do observations of children. Refer to the outline of observation methods in this chapter and examine your own methods. What methods are you using? If these are narrative methods, what type are they? How can you improve your observations and make them more useful?

2. Examine the screening instruments being used in your program, and, if possible, compare them to others. Are the screening instruments your program uses beneficial in terms of the questions presented in this chapter? If not, what will you, as a professional, do about your concerns? Would you bring your concerns to a staff meeting? How would this be put on the agenda? Outline what you would say in a letter or at a meeting.

3. Examine the forms you are using in terms of the questions presented in this chapter. Using blank copies, try to redesign a form to make it more practical and usable. Experiment with designs for combining the two forms into one format.

4. Do one child observation as a running record, using objective and descriptive narration. Submit it to your instructor or supervisor,

Resources and Suggested Readings

Beatty, Jan. *Observing Development in the Young Child,* 4th ed. Upper Saddle River, NJ: Prentice-Hall/Simon & Schuster, 1998.

Benjamin, Ann. "Observations in Early Childhood Classrooms: Advice from the Field." *Young Children,* 49, 6 (1994): 14–20.

Berk, Laura E., & Winsler, Adam. *Scaffolding Children's Learning: Vygotsky and Early Childhood Education.* Washington, DC: National Association for the Education of Young Children, 1995.

Billman, Jean, & Sherman, Janice. *Observation and Participation in Early Childhood Settings.* Boston: Allyn and Bacon, 1996.

Bondurant-Utz, Judith, & Luciano, Lenore B. *A Practical Guide to Infant and Preschool Assessment in Special Education.* Boston: Allyn and Bacon, 1994.

Bredekamp, Sue, & Rosegrant, Teresa, eds. *Reaching Potentials: Appropriate Curriculum and Assessment of Young Children,* Vol. 1. Washington, DC: National Association for the Education of Young Children, 1992.

Brewer, Jo Ann. *Introduction to Early Childhood Education, Preschool through Primary Grades.* Boston: Allyn and Bacon, *1995.*

Curtis, Debbie, and Carter, Margie. *The Art of Awareness: How Observation Can Transform Your Teaching.* St. Paul, MN: Redleaf, 2000.

Dodge, Diane Trister; Colker, Laura; & Heroman, Cate. *Connecting Content, Teaching and Learning: A Supplement to the Creative Curriculum for Early Childhood*, 3rd ed. Washington, DC: Teaching Strategies, 2000.

Garlick, Betty. *Evaluating Children's Progress through Observation.* Paper presented at Michigan State University, February 1, 1980, p. 1.

Head Start Bureau, Administration for Children and Families, Department of Health and Human Services. *Head Start Bulletin No. 43, Screening and Assessment in Head Start.* Washington, DC: U.S. Department of Health and Human Services, 1993.

Head Start Bureau, Administration for Children and Families, U.S. Department of Health and Human Services. "Head Start Outcomes Framework." *Head Start Issue 70, Screening and Assessment in Head Start.* Washington, DC: Department of Health and Human Services, 2001, pp. 44–50.

Head Start Bureau, Administration for Children and Families, U.S. Department of Health and Human Services. *The Head Start Path to Positive Child Outcomes.* Washington, DC: U.S. Department of Health and Human Services, 2000.

Head Start Bureau, Administration for Children and Families, U.S. Department of Health and Human Services. *Observation and Recording: Tools for Decision Making.* Washington, DC: U.S. Department of Health and Human Services, 1998.

Hills, Tynette W. "Assessment in Context—Teachers and Children at Work." *Young Children,* 48, 5 (1993): 20–33.

Isenberg, Joan P., & Jalongo, Mary R. *Major Trends and Issues in Early Childhood Education: Challenges, Controversies and Insights.* New York: Teachers College Press, 1997.

Kamii, Constance, ed. *Achievement Testing in the Early Grades: The Games Grown Ups Play.*

Washington, DC: National Association for the Education of Young Children, 1990.

McAfee, Oralie, & Leong. Deborah. *Assessing and Guiding Young Children's Development and Learning.* Boston: Allyn and Bacon, 1994, p. 111.

Meisels, Samuel J. *Developmental Screening in Early Childhood: A Guide,* 3rd ed. Washington, DC: National Association for the Education of Young Children, 1985, 1989.

Meisels, Samuel; Dichtelmiller, Margo; Jablon, Judy; & Marsden, Dorothea. *The Work Sampling System,* 4th ed., and *Work Sampling System for Head Start.* Ann Arbor, MI: Rebus, Inc., 2001.

Meisels, Samuel; Dombro, Amy; Marsden, Dorothea; Weston, Donna; & Jewkes, Abigail. *The Ounce of Prevention Scale.* Pearson Education, Inc., publishing as Pearson Early Learning New York, NY.

Petersen, Evelyn. "Individualizing for Every Child: Can We Do It?" *Children and Families Magazine,* 17, 4 (1998): 30–37.

Petersen, Evelyn, ed. *Individualizing for Each Child...You Can Do It.* Videocassette. Bloomfield Hills, MI: The Program Source International, 1999.

Teaching Strategies, Inc. *The Creative Curriculum Developmental Continuum Assessment Toolkit for Ages 3–5.* Washington, DC: Author, 2001.

Websites

www.ericeece.org   ERIC, the Educational Resource Information Center/Elementary and Early Childhood Education Clearinghouse at the University of Illinois, 805 West Pennsylvania Avenue, Urbana-Champaign IL 61801, provides information about current research and developments in the field of education and maintains a wide selection of materials on screening and observation

www.headstartinfo.org   Head Start publications and information

7 Interest-Based Curriculum

Horizontal Planning

In the next three chapters we are going to explore ways to organize curriculum information so that it can be used systematically and effectively in reaching goals and in helping children reach outcomes. In doing this, we will be looking at ways teachers translate ideas from thought to paper, and from paper to appropriate children's learning experiences. These processes often incorporate systems.

To *organize* is to see something in its entirety, and then to perceive ways to break it down into smaller parts that can be categorized or ordered, and then more easily and systematically used. We will be exploring ways to organize and use each of the two broad types of early childhood curriculum information, but first we need to see the task in its entirety.

All Curriculum Information

To see the "big picture" of early childhood curriculum ideas and information, one must think about where teachers get information. Teachers get curriculum information from personal living and teaching experiences, as well as from books, magazines, and handouts. Teachers get curriculum ideas from other teachers, supervisors, and friends, and from workshops and conferences they've attended. They also get curriculum information from the children themselves, from parents and elders, and from the cultures of the communities in which they live. Information and ideas are obtained from events occurring in communities, and from the seasons, climate, and geography of one's setting.

The more years one teaches, the more curriculum ideas and information one collects. The interesting thing about this is that one wants to use *all* of these good ideas when working with children. So, teachers save ideas in folders, in envelopes, in cupboards, and in boxes under the bed, discarding nothing. Sometimes the amount of curriculum information collected is so overwhelming that they feel smothered. Teachers want to use the ideas but there are so many, they don't know how to begin. The situation might look something like a mountain of information, under which teachers are struggling to function (see Figure 7.1).

So how do you break down this mountain into manageable parts you can organize? Think about the way you ask children to organize the task of putting away unit blocks after an active hour of construction, when they are spread out all over the rug. Children think this task is enormous, because they actually believe that there are three times as many blocks as when they started to play.

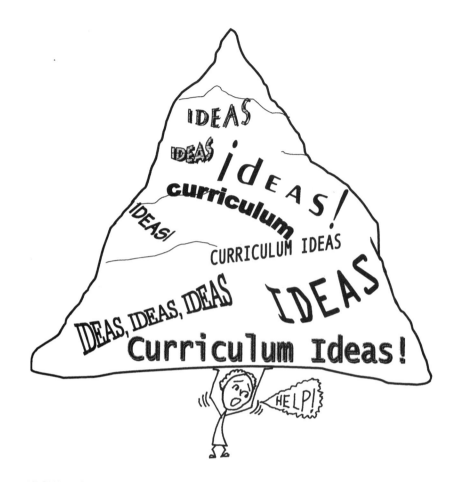

FIGURE 7.1   A Mountain of Ideas

(Young children cannot "conserve" very well; the blocks are spread out, so they believe there are more.) What is the first thing you ask children to do that will help them in this task?

Perhaps you suggest that they sort the blocks into their different types, putting them into small piles—square ones, long rectangles, short rectangles, and so on. Now that the task has been broken down into smaller parts, the job doesn't look so big. It becomes easy and fun to do. Some children carry the piles and some arrange them on the shelves, matching them to perceptual cues taped or drawn on the shelves. Teachers can begin to organize their mountain of curriculum information in the same way. There are only two basic kinds of curriculum information in that mountain, so let's split the mountain into two, more manageable halves, as shown in Figure 7.2.

Recall that Chapters 1 and 6 stated that all curriculum information is composed of two broad types: interest-based information and skill-based information. The *interest-based information* is made up of both thematic and emergent curriculum ideas, because in both cases, the ideas are based on the interests of the teachers and the children. In this chapter we will learn more about these two

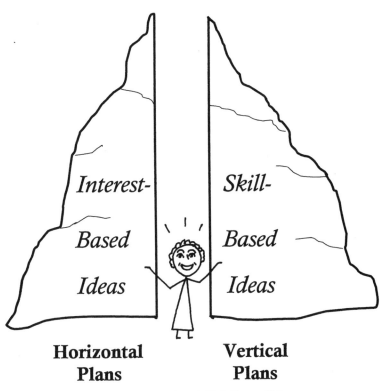

FIGURE 7.2   Interest-Based and Skill-Based Ideas

types of curriculum information, and find ways to effectively organize and use them to benefit children and meet curriculum goals. In Chapter 8, we'll organize skill-based information and explore a system for scaffolding it and using it effectively. Now, we need to find ways of organizing interest-based information, starting with thematic curriculum.

Systems for Using Thematic Curriculum

Most teachers already have a system for breaking down and organizing theme-based curriculum information that works very well, even if they may not realize that they're using a system. Teachers list a variety of themes or topics that they believe will interest children and provide springboards for the development of factual content and knowledge. (Recall that knowledge was one of the four types of learning to consider in curriculum development.) Teachers arrange the themes in a logical order, from the beginning to end of the program year, usually matching the themes to things the children are feeling or experiencing as the year proceeds. It's called a *horizontal plan* because it can be represented in a horizontal time line in which themes and subthemes or thematic units appear as consecutive milestones along the time line. A drawing to represent the horizontal plan (see Figure 7.3) can help teachers see how they are organizing and managing thematic information.

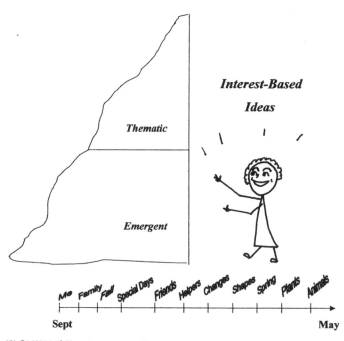

FIGURE 7.3 Interest-Based Horizontal Planning

In the process of choosing topics, some teachers draw *preplanning webs*, putting a primary topic of interest in a middle circle, and drawing lines to other circles containing related topics that might develop into subthemes, emergent curriculum, or projects. *Webbing* is another way that teachers organize and manage thematic information. Webbing sometimes helps teachers to prioritize the potential themes and subthemes or units, keeping the ones that may generate the most interest and investigation, and discarding others. You will see a planning web later in this chapter.

For effective utilization, whether they come from the teacher's lists or planning webs, themes should appear in a written, long-range plan for the year. One way to represent this plan is the drawing in Figure 7.3. Another way in which helpful detail can be added is in a written outline in which both thematic and emergent curriculum is organized so that effective implementation can happen.

Horizontal Plan Outlines

It is necessary to discuss the importance of writing an outline of the teacher's horizontal plan for using interest-based curriculum. An outline requires teachers to organize and order their curriculum information. Outlining also has many advantages for children and staff:

1. Outlines are flexible; flexibility is a must for early childhood teachers.
2. The outline format presents a natural, gradual flow of ideas.
3. Outlines clearly show overall themes or goals, as well as primary themes and subthemes.

4. Thematic units can easily be changed to match children's needs and interests.
5. Emergent curriculum resulting from new interests can be easily incorporated.
6. No dates or weeks for themes are rigidly set in stone; time frames are flexible.
7. Outlines help teachers do advance planning.
8. Staff can move along the horizontal plan outline without deadlines, staying in tune with the changing developmental needs and interests of children and the group.

In the example of horizontal planning seen in Figure 7.4, the overriding goals are the child's self-esteem, caring about others, and caring about the world in which he or she lives. Themes relating to these three goals recur throughout the year, incorporating activities that make children feel special and competent, helping them understand and be proud of their own capabilities, and helping them understand others and the world around them. The unspoken but implied question is, "Who am I and how do I fit in?" As children proceed through the year, they begin to have some answers that are age appropriate.

Notice the seven major headings in the outline of Figure 7.4. Parts I, II, and III, "Me and My World," "My Expanding World," and "Special Days in My World," emphasize self-esteem. Parts IV and V, "Learning More about My World," emphasize caring about both self and others. Parts VI and VII, "Sharing My World," focus on caring about the world. The seven parts of the outline in Figure 7.4 match the seven time blocks in Appendix A of this book.

In all seven parts of the outline and the time blocks, Self, Caring, Changes, Health (including nutrition), and Safety are recurring subthemes. Health and safety are integral parts of caring about oneself, and coping with change is a necessary life skill that is also important to self-esteem. You will also find many themes relating to caring about others—family, friends, and adults who help or teach the child, as well as animals in the child's world.

Many of the learning experiences in the various categories of Appendix A will show a strong emphasis on self-concept and positive social skills. For example, there are entries about weighing and measuring children, being proud of their bodies, "I Can" activities, doing group projects, and discussing family, friends, and adults who the children care about and who help them learn and grow.

It should be noted that the horizontal plan in Figure 7.4 was developed for a program in northern Michigan and reflects the seasons, common events, plants, and climate of that geographic area. If the program were in Anchorage, Alaska, the themes occurring in the different months of the year would include berry picking, hunting, skinning and drying fur, salmon fishing, smoking salmon, and native plants and roots to harvest and eat. The themes about homes and families would include Native elders, tribes and extended families, and ancestors' homes. Themes must always reflect the values and cultures of children and families in the program. Caution should be used in purchasing "theme books" unless they are used only as curriculum supplements.

FIGURE 7.4 *Example of a* Horizontal Plan

I. Me and My World (September/October)
  A. Me
     1. My body
     2. My health and fitness
     3. My senses
     4. My feelings
     5. My safety
  B. Families
     1. My family
     2. Brothers and sisters
     3. Other families
  C. Homes
     1. My home
     2. Other kinds of homes
     3. Family fun (leisure interests, hobbies)
     4. Family routines (rules, eating sleeping, beds)

II. My Expanding World (October/November)
  A. Friends
  B. Changes
     1. In air, weather, sky
     2. In the water around us
     3. In things that grow in the earth around us
  C. Foods
     1. Of the orchard (fruits and seeds, apples)
     2. Of the water (lakes or sea)
     3. Of gardens or farms (squashes, pumpkins)
     4. Breads—food everyone eats

III. Special Days in My World (November/December)
  A. Changes in seasons and special days
  B. Hunting and gun safety
  C. Holidays—what they mean to us
     1. Family fun and family traditions
     2. Friends and company
     3. Shopping and gifts
     4. Traveling

IV. Learning More about My World (January/February)
  A. How I learn best
     1. My senses; my questions
     2. Experiments and changes
  B. Shapes are all around us
  C. Staying healthy keeps me learning
  D. Learning from friends

V. Learning More about My World (February/March)
  A. Adults help me learn (include snow plowers, trash collectors, linemen, etc., not just professionals)

(continued)

FIGURE 7.4   *continued*

B. Important places where I learn
C. Staying safe and healthy as I learn

VI. Sharing My World (March/April)
   A. My world is always changing
   B. Seasons and timelines
   C. Changes in the environment

VII. Sharing My World (April/May)
   A. Plants grow, change, and share my world
      1. Baby plants (seeds, cuttings, care)
      2. Big plants (trees, flowers, food plants, care)
      3. Plants help us and need our help
   B. How animals grow, change, and share my world
      1. Animal babies (and human babies)
      2. Animal "clothes" or coverings (and ours)
      3. Animal homes (and ours)
         a. Animals that fly
         b. Animals in the sea, water, and mud
         c. Animals in the woods, forests, and meadows
         d. Animals in the desert and mountains
         e. Animals on farms or in zoos
      4. Animals help us and need our help

In actual practice of the Figure 7.4 plan, themes often led to emergent interests. "Community Helpers" led to emergent curriculum about tools and work vehicles; "Holidays" led to transportation and travel curriculum; "Shapes Around Us" led to heart shapes and to healthy hearts, in which materials from the American Heart Association were used to develop curriculum.

The outline format allows teachers to include, expand, and build on emerging interests in long-range and daily lesson planning. The pace of steps in covering the topics on an outline may be altered in doing this, but changes in pace do not detract from the goals and direction of the teacher's plan. Flexible time frames in an outline system are easier to work with than specific dates, and are more developmentally appropriate.

Themes: Making Choices

Although teachers draw their ideas for themes from many sources, best practice dictates that they should choose themes that are the most relevant to program priorities and to the children and families with whom they work. Thematic content should reflect the changing interests of children and families, community events, the program's and teacher's values, cultural values and considerations, and the geography and climate that influence curriculum choices. Usually, simple themes are explored at the beginning of the year, and become more complex as the year progresses, matching children's development.

Sometimes teachers need to hold their own interest in a particular theme in check until the children's interests and the values of the theme are realistically evaluated. In other words, teachers should avoid the temptation to choose a theme because they think it's "neat" or "cute." Teachers should be honest with themselves about the benefits to children of the themes they choose. Before making a decision, it is wise to evaluate a potential theme by writing down specific things children might learn or gain from experiences connected with it.

Themes that might cause children to act aggressively should be very carefully evaluated. For example, in many groups of 3- and 4-year-olds, dinosaur themes would not be appropriate, and knowledge about dinosaurs in the long distant past would be too abstract. This theme is usually more effectively used with 5- to 8-year-olds.

In the system for organizing thematic information, the teacher's thinking and planning about interest-based curriculum proceeds from ideas and anticipatory webs to a written representation or an outline, and from there, into actual use in lesson plans. (Ideas that don't get into lesson plans are usually not used.) Lesson plan forms (Chapter 5) have spaces where thematic experiences can be entered. These experiences are most often seen in adult-directed time entries (both large and small group) and in spaces on the lesson plan form that describe what happens in free-choice time.

It's important, however, not to become a perpetuator of "theme overkill." If your theme is the color green, that does not mean that every single thing you do that week must relate to the color green. Many activities are not meant to enhance themes, but to meet individual needs or goals. Teachers provide other hands-on materials and activities every day, simply because children love them and learn from using them (blocks, art media, water/sand, dramatic play, wheel toys, etc.). Themes should not be overwhelming; they should be integrated into the day in the same way that certain colors of thread are repeated in a pattern, adding richness, cohesiveness, and interest to a design.

TIP

Teachers should have the long-range written plan for thematic curriculum posted or nearby when doing lesson plans. When the written outline or the time line is in view, it is easier to see other thematic or emergent possibilities that might be incorporated in the future. The overall direction of the plan also helps teachers do advance planning for thematic units, such as arranging for visitors or field trips or making notes on special items and artifacts the teacher may want to gather for children to use with a theme or a project.

Systems for Using Emergent Curriculum

Emergent curriculum is the other kind of interest-based curriculum content. Emerging curriculum can be sparked by children's interest in a teacher's theme or subtheme that they want to investigate. Teachers would expand the original theme to meet children's interests, perhaps even encouraging children to develop investigative and collaborative projects. Projects are still another way teachers organize, systemize, and use interest-based curriculum information efficiently.

Children's interests can also emerge in other ways, from spontaneous incidents or "teachable moments" that happen in the classroom. For example, a fuzzy, brown caterpillar crawling along the window sill might spark excitement and emergent curriculum about caterpillars. To respond, the teacher might have the children build a terrarium so they could observe the caterpillar more closely. The children might draw, paint, or construct caterpillars, or move like caterpillars to music, or read the book *The Hungry Caterpillar*. While this is happening, the teacher would need to find out what prior knowledge and new questions children have about caterpillars, and decide whether this topic would generate enough interest to be a new theme or project to add to the horizontal plan. A continued high-interest level would be the deciding factor.

Projects

Both emergent and thematic curricula are vehicles for expanding knowledge or factual content about a subject. Some types of emerging interests last only a day or two, and some, if they become investigative projects, may go on for two or three weeks or, with older children, for months. Projects should continue for as long as children's interest and learning remain high.

In addition to gaining more knowledge as they work on collaborative projects, children learn and practice many skills: investigation, group discussion and problem solving, data and artifact collection, creative representation, construction, comparison and evaluation, and written or dictated summations of what has been completed or learned. Field trips are taken, and interviews take place with people who have expert knowledge about the subject.

One October, in a kindergarten classroom I was observing, the children were decorating the room for Halloween and developed an enthusiastic interest in bats. In this case, the teacher and children did a planning web and the teacher listed the children's questions about bats, the things they wanted to investigate. Because of children's emerging interest, the study of bats became emergent curriculum, and was added to the teacher's themes and interest-based curriculum content. Through children's individual and collaborative group investigations, many skills were practiced, including Internet information searches.

Two children, with the help of a parent volunteer, did a simple Internet search that led to a list of activities from which children learned many more facts about bats, and found crossword puzzles and games relating to bats that they could use. Other children found pictures or photos of bats, and drew, painted, or created paper bats that were hung upside down from tree twigs. Others found stories and books to share with the group. One child asked parents to help contact a taxidermist who brought the children a stuffed bat they could examine closely. With the facilitation of the teacher and other adults, children answered their own questions about bats, starting with whether it was a bird, since it could fly, or a mammal, since it was furry. Representation through construction, drawings, and writing helped document what was learned. The teacher's daily journal about the project was further documentation of the curriculum goals that were met.

Planning Webs

Just as children represent their learning with drawings, teachers' drawings of web plans represent ways to organize and systematically use emergent, interest-based curriculum. For example, if a teacher in Michigan used the theme of "Fall," the emerging interests of children might grow from the experience of visiting an apple orchard. Apples may have been a subtheme of "Fall" in a thematic web plan. Other subthemes would also be seen—such as seeds, fall leaves, pumpkins, and harvest foods. These subthemes might lead to other topics, such as traveling seeds and harvest celebrations. Webs can be used as a system of organizing planning. They can also be used to keep track of emerging curriculum and its direction as it develops.

Suppose apples became a motivating interest. The teacher would ask questions to determine what children know about apples and what they want to find out. An anticipatory or preplanning web might show children's interests in investigating types and colors of apples, harvesting and storing apples, foods made from apples, apple trees, other fruit trees, fruit tree flowers, and ways to protect fruit trees from damage. A project-planning web would organize the curriculum as it developed during investigation.

Even if the theme of apples were not developed into a project, teachers could build daily curriculum on the emerging interests of children about apples by adding more materials to the setting and more activities to the lesson plan. Learning experiences might include stories about apples, art creations about apples, creative representations made with apples, sorting, ordering and categorizing apples, cutting up apples for snack, or making apple crisp or apple sauce and describing the process in a dictated experience story. The teacher would simultaneously integrate skill-based experiences into the lesson plans.

The apple theme and its emergent curriculum would work well in Michigan, but would not work at all in programs whose economic geography doesn't include apples and fruit orchards. Successful themes and emergent projects must be meaningful and culturally relevant to children and families.

One example that would probably work for most programs is the study of dirt or soil. This interest might emerge from the children's interest in mud and dirt in the outdoor play area that is often tracked into the center. A multitude of topics can be imagined when teachers list questions representing children's interests. If the questions spark even more interest, the children and teacher would begin a project, organizing the emerging curriculum with a planning web (see Figure 7.5), such as the following:

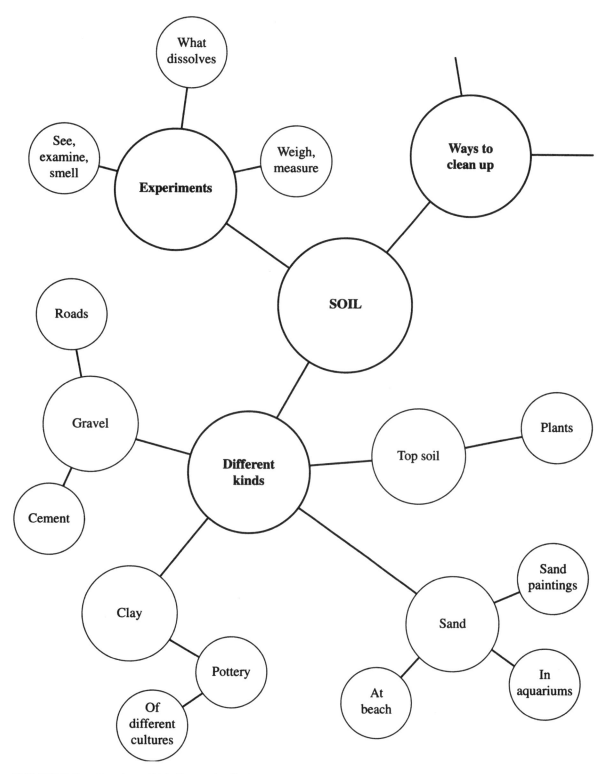

FIGURE 7.5   Teaching Web Example: Soil

Questions

1. How do we clean up mud and dirt?
2. Will different kinds of soil or dirt clean up differently?
3. What kinds of soil can we find? (sand, topsoil, clay, gravel-mix)
4. What experiments can we do with soil? (see with magnification, smell, weigh, try to dissolve, see what disappears into it)

Examining topsoil could lead to planting seeds and finding out what they need to grow. Examining clay could lead to exploring different kinds of clay and making things from clay. This in turn could lead to Internet searches about pottery and examining pottery of different cultures. A web keeps the information and investigations organized so curriculum can expand in meaningful directions.

Teachable Moments

It is easy to see that a great deal of emergent curriculum springs from the teacher's ability to respond to children in *teachable moments*. The ability to "think on your feet," respond to children, and then expand on learning in appropriate ways whenever a spontaneous moment occurs is the mark of an excellent early childhood educator. What I have found in the field is that teachers who consistently demonstrate this ability are also teachers who create careful and comprehensive lesson plans. Their plans demonstrate both interest-based and skill-based planning, long-range and monthly goals, and daily objectives.

Some of you might wonder how such careful planners could also be spontaneous teachers. Detailed and comprehensive planning might also characterize a person who has rigid expectations, or one who lacks the creativity and divergent thinking skills necessary to respond spontaneously to incidental teaching moments. Assuming that a person who creates careful lesson plans is one who *never* could be spontaneous is just as biased as assuming that a "free spirit" sort of teacher will *always* be able to respond to teachable moments. Conclusions on this interesting issue, if any, must be based on real experience and not on assumptions.

The best way to explain what I have seen in practice—that most teachers who do detailed lesson plans are also those most likely to risk changing their plans to capitalize on a teachable moment—is the way a college instructor once explained it to me as a student: Those who have a strong, healthy tree with strong roots and strong primary branches are those who are the most likely to go out on a limb.

Strong horizontal and vertical planning systems—time lines, outlines, webs, and projects—are the strong roots and the tree of the teacher's curriculum. Teachers who have mastered these elements can always risk going out on a limb or a smaller branch (leaving the lesson plan to capitalize on teachable moments) because the tree is strong and will always be there for them, whenever they want to return.

Summary

In this chapter we have discussed emergent and thematic curriculum, both of which are composed of interest-based information for curriculum. We have seen that much more content learning can occur when teachers expand and build on the children's interests, develop themes and projects based on these interests, and put their plans in written form. Daily lesson planning and advance planning are easier to accomplish when one has a written horizontal plan for the year.

A horizontal plan in outline form was suggested because of its many advantages. An outline format is more flexible and more in tune with the changing interests of children than plans that are dependent on rigid time lines and dates. Horizontal planning among teachers can and should differ on the basis of personal values; program priorities; the interests of children, parents, or the community; and the geographic nature and culture of the program's location.

Emergent curriculum content often springs from spontaneous incidents that spark high interest in children. Teachers organize this content with lists, webs, and projects.

Themes and emergent activities should make an ongoing written appearance in lesson plans, but not be overwhelming. Many activities chosen for daily and weekly lesson plans will mesh with and reinforce a theme. However, other activities in daily lesson plans are chosen because they help the children learn particular skills. These skill-based activities, occurring regularly throughout the year, are another very important kind of curriculum planning that proceeds simultaneously with horizontal planning. Skill-based information is the *vertical* part of the curriculum, which is the subject of the next chapter and the other half of the mountain of information we are organizing.

Self-Study Activities

1. Critique a thematic unit you have written or used in terms of the children's parents and the community in which you live. Would adults be interested and supportive of your choice?

What additional ideas might they want you to add?

2. Choose one thematic unit that you have done. Now imagine your program and class-

room in an entirely different geographic location and climate, and find ways to modify your web or thematic unit to fit that new culture. For example, what would change if you lived in the desert of the Southwest, or in Anchorage, Alaska?

3. Develop a horizontal plan outline for the year.

Resources and Suggested Readings

Barbour, Nita, & Seefeldt, Carol. *Developmental Continuity across Preschool and Primary Grades: Implications for Teachers.* Wheaton, MD: Association for Childhood Education International, 1993.

Becker, Joni; Reid, Karen; Steinhaus, Pat; & Wieck, Peggy. *Themestorming: How to Build Your Own Theme-Based Curriculum the Easy Way.* Beltsville, MD: Gryphon House, 1994.

Berry, Carla F, & Mindes, Gayle. *Planning a Theme-Based Curriculum: Goals, Themes, Activities, and Planning Guides for 4's and S's.* New York: Goodyear Books/HarperCollins, 1993.

Brewer, Jo Ann. *Introduction to Early Childhood Education—Preschool through Primary Grades.* Boston: Allyn and Bacon, 1995.

Cromwell, Ellen S. *Early Childhood Education: A Whole-Child Curriculum for Ages 2–5,* 2nd ed. Boston: Allyn and Bacon, 2000.

Fortson, Laura Rogers, & Reiff, Judith. *Early Childhood Curriculum: Open Structures for Integrative Learning.* Boston: Allyn and Bacon, 1995.

Helm, Judy, & Katz, Lillian. *Young Investigators: The Project Approach in the Early Years.* New York: Teachers College Press, 2001.

Jones, Elizabeth; Evans, K.; & Rencken, K. S. *The Lively Kindergarten: Emergent Curriculum in Action.* Washington, DC: National Association for the Education of Young Children, 2001.

Jones, Elizabeth, & Nimmo, John. *Emergent Curriculum.* Washington, DC: National Association for the Education of Young Children, 1994.

Katz, Lillian, & Chard, Sylvia C. *Engaging Children's Minds: The Project Approach.* Norwood, NJ: Ablex, 1989.

Kieff, Judith E., & Casbergue, Renee. *Playful Learning and Teaching: Integrating Play into Preschool and Primary Programs.* Boston: Allyn and Bacon, 2001.

8 Skill-Based Curriculum

Vertical Planning

PART I: THE SYSTEMATIC MANAGEMENT OF SKILL-BASED ACTIVITIES

The two interest-based parts of curriculum information that make up the teacher's horizontal planning emphasize interesting factual content that adds to the child's body of knowledge. The vertical curriculum emphasizes skill-based planning that helps children develop many cognitive and psychomotor skills, language skills, and process thinking skills. These skills also help children to construct their own knowledge.

Planned activities based on vertical curriculum information include many types of problem-solving experiences such as observing, describing, counting, measuring, experimenting, evaluating, and comparing. Activities also include matching, grouping, ordering, pairing, and cause-and-effect experiences. In addition, the vertical curriculum consists of language and literacy experiences, many large- and fine-motor activities, and perceptual and memory experiences that are both auditory and visual.

Helping children develop a balance of these skills, and teaching these skills at the right time, developmentally, for each child, is a tall order. It was these two issues that motivated me to develop the vertical curriculum planning system in this chapter. At the end of each year, when my 4-year-olds went on to kindergarten, I wondered if I had really done my best to provide a balance of practice in all of the skills children needed. Was I doing too much in the creative arts, language, dramatic play, and natural science, and not enough math and literacy? Were the children competent in all motor skills? I also wondered if I was presenting some skill-based experiences too early or too late for the diverse developmental levels in my group. I wanted to be positive that I was introducing and scaffolding skill-based experiences at the right times, and presenting a balance of all types of skills. I wanted a system to help me do this so that every child would benefit.

To develop the system, I researched past lesson plans to list all the kinds of skill-based experiences I had done over a four-year period, and sorted these activities into five types. Next, I took each skill-based activity in each of the five groups and broke it down into step-by-step parts, leading from simple to complex, or beginning to mastery. The Montessori approach for using materials inspired me in this task. When I was finished, the data I had gave me the foundation of the management system I developed and used successfully with 3- to 5-year-olds (e.g., the system presented in this book). With this system of organizing the vertical curriculum, every daily lesson plan can provide a balance of all skill-based activities, and each skill-based experience can be introduced and scaffolded at the right time, developmentally, for the children.

In Part I of this chapter, the emphasis is on developmental sequencing and why it is important in skill-based planning and scaffolding. In Part II, you will learn about the system and how to use it to organize and scaffold skill-based experiences. Because *this is not "curriculum" but a system—a way to organize and use curriculum information*—it can be to used simultaneously with other curriculum modules or planning tools such as the Head Start Outcomes Framework.

Why a Management System Is Needed

Some of you might believe that a management system for vertical curriculum is unnecessary. If teachers do a really great job of offering a rich and varied learning environment, encourage children to use all learning centers, and give them ample time to use the materials, shouldn't the problem of increasing the children's skills take care of itself? You might think that all children will gain mastery of all skills simply by working with appropriate materials and activities each day.

Experience reveals that this is not usually true. Some children who are actively involved in all areas of the setting do get enough practice in the skills the teacher wants them to develop. Many other children, however, do not get enough guidance, reinforcement, and practice in every skill area to reach their full potentials.

One reason for this is the preferences of children during free-choice or child-initiated time. Some children want to spend most of their time in the art or manipulatives areas. Perhaps they avoid the large-muscle area and blocks and their opportunities for building other skills. Other children might be particularly inventive, skillful, and verbal in using the literacy and dramatic play areas, but may spend very little time in the fine-motor and manipulatives areas.

Another factor that inhibits the ability of children to gain enough practice in all the skills they need is inherent in the makeup of many of today's early childhood classrooms, which are becoming more diverse in nature. Diversity creates a need for greater attention to individualized teaching.

In addition to the chronological mixture of children appearing in early education classrooms, children enter today's centers with more diverse backgrounds and skill levels than they did a decade ago. Although some children have reaped the benefits of skilled parenting, others have stressful home lives or may come from abusive homes. Many more children in today's centers have been identified as having special needs, learning deficits, and disabilities.

The children being served, whether they are in mixed groups or homogeneous age groups, present far greater challenges in individualized teaching than they did in the past. Groups of young children with different ages, backgrounds, needs, and skill levels need ample time to explore materials and need adults to encourage and help them practice skills.

To help today's children reach their full potentials, teachers now need to develop and use better management systems for planning the vertical curriculum. A planning system can ensure that all basic skill areas are covered, that skill practice activities are introduced gradually throughout the year, and that they are practiced in meaningful ways that mesh with ongoing themes and interests. To use this kind of system, it is necessary for teachers to understand fully what is meant by skill-based and developmentally sequenced activities

Skill-Based Activities

There are certain skills that every teacher wants children to master before they leave the program. These are skills agreed on in the early childhood field as appropriate to the development, limitations, and capabilities of the children with whom the teacher is working. They are probably skills that the early childhood program and the children's parents believe are important for teachers to teach. These skill-based activities should consistently appear in daily lesson plans.

Observers will see specific skills being worked on when children practice tearing or cutting; practice walking on a balance beam; or practice sorting and matching items by category, color, shape, or size. Sometimes the practice of a specific skill will take the form of a literacy activity, such as dictation by the child about a painted creation, or about a block structure, or in a personal journal. Sometimes the practice of a problem-solving skill might be accomplished by having children plan a field trip, prepare and eat vegetable soup, measure and graph objects, or do a science experiment and tell what happened.

Planning developmentally sequenced skill-based activities throughout the year that reflect a daily balance of all skill areas is the challenge of vertical curriculum planning. To examine management ideas that will help teachers cope with this challenge, we need to take a deeper look at what *developmentally sequenced* means.

Developmentally Sequenced Activities

Developmentally sequenced activities are those activities that are planned in order to mesh with the ongoing and changing development of children as they grow and learn. Activities are always planned to provide children with success; children should practice skills that match their skill levels. But learning activities should also provide an element of challenge; children should grow gradually more skillful.

Descriptive praise from adults often motivates children to expand on a creation, try again, or try something new. But scaffolding, combined with praise, can actually be more motivating. Scaffolding opportunities for teacher-child interaction are a natural part of developmental sequencing (e.g., the sequenced activities themselves are already scaffolded). When teachers understand developmental sequencing and can predict the next step in the sequence of a particular skill, it is much easier for them to use appropriate dialogues to scaffold learning experiences. This encourages children to try more advanced skills and to use thinking processes that will lead to mastery and expected children's outcomes.

--*-*

Very little written guidance has been available to early childhood teachers for addressing the comprehensive daily planning of developmentally sequenced skill-focused activities. Teachers who do this sort of planning do it on the basis of fundamental child development knowledge and what they have learned from their own observations and experience.

Sometimes, the only guidance teachers have are lists of various skills that are found in assessment instruments. These lists usually show skills in terms of achievement-level milestones: "Can cut paper with scissors on straight line," "Can pair two items by a common relationship," "Can remember and follow two oral directions," "Tries several methods to solve a problem and is persistent." These achievement-level milestones are used as indicators to help teachers see "where each child is," either in achieving mastery or in needing help. These tools may tell the teacher something about skills individual children need to practice, but they do not give specific help to teachers in *breaking down these skills into sequenced hands-on activities that can be entered in daily plans from the beginning to the end of the year*

Early childhood texts often provide lists in which skills are broken down into gradual steps on the basis of fundamental child development knowledge. Texts may list milestones in many areas of development. Each milestone may also describe a skill at a certain level of development, but the information provided rarely tells teachers how to help individual children to *arrive* at that particular milestone.

A textbook might say, "By four years, most children can make one full cut with scissors but have trouble cutting on a straight line." This information tells generally what to expect from 4-year-olds, but it does not tell teachers what to do with a group of 4-year-olds to help them progress to mastery if many children are at different skill levels. *There is not enough detail about developmental sequencing to tell the teacher how to practice precutting skills or scissors skills with diversely skilled 4-year-olds on a daily and weekly basis.* To do this kind of individualized planning, the teacher needs *sequential* information about the skill of cutting.

Early childhood teachers often buy tradebooks that purport to include complete curriculum-planning activities for the program year. These should be examined very carefully. Some of the ideas included in such books are excellent. However, if a book simply proposes that "cutting and pasting" should be done during the first three months of the year, it does not give teachers enough sequential information to allow them to address individual differences in children's skill levels. Similarly, a book that directs the teacher to do specific activities for the entire group of children for each day of each week of the year will not help teachers who want to address *individual* needs and differences.

--*-*

To sum up, developmental milestones are good guidelines for long-range objectives, but they do not tell teachers how the child learns each skill, gradually, bit by bit, by practicing an activity that the teacher incorporated into his or her ongoing lesson plans. To do lesson planning that incorporates sequenced skill practice, and scaffolding opportunities, teachers need to look at what should be happening for children *in between the developmental milestones,* instead of focusing on the milestones themselves. By the same token, in order to do daily and weekly lesson planning that effectively addresses individual differences, teachers need to plan skill-based activities that help children practice all the steps that come between the milestones. When teachers do this kind of thinking and planning, they are doing developmental sequencing of skill-based activities, or *vertical planning*.

--*-*

Unfortunately, many teachers simply plan their skill-focused activities on the basis of "What do I feel like having them practice today?" or "What haven't we practiced lately?" Some teachers may even choose a skill that a child is to have mastered by the end of the year and simply start practicing the "finished skill" the first week of school and practice it every day thereafter.

Teachers do not intend to plan skill-focused activities at inappropriate times, but may not be aware of more appropriate alternatives. In discussing these alternatives, it would be helpful to examine what one might call *natural* developmental sequencing, *guided* developmental sequencing, and *planned* developmental sequencing.

Natural Sequencing

An example of natural developmental sequencing is the gradual sequence in which a baby learns to control and strengthen the muscles and movements of its body in order to learn to walk. If you allow a baby safe and normal opportunities to move about, and do not unduly restrict movement, the baby will learn to lift its head, then learn to roll over, then gradually learn to sit without support, then learn to creep and to crawl, then learn to pull itself up to stand with support, then learn to stand without support. Then, finally, after learning to walk a few steps by holding on to an object or a person, the baby will learn to walk independently.

Guided Sequencing

Guided developmental sequencing occurs in several ways during free-choice time in most early childhood programs. In a center for 3- and 4-year-olds, if adults offer crayons, markers, and paper every day, and if they encourage and praise the open-ended use of these materials, the children who use them will gradually improve their skills in using crayons, markers, and paper. By the end of the year, they may be able to do a drawing and print their first names with a large pencil, a crayon, or a marker. This method allows children's skills with crayons and markers to develop gradually and comfortably at the developmental pace of each child, but the skills are encouraged and reinforced, or "guided," by adults.

Similarly, in programs following appropriate practices in the field, adults guide the developmental sequence of painting skills by emphasizing the process of painting, not the product that might emerge. They guide by offering bright, thick paint and large brushes. They encourage children to experiment with paint, and the children start by mixing the colors up and covering the entire paper. Then, as adults continue to offer painting experiences, the children start to separate some colors and leave some empty space. Next, they enclose some spaces with planned strokes and begin to see emerging shapes. Soon, children paint planned shapes, and finally they learn how to plan and put together some of their painted shapes and spaces so that a "picture" recognizable to adults emerges. Daily painting opportunities provide guided developmental sequencing for the skill-focused activity of painting.

A third example of guided sequencing can be seen in the use of unit blocks. When early childhood teachers provide unit blocks, the time and space to use them regularly, and the praise, encouragement, and questions that nurture further skill development (scaffolding), they are providing guidance to the developmental sequence of skills that children acquire and master during block building. (See discussion of scaffolding in Chapter 2.) When teachers see block building as a skill-focused activity that can be practiced and encouraged with attention, questions, and accessories (scaffolding), they are guiding the developmental sequence that occurs when children use blocks.

Planned Sequencing: Motor Skills

Think about the example provided earlier of guided sequencing with crayons, markers, and paper. There's a way for teachers to expand their teaching methods to do "planned sequencing" of this skill-based activity.

If the opportunity to use crayons and markers were offered only as a guided activity during free-choice time, some children who might need extra practice in this skill might not choose this area or activity very often; they might not get the practice they need. However, if the teacher could identify which children were not using this area and these materials, and which of these children needed more opportunities to practice the skill of using crayons and markers, then the teacher could plan ways for those children to practice this skill.

The teacher could provide this practice by planning for it to happen regularly in a scheduled, short, small-group time for all the children. This method would not single out any children as being less skillful than others. All the children in a small group could enjoy scribbling or drawing, regardless of skill level. The children could tell the adult about their drawing, and the adult could write down their dictation and date the drawing, nurturing literacy skills. In 10 minutes, children in a small group could make two drawings, one to take home and one for the teacher to keep in the portfolio. This plan would give the teacher an ongoing method to assist the children who need individual scaffolding, as well as a way to observe children's progress in the skill of handling crayons, markers, and paper.

--*-*

Here is a second example of planned sequencing. In a mixed-age group of 3- to 5-year-olds, children may start the year at ages 3½ or 4 and end the year at ages 4½ or 5. Teachers may want children to end the year with the ability to use scissors to cut on a line or to cut out a large, simple shape.

Most 3- and 4-year-olds are not adept with scissors when they enter preschool programs. They should not all be expected to start practicing cutting with scissors at this time, and certainly should not be expected to cut pictures from magazines, in which the thin paper slips and bends. The developmental sequence of mastering skills leading to the use of scissors should be planned, and should begin with experiences that strengthen the hand muscles, like using clays and playdough, tongs, hole punches, and pinch clothes pins. The next step in the sequence is to plan many experiences in tearing paper, so that the child's hands learn the feeling of opposition, and so that the fingers learn how to begin controlling the medium of paper.

TRY THIS NOW

To understand exactly what is meant by the "feeling of opposition" and "controlling the medium of paper," get a scrap piece of paper right now and tear it in half. You will see that your two hands did opposite things: One hand moved away from you and one toward you. Now, try to tear the scrap paper into a shape. Again, your hands do different things as you turn the paper and control it as you tear it.

In cutting with scissors, the hands also do different things. One hand holds and turns the paper, and the other hand cuts. Enjoyable activities in tearing various papers and sometimes using glue to make torn paper collages will lead naturally to children's interest in tearing shapes out of paper. When the child can tear out shapes, he or she has learned that the hand that holds and turns the paper being torn does something different than the dominant hand, which will eventually do the cutting.

This is why experiences in tearing paper should be planned to precede the use of scissors, especially if the practice of this skill is to occur in a scheduled small-group time in a mixed-age group. During free-choice time, children who are already adept at using scissors will have plenty of opportunity to use their skills. But in a mixed-age group during small-group time in the first month of the year, tearing paper (not using scissors) should be the planned, developmentally sequenced activity, because it will be successful and helpful to every child in the group. Those who are more adept with scissors will not mind tearing (all children love to tear paper), and the activity of tearing and turning the paper will still help children who can cut to improve their scissor skills.

Skills in using the scissors themselves can also be developmentally sequenced and planned. Appropriate vertical lesson planning should gradually incorporate the following steps in the skill-based activity of using scissors:

1. After tearing experiences, children practice snipping the edge of the paper.
2. Next, they practice cutting into the paper, making fringes.
3. Next, they practice cutting the paper apart at random.
4. Then, they practice cutting it apart by following a straight line drawn on the paper, and then a curved line.
5. Next, they practice cutting on a line drawn on paper which incorporates angles or zig-zags.
6. Then, they practice cutting out a large circle or oval of paper by following a continuous line.
7. Finally, they practice stopping and changing direction with the scissors as they follow a line that is not continuous; for example, they might practice cutting out a square or triangle.

The developmentally sequenced steps listed here for the skill of cutting with scissors could easily be put into monthly or daily lesson plans in a planned, consecutive, and gradual order for practicing and learning, as they are in Appendix A.

Most skills that teachers want children to attain by the end of the year can be practiced in guided developmental sequences, starting simply and gradually becoming more challenging or complex. Motor, perceptual, memory, language, and problem-solving skills can all be practiced gradually, with scaffolded developmentally sequenced activities that match children's changing skill levels.

Planned Sequencing: Perceptual Skills

Match, Find, and Label.   Here is an example of a perceptual activity that can be sequenced for the purpose of scaffolding and lesson planning. Young children begin to internalize the concept of the shape of a triangle or square through real experiences, such as playing a triangle instrument or sitting on a carpet square. Learning that adults have names for colors and shapes and that they want children to learn these names is comfortable and acceptable to children, who want to please adults and who want praise for their accomplishments. However, learning colors and shapes (and many other such concepts) should proceed in planned, sequenced, "match, find, and label" activities that move from concrete to abstract (a sound child development principle).

Here's the way sequenced methods could be used in teaching a child about a square. The first step in the perceptual skill of learning a shape is for the child to experience the shape with his or her senses, physically and kinesthetically. The adult would start the year with meaningful verbal comments whenever a child is using or handling something square—a carpet square, a square cracker, a window square, or a square enclosure made of blocks.

The adult would also use questions in small-group or one-on-one time to help a child understand the concept of a square shape, starting with, "Can you find one that is the same shape as this one?" The child would be matching the shape, not naming it. Later, the adult would name the shape, saying, "Can you find a square one like this?" The child would find a square and also hear the name, which would be the "finding" stage. Later, the adult would be able to ask the child to look at a group of various shapes and tell which ones were square. When the child can isolate and name the shape, he or she has reached the "label" stage. After the match, find, and label stages, the child's learning about a square does not stop; it continues to develop.

Beyond Match, Find, and Label.   What has been learned about a square with practice in hands-on perceptual experiences now becomes committed to memory. At this point, when an adult asks what a square is, the child will be practicing a *memory skill* as well as a *perceptual skill* whenever he or she tells the teacher the name of the shape. The concept of that shape is something the child has already learned through hands-on perceptual experiences.

Further, when the child uses this learning about what a square is in creating a pattern or design, the child is synthesizing the information from hands-on experiences in both perceptual and memory activities and putting this information to a new use. He or she is now demonstrating a *problem-solving skill.* When the teacher sees the child using information in this new way, it shows a change in behavior; not only has the child "learned" what a square is but the child is now using and integrating new problem-solving skills, along with formerly acquired learning, *to construct new knowledge* about the square.

This particular example, skill practice with shapes, was given to illustrate something interesting that happens when teachers do long-range planning for certain skill-focused activities. At the beginning of the year, activities in which children practice recognizing shapes would be categorized as perceptual activities. But as the year progresses and children integrate their learning, skill-based activities concerning shapes would encompass other skill areas. Tracing shapes would be a motor activity, remembering names of shapes would be a memory activity, and creating designs with shapes would be a problem-solving activity. Remember this point when we begin to look at the management plan for vertical activities that will be presented in this chapter.

--*-*

Similar developmental learning sequences can also be used in teaching 3- to 5-year-olds the colors. Again, the learning activities or experiences should move from concrete to abstract and from matching to finding to labeling. For example, a child learns what *red* is by actual experience with things called *red*—

by playing with paints, playdough, and other things that are red; by consuming foods and liquids that are red; or even by seeing that blood from a cut is red.

The child would see and handle real red objects first (real red apples), then see the color red in pictures of these real objects (pictures of red apples), and then recognize the color red in more abstract symbols for the objects (pictures of red spheres or circles).

Young children may also eventually be able to learn *red* by an inappropriate method—the method of rote practice. But in the field of early childhood, educators want children to develop the lifelong skill of learning to love learning. This is done not with rote practice, but by helping children gain skill mastery through meaningful, enjoyable learning experiences and active engagement in planned, guided, and spontaneous hands-on activities.

PART II: A SYSTEM FOR SKILL-BASED PLANNING

It's time to revisit the illustration of the mountain of curriculum information. In Chapter 7, we divided the mountain in half and discussed the systems teachers can use to organize and implement interest-based curriculum. Now we need to break down the "skill-based" half of the mountain into more manageable parts. When we have smaller parts, they will be easier to use systematically in curriculum planning (see Figure 8.1).

Now that the half-mountain has been separated into five smaller parts, we need a system for using the information in each part. All the activities that take place in an early childhood classroom will fall into the five general categories that are seen in the five parts of the half-mountain. We will now learn how to use the

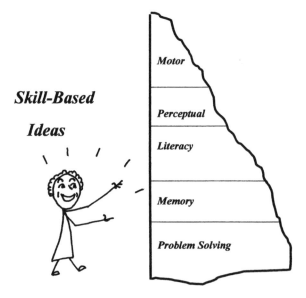

FIGURE 8.1   Vertical Planning

concepts of developmentally sequenced activities and planned sequencing from Part I of this chapter to organize and use each of the five categories in the half-mountain for curriculum planning. Do you recall that in Part I of this chapter, the developmental sequencing of skill-based activities was called *vertical planning?*

Vertical Planning

Using the interest-based information in Chapter 7 was called *horizontal planning*; using skill-based information is called *vertical planning*. Early childhood educators actually use both types of information simultaneously when they do daily lesson planning. This complex planning can be seen more easily in the diagram shown in Figure 8.2.

Here are typical items that might be entered in a lesson plan after children visited an apple orchard to pick apples. Some activities would take place in group time and some during free-choice time; some do not relate to the theme,

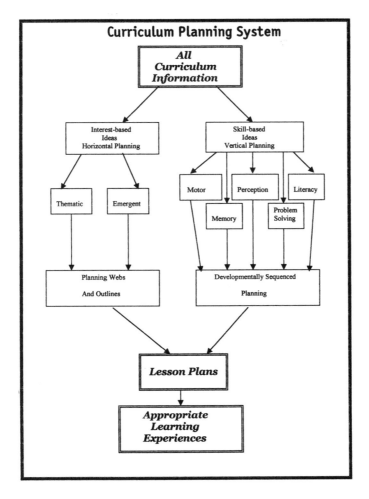

FIGURE 8.2   Curriculum Planning System

which is appropriate. In the parentheses you will see which major skills are being practiced during each of the activities.

Remember the trip to the apple orchard. Do an experience story. (memory, language/literacy)

Discuss plans to make applesauce. What do we need? How might the apples change? (language/literacy and problem solving)

Sort apples by color. (perceptual, problem solving)

Sort apples by size and order them smallest to largest. (perceptual, problem solving)

V E R T I C A L

Cut up apples for snack. (physical/fine motor)

Count the apple seeds. (math/problem solving, fine motor)

Observe and describe apples. (use senses: feel, smell, taste, look) List the words. (perceptual, language/literacy, science/problem solving)

Do an obstacle course activity with mats, tunnel, and balance beam. (large motor/physical)

Play sound matching games. (auditory perception, memory)

Make a torn-tissue paper collage. (fine motor/physical, creative problem solving)

Do fingerpainting. (fine motor/physical, creative problem solving, perceptual)

Build with blocks. (creative problem solving, fine motor, language)

Apples ——————————— HORIZONTAL ———————→

This partial list of lesson plan entries shows that both skill-based and thematic curriculum are integrated and occur simultaneously in written lesson planning. In addition, this schema shows that children's learning experiences can be represented as a list of skill-based activities that is built on a main theme, and built upwards from it—for example, the vertical curriculum proceeds vertically from each point or theme in the horizontal (time line) curriculum, hence the term *vertical planning*.

Learning Domains Addressed in This System

Do you remember that the Head Start Outcomes Framework listed eight categories or learning domains in which positive outcomes are expected for 3- to 5-year-olds? In the system for managing skill-based information that is presented in this book, however, only five categories or learning domains are addressed: *Motor* (fine and large motor), *Literacy* (including language), *Problem Solving, Perceptual* (auditory and visual), and *Memory* (auditory and visual).

Although the differences between the systems in this book and the Outcomes Framework will be compared, you should remember that the purpose of this chapter is not to show teachers how to plan for eight areas of the Head Start Outcomes. The purpose is to *present a system for organizing skill-based curriculum* so that it will be efficiently used to benefit children in *any* kind of early childhood program. This system, however, can easily be used to help Head Start teachers plan learning experiences that match Head Start Outcomes Framework indicators and elements in all learning domains.

The "Social-Emotional" and "Approaches to Learning" domains listed in the Head Start Outcomes Framework will not be specifically addressed in this chapter, because these two areas are not domains in which skills can easily be broken into predictable steps (developmentally sequenced) and scaffolded to attain outcomes. These outcomes are more influenced by interactions with others than with engagement in specific activities.

Positive "social-emotional" outcomes and "approaches to learning" outcomes are the goals of every good early childhood program. These goals are easily reached in programs where staff love working with children and their parents, understand developmentally appropriate practice, provide positive guidance and reinforcement, and plan positive experiences where children can play and work independently and in groups. When those factors are consistent, expected social-emotional and attitude outcomes will occur gradually and naturally for most children. If any children have special needs in the approaches to learning and social-emotional, however, staff must provide individualized interactions and experiences to help children achieve positive outcomes. The following diagram will show how the five categories or learning domains in this book (*A Practical Guide...*) overlap and relate to the domains in the Head Start Outcomes Framework (*Outcomes*).

References	*Learning Domain Category*				
A Practical Guide	Motor	Literacy	Problem Solving	Perception	Memory
Outcomes	Physical	Language & Literacy	Math/Science/Creative	_____	_____

The content of the domain elements and indicators for "Motor" and "Physical" are the same in both references, although in this book the elements and indicators are called *learning experiences*. The content of both references in "Language" and "Literacy" is the same, but in this book only one category is used (the heading "Literacy") for both of these domains. "Problem Solving" as used in this book's system of curriculum planning includes the content of "Math, Science, and Creative" domains. I have included "Perception" and "Memory" as additional domains for two important reasons.

One is that the daily learning experiences planned by early childhood teachers are inherently laden with perceptual and memory skills; children continually practice and gradually improve these skills in natural and enjoyable ways. The second reason is that these domains have great impact on outcomes in the other learning domains, particularly in the Head Start Outcomes Literacy domain elements of Phonological Awareness and Print Awareness. For example, auditory and visual perception skills are very necessary to children's abilities to discern fine differences in real objects and the representation of objects with symbols. Children need developmentally sequenced practice in auditory and visual perception in order to eventually hear and see the fine differences in letters and their sounds. Auditory and visual perception skills help children reach outcomes in language and literacy that are particularly important to success in reading. Sensory perception is highly related to physical and cognitive development, and is also complementary to the skill development of children with certain learning styles; some children need more sensory stimulation than others.

Conscious memory is very much related to all learning domains, particularly language, literacy, perception, and problem solving. Although memory skills are often thought of as cognitive skills, both auditory and visual memory skills can be broken down into developmentally sequenced steps and practiced. With planned learning experiences and adult facilitation or scaffolding, children can improve both their visual and their auditory memory skills.

In the system of organization being presented in this book, it is not necessary to compartmentalize the science, math, and creative domains. Early educators value and include a variety of creative experiences in daily plans, so expected outcomes in the creative area are easily attained, and a separate category is not necessary in presenting this system. In addition, creative or divergent thinking processes are much like the process thinking of science and math. Creative thinkers, like scientists and mathematicians, are divergent thinkers. Divergent thinkers know there are many ways to solve a problem or answer a question, not just one way. When confronted by an obstacle, they think of new ways to work around it. When teachers foster creative, divergent thinking, they are helping children learn an important life skill.

What educators are really teaching in curriculum for young children is not "science," "math," or "creativity," but the ability of children to *think* and to process information so that they can use it to construct their own knowledge or express their own ideas. Another label for this process is *problem solving*. This is why learning experiences in science and math and all the elements related to them, including the divergent thinking which is the basis of creativity, are called *problem solving* in this book's system of vertical curriculum planning.

To make this point very clear, here is an example of the scientific process. Children, who are natural scientists, constantly use these steps to discover things as well as to express themselves in many ways.

1. Observe intently. Handle, examine, use senses.
2. Hypothesize, imagine, guess. What are the alternatives? Plan what you could do.
3. Experiment and manipulate.
4. Discover what happens.
5. Evaluate; possibly modify. Experiment again. (Second experiments are sometimes omitted.)
6. Conclude. Express what has happened. Tell why you think it happened.

In science or math, children express themselves with oral or dictated descriptions or conclusions; in the creative process, they express themselves through creating with open-ended media. When children use any type of art media, such as paint, to create something on paper, they are also using divergent thinking processes. They imagine, plan, experiment, and evaluate. If they discover something that inspires them to change or modify the creation, they experiment again until they conclude that it is complete. The same kinds of process thinking occurs in creating music and dance.

Children use these basic steps (with slight modification) in any kind of problem solving—making something with clay, negotiating a compromise with a peer, experimenting with fingerpaint, figuring out the math to complete two block towers of equal height with different kinds of blocks, making something at the workbench, or doing a simple science experiment. For all these reasons, the learning domains of science, math, and creative process thinking are simply titled *problem solving* in the system in this book. Curriculum planning in problem solving should include science, math, and creative experiences. Now let's find out more about how the system works.

A Planning System That Incorporates Sequenced Time Blocks

Developmental sequences which support scaffolding in the development of motor, perceptual, literacy, memory, and problem-solving skills for 3- to 5-year-olds are presented in Appendix A of this book. In Tables 8.1 and 8.2, we will look at, in detail, the first two of the seven Time Block tables in Appendix A. These tables not only provide teachers with a system for vertical planning, but provide scaffolding support that is specific to skills.

Each skill-based activity in the Time Blocks is developmentally sequenced. This means that each one progresses from simple to complex. If teachers use the sequences in these tables thoughtfully, they can predict the next steps toward expected outcomes. In this way, the tables will enable teachers to more easily plan or use appropriate dialogues and scaffolding to help children reach outcomes and to continue to develop mastery in learning domain skills.

TABLE 8.1   *Skill-Based Activities—Me and My World*
               Time Block 1 (September–October)

MOTOR	PERCEPTUAL
LARGE GROUP **Body Movement:** Copy and/or create to music, songs, chants, rhymes. Act out prepositions. **FREE CHOICE** **Using Blocks:** Use unit and large hollow blocks. Stack, lay, carry, build. **Active Play Inside/Outside:** Use all types of locomotion, including wheel toys. Follow line or path with body or toy. Practice climbing and rolling. Jump with both feet. Toss, catch, and pass with big, soft beanbags, or paper-stuffed pillowcase. Use hammer with pegs or *soft* wood or Styrofoam. **Clays and Playdough/Sand and Water:** Use freely; fill, pour, float, sink, mold and dig. **Dressing and Undressing:** Practice with outer wear, dress-up, and zipper/button toys. **Art Media:** Use crayons, markers, chalk, paper. Use easel paint and fingerpaint. Paint at tables. Use varied collage materials. **Manipulatives, Table Toys, Floor Toys:** Use large, easy puzzles. Use large pegs/pegboards. Use large lego blocks. String large beads. Use stack and nest toys. Use shape box toys. Use snap and bristle blocks. **SMALL GROUP** **Games:** Follow object with eyes. Tear paper at random. Use tongs and pinch clothespins. Trace simple templates with fingers; free form, one line. Practice pouring water. Practice any manipulatives. **Meals and Snacks:** Pour, pass, serve, spread. Clean up, brush teeth.	**LARGE GROUP** **Music and Circle:** Use instruments. Recognize body parts. Listen to sounds and identify some. Notice what we are wearing. **FREE CHOICE** **Blocks:** Use all types. Handle and match types. **Exploring with Senses:** Use clays, playdough, water, sand, earth. Explore and match textures. Handle and match recycled items. Handle collage items. Match familiar objects. Use various paints. Compare colors used in art media. Notice smells, tastes. **Manipulatives, Table Toys, Floor Toys:** Use simple, large puzzles/parquetry. Use face–body parts activities. Match textures. Match familiar silhouette shapes. **Cleanup:** Use pictures and perceptual labels. Recognize sound cues. **SMALL GROUP** **Games:** Compare sounds: high, low, loud, soft. Tell direction of sound source.* Compare ourselves regarding sizes, hair, eyes. Guess a hidden object by touch alone. Match some primary colors. Compare objects: big, small, like, unlike. Match like objects. Examine/match circles and ovals. Identify simple sounds.* Recognize familiar shape silhouettes. **Meals and Snacks:** Perceive colors, textures, tastes, smells, temperatures.

LITERACY

LARGE GROUP
Literature:
Hear stories and books.
Do fingerplays and rhymes.
Do songs and chants.
See flannelboard stories.
Use/talk with puppets.

Conversations:
About work and play choices.
About plans and routines.
On simple rules for safety.
About friends and names.
On things that make us happy or sad.

Body Language:
Move to music.
Imitate animals and nature.
Act out prepositions with music, rug
    squares.

FREE CHOICE
Talk/Listen/Do:
Use books and pictures.
Use people's names.
Name items and equipment.
Talk about healthful ways.
Use friendly words.
Use, talk about safe ways and rules.
Play with puppets.
Talk about art and creations.
Use picture recipe to make playdough.
Use tape recorder.
Use listen station.
Use play telephones.
Examine computer.

Dramatic Play:
Converse spontaneously.
Use materials creatively.

Writing Center:
Do creative "writing" and communicating.

SMALL GROUP
Games:
Discuss me, my home and family.
Start a "me" book.
Discuss pictures about feelings.
Discuss work and play choices.
Use puppets together.
Discuss health and safety.*
Read a picture book.*
Discuss visitors/helpers. *
Discuss outdoor walks.*

Meals and Snacks:
Discuss and name foods. Tell preferences.

MEMORY

LARGE GROUP
Learning Together:
Copy adult modeling.
Imitate in simple games of "Do What I
    Do."
Hear and talk about stories.
Sing songs in unison and call and response.
Enjoy and learn fingerplays.
Try counting by rote up to 5 in songs,
    rhymes, birthdays.
Learn daily schedule, routines, limits.
See picture sequence of daily schedule.
Use names of friends in songs, rhymes,and
    games.
See own name in print.

FREE CHOICE
All Area Learning:
Learn names of areas, materials, and
    equipment.
Learn how we use materials and
    equipment.
Learn names of friends.
Learn limits, expectations, and routines
    with practice and helpful visual cues.
Learn helpers' jobs with practice and
    helpful visual cues.
Use healthful habits at snacks and meals,
    when toileting, and in cleaning to
    prevent spread of germs.
Use safety habits with materials,
    movements, fire drills.

Cleanup:
Learn adult cue to start.
Learn where things go.

SMALL GROUP
Games:
Talk about fire and tornado drills.
See sequenced pictures of the daily
    schedule.
Recall today and what I liked best.
Repeat own and each other's names in
    rhythmic chant.
Remember summer and family fun.*
Recall one or two objects when these
    are removed from a group and hidden.
Guess names of areas from adult clues.
Sometimes recognize own printed name.
Recall some friend's names.

Meals and Snacks:
Learn the routine.
Copy positive social language.

PROBLEM SOLVING

LARGE GROUP
Conversations:
On work/play choices from day's options.
On the schedule of the day.
About nature, the weather, and its changes.
About our body parts and their use.
    (demonstrate).
On what makes us feel happy or sad.

FREE CHOICE
Blocks:
Stack, lay, connect.
Observe differences in structures.

All Area Learning:
Begin to know areas and materials by use.
Make work/play choices.
Begin to plan the use of time.
Ask questions and use senses to gain
    information.
Negotiate turns with materials.
Explain wants and needs with words.
Match, sort, and tub materials.
Manipulate materials.
Examine computer.
Observe properties of sand, water, paint,
    playdough/clays.
Observe changes resulting in mixing
    colors.
Make playdough; measure, mix; see
    changes.

Dramatic Play:
Choose items for role-play and pretend.
Plan and carry out play.

Science and Math:
Observe and handle nature items.
Observe our plants and animals.
Measure and weigh ourselves.
Estimate in pouring and filling.

SMALL GROUP
Games:
Discuss play choices and plan one choice
    for next time.
Tub and sort items.
Count own body parts.
Count heads and noses of those in group.
Blow bubbles with individual cups/ straws;
    observe and tell.

Meals and Snacks:
Set table with one-to-one match.
Help prepare snack when possible.
Problem-solve when using utensils.
Estimate in pouring, filling.

TABLE 8.2 *Skill-Based Activities—My Expanding World Time Block 2 (October–November)*

MOTOR	PERCEPTUAL
LARGE GROUP **Body Movement:** Copy and/or create to music, songs, chants, rhymes. Act out prepositions. **FREE CHOICE** **Using Blocks:** Use unit and large blocks freely. **Active Play Inside/Outside:** Use varied locomotion, including wheel toys. Follow line with body or toy. Try balance beam, laid flat. Use steps/rocking boat. Use indoor climber. Use mats to jump and roll. Balance on one foot; try to hop. Toss/catch large, light items. Jump over a low rope; rake, jump in leaves. Use hammer and soft materials or pegs. **Clays and Playdough/Sand and Water:** Use freely; add variety. Pour, fill, float, sink, dig, mold. **Dressing and Undressing:** Outer wear, dress-up, and zipper/button toys. **Art Media:** Use crayons, markers, paper, scissors. Do varied painting, fingerpaint, collages. Try spray painting. Try dripped-glue designs. Try hole punch designs. Try rubbings from nature. **Manipulatives, Table Toys, Floor Toys:** Use all appropriate manipulatives freely. **SMALL GROUP** **Games:** Tear paper with purpose. Use simple templates with curves; one line. Fold paper; either one or two folds. Learn about eye dropper painting. String paper tubes, big pastas, or cereals. Snip or fringe with scissors. Practice any manipulatives. **Meals and Snacks:** Pour, pass, serve, and spread. Carry, clean up, brush teeth.	**LARGE GROUP** **Music and Circle:** Use instruments. Match sounds of like instruments. Identify other sounds. Compare ourselves; sizes and other characteristics. Guess hidden objects by touch alone. Notice what we wear. **FREE CHOICE** **Blocks:** Use all types. Handle, match, and find types. **Exploring with Senses:** Use clays, playdough, water, sand, mud. Match textures and recycled items. Mix and match paints. Do more smelling and tasting. Sort items found in nature such as leaves, stones, seeds. Use some musical instruments in play. **Manipulatives, Table Toys, Floor Toys:** Use materials fully. Use blocks, flannel pieces, beads, pegs, and parquetry to create own patterns. **Cleanup:** Use perceptual labels. Recognize sound cues. **SMALL GROUP** **Games:** Match primary colors, unnamed. Hum together; match a pitch. Recognize a voice. Identify familiar sounds on tape. Match familiar shapes. Match simple objects to their pictures. Reproduce easy three-part patterns with model in view using cubes, beads, or other objects. Find or match circles, ovals, squares. Guess objects by touch.* Match big and small objects. **Meals and Snacks:** Perceive and discuss tastes, smells, textures, colors. Perceive that some foods have shapes.

LITERACY

LARGE GROUP
Literature:
Hear stories and books.
Do fingerplays and rhymes.
Do songs and chants.
Use flannelboard and puppets.

Conversations:
About choices and plans.
On rules for our room and group.
About feelings and fears.
About friends and names.
About new toys and equipment.

Body Language:
Move to music.
Use gestures and imitations.
Try signing a simple word or phrase.
Add to actions with prepositions.

FREE CHOICE
Talk/Listen/Do:
Use books/pictures.
Use names of people and materials.
Use and talk about healthful ways.
Use friendly words.
Use and talk about safe ways/rules.
Use puppets and flannelboard.
Answer open questions.
Do artwork dictation.
Try new recipe cards.
Use the computer.
Tape record/listen.
Use play telephones.

Dramatic Play:
Use new props and materials.
Converse spontaneously.

Writing Center:
Create original communication.
Try new materials.

SMALL GROUP
Games:
Continue "me" book as a personal journal.
Discuss foods, health, safety.*
Discuss feelings of self and others.
Discuss visitors, trips, and walks.*
Discuss our plants and animals.
Begin simple dictation or experience stories.

Meals and Snacks:
Discuss and describe food. Talk with peers and adults.

MEMORY

LARGE GROUP
Remembering Together:
Copy adult modeling.
Imitate in simple games of "Do What I Do."
Hear stories and songs.
Do fingerplays/rhymes.
Know what comes next in schedule.
Try rote counting to 5 in nonstereotyped songs, rhymes.
See and discuss pictured sequence of routines such as fire drills, meals/toothbrushing.
See visual cues for limits/rules and helper jobs.
Know many names of friends and adults.
Recognize and name familiar sounds. See own name in print (name tag, creations).
Remember summer or past events.
Remember fun times with friends/family.
Recall name of a person hidden when adult gives clues.
Repeat simple oral or clapped rhythm.

FREE CHOICE
All Area Learning:
Know names of areas, equipment, and materials.
Know how to use these appropriately.
Use names of friends.
Know rules and expectations.
Remember helpers' jobs; use visual cues.
Practice health habits.
Practice safety habits.

Cleanup:
Remember light or sound cues.
Know where things go.

SMALL GROUP
Games:
Recall two things I did today.
See, match own name in print.
Remember walks, trips, visitors.*
Recall two or three objects removed and hidden.
Recall/do 1–2 tasks while seated.
Find one primary color when named.
Find circles and ovals.
Repeat a simple clapped or oral rhythm.

Meals and Snacks:
Remember the routine.
Use positive social language.
Begin to talk about food groups.
Talk about foods for healthy teeth.

PROBLEM SOLVING

LARGE GROUP
Conversations:
About work and play choices.
About the daily schedule.
About weather changes and how these tell us seasonal changes.
On rules developed by the group.
On "last time" or "next time."
On body parts and their use.
About ways we can relax.

FREE CHOICE
Blocks:
Stack, lay, connect, enclose.
See parts of whole.
Compare differences in structures.

All Area Learning:
Know areas by use.
Make work/play choices.
Ask questions and use senses to gain information.
Negotiate wants, needs, and turns with words.
See step-by-step process in use of media and manipulatives.
Begin to see parts of whole in puzzles, designs.
Match, sort, and tub materials. Use computer.
Try new multisensory media; colors, clays.

Dramatic Play:
Plan and carry out play.
Do safety and health habit role-play.

Science and Math:
Notice and handle new items; count some.
Observe/tell about nature and our plants and animals.
See changes mixing, cooking and grinding.
Use the balance scale and measuring tools.

SMALL GROUP
Games:
Use minilight and a magnifier to examine nature items found.
Blow bubbles with individual cups/straws; add drops of food color; observe and tell.
Sort nature items in two ways.
Graph selves by size or in other ways.
Guess, find out what floats or sinks in cup of water.
Match three or four items one to one.

Meals and Snacks:
Continue to help in set up and preparation.
See changes in foods experiences.

TIP

Head Start teachers should note that the Head Start Outcomes Framework domain elements and their indicators are *also* developmentally sequenced, making them easy to integrate with the skill-based planning systems presented here. Many learning experience examples that are sequenced in the monthly time blocks of Appendix A will match specific Head Start Outcomes domain elements and indicators.

When teachers examine the information in Tables 8.1 and 8.2 (and later in Appendix A) they will find that most of the skill-based activities they want to scaffold with children on a daily basis are already sequenced and included in the seven time blocks. Each time block is approximately four to five weeks in length. These time blocks can be thought of as navigational charts for vertical planning in seven consecutive periods of a nine-month program year. They will provide a system for organizing vertical curriculum information into one long-range plan, containing seven four- to-five-week plans. This system can help teachers place already sequenced skill-based activities into daily lesson plans more easily and quickly.

Tables 8.1 and 8.2 will give you examples of sequenced activity ideas that could be used in lesson plans during the first eight weeks of the program year. We'll use them here to learn about the planning system and how it works.

General Notes on Format

The first thing you will notice about Tables 8.1 and 8.2 is that each of these time blocks is organized into five categories under the headings "Motor," "Perceptual," "Literacy," "Memory," and "Problem Solving." Seeing these five categories of skill areas simultaneously as each time block is viewed helps teachers remember to plan a balance of activities in all five skill areas. This format helps the teacher see all the learning domains that are important for children, not just those the teacher enjoys most.

The next thing you will notice is that a comprehensive list of already sequenced, skill-based activity examples is suggested in every one of the five skill categories. If teachers choose activities from each of these five categories regularly each day over the course of a month or five weeks, they will be providing a balance of practice in all learning domains in their lesson plans.

When you examine these two tables you will see that in the "Motor" category, both small- and large-motor activities are listed. In the "Perceptual" categories, tactile, auditory, and visual perception experiences are included. Both visual and auditory memory activities are included in the "Memory" category. Comprehensive lesson planning for young children should include all these areas of development.

--*-*

Each of the five categories are further divided into three subcategories: "Large Group," Free Choice," and "Small Group." This has been done to precipitate easier and quicker placement of these examples (or alternative activities of the teacher's choice) into a daily lesson plan. The title "Free Choice" is used because of its brevity. (*Free choice* means that children will make choices of materials that may have been preplanned by the teacher with specific goals in mind.)

Meal and snack activities are listed under "Small Group" because, whenever possible in early childhood programs, children do eat in small groups, where conversation and learning are guided by an adult. Teachers who do not schedule a daily small-group time can still use the "Small Group" examples presented in the tables. For example, the small-group activities in the tables could be used with individuals or small groups during free-choice time or at other times in the program day.

--*-*

The activity lists in the tables are not all-inclusive. To present this planning system, it is necessary to provide examples of developmentally sequenced skill-focused activities in five major skill areas. In Tables 8.1 and 8.2, however, and in the complete set of Time Blocks provided in Appendix A, what is emphasized are the *sequential steps* in practicing each activity or skill, not the specific methods or materials the teacher would use in implementing the activities.

The steps in skill sequencing and the method of organizing the activity examples are far more important than the examples themselves, because it is the steps and the method that give teachers a system for organizing and using their own ideas in the vertical curriculum. As they become familiar with the system, teachers are urged to add their own ideas and skill sequences, and to modify the examples that are presented.

For example, a kindergarten teacher might have different long- and short-range goals and objectives than a teacher of 4- and 5-year-olds, but kindergarten goals could still be broken down and sequenced, and the method presented here could still be used to reach outcomes.

--*-*

As we further examine these two tables, we will be discussing several aspects that will help teachers use the system effectively. You might ask: Why are some activity ideas general and some specific? What are the reasons they are placed in certain categories or sections? What do I do first? How fast should I move through a time block? How can I individualize this system?

General and Specific Activity Ideas

Most activity examples listed are general in nature so that teachers can modify and personalize the activities they choose. Look at Table 8.1. In the "Motor" category, one "Large Group" activity is to "Copy and/or create to music, songs, chants, rhymes." In motor, free-choice time, another is "Use crayons, markers, chalk, paper." In the "Literacy" category, one large-group activity is "Hear stories and books"; another is talk "about plans and routines." Specific music, books, materials, and "plans and routines" would be up to the individual teacher.

Some activities are seen in every time block, such as "Copy adult modeling" in the "Memory" category. This is because children at every age and stage will remember and copy adult modeling. Remember that whenever adults model, children are practicing memory skills.

Please look at the examples in the "Small Group" sections of Tables 8.1 and 8.2. Specific activities have been included here, either to help children practice skills that are important to horizontal and vertical plans or because they are skills that are best practiced with adult guidance. During planned small-group time, children usually practice skills that teachers want to observe closely, or skills with which teachers may want to assist through dialogue and scaffolding.

Manner of Sequencing

Let's examine the manner of sequencing that has been done in the tables by looking at some examples. In Table 8.1, "Motor, Small Group," you will see "Tear paper at random." In Table 8.2, "Motor, Small Group," you will see "Tear paper with purpose" as well as "Snip or fringe with scissors." In Table 8.1, "Motor, Free Choice," you will see "Follow line or path with body or toy" (such as a taped line), and in Table 8.2, "Motor, Free Choice," you will see "Try balance beam laid flat." (If you would look at the Time Blocks that follow Table 8.2 [Tables A.3 to A.7, "Motor," in Appendix A], you would find continuous steps in the sequential development of skills with both scissors and the use of the balance beam.)

Look at the "Perceptual category in Table 8.1. In "Small Group," you will find "Tell direction of sound source." In Table 8.1, "Perceptual, Large Group," you will find "Listen to sounds and identify some." In Table 8.2, these activities are more challenging. See Table 8.2, "Perceptual, Small Group," "Hum together; match a pitch," "Recognize a voice," and "Identify familiar sounds on tape." In Table 8.2, "Large Group," see "Match sounds of like instruments" and "Identify other sounds." (These experiences match indicators in the Head Start Outcomes Literacy domain in Phonological Awareness.)

Please compare Tables 8.1 and 8.2 in the "Literacy" category to see how conversations and materials become slightly more complex in Table 8.2. For example, in the "Free Choice" section, children move from examining the computer in Table 8.1 to *using* the computer in Table 8.2. They move from naming equipment to *using* the names of equipment; children move from telling about their art to *doing* simple dictation about their art.

In "Literacy, Large Group, Literature," children move from seeing and hearing the teacher do flannelboard stories in Table 8.1 to using flannelboards themselves during "Large Group" and "Free Choice" in Table 8.2. In "Literacy, Large Group, Conversations," children move from discussing simple safety rules in Table 8.1 to talking about and planning rules for the group in Table 8.2. (These experiences match indicators in the Head Start Outcomes Literacy domain in Book Knowledge and Early Writing.)

Similar examples can easily be found by examining the sequences in the "Memory" and "Problem Solving" categories. In Table 8.1, "Memory, Free Choice," children "Learn helpers' jobs with practice and helpful visual cues." In Table 8.2, "Memory, Free Choice," they "*Remember* helpers' jobs." Now compare the "Problem Solving" category in the "Blocks" section of "Free Choice" Tables 8.1 and 8.2. See that children move from "Stack, lay, connect" and "Observe differences" in Table 8.1 to "Stack, lay, connect, *enclose,* and "See parts of whole" in Table 8.2. If you examine all seven tables or Time Blocks, you will see that all the sequenced steps of skill development in block building have been listed.

As these tables are used throughout the year, each activity becomes more challenging, meshing with teachers' scaffolding and with children's growing skills. For example, in Table 8.2, "Memory, Small Group," you will see "Recall/ do 1–2 tasks while seated." In Time Block 7, seven months later, you will see "Recall/do 3 tasks that require movement." Recalling tasks while moving about is a more complex memory skill than recalling and doing tasks while sitting still. Careful sequencing was attempted in every section of these tables, not only in teacher-directed sections (large group and small group) but also in the work that teachers do with children in free-choice time.

Placement of Activities within Categories

The placement of activities in the particular subcategories of "Large Group," "Small Group," and "Free Choice" in these tables is based on my own experience with 3- to 5-year-olds. These were the places and times where these activities fit best for me. However, every teacher has an individual style and works with different kinds of groups. The Time Blocks are not a "canned curriculum" but a system of organization for lesson planning. When teachers become familiar with this system, they should experiment with their own sequenced activities, and their placement in lesson plans.

You should, however, be provided with some insight into the reasons for the placement choices seen in the subcategories of these tables ("Large Group," "Small Group," and "Free Choice").

Please examine Table 8.1, "Literacy." In "Large Group," suggestions are made to talk about friendships, safety, and routines. In "Small Group," the skill-based activities suggested are "Discuss me, my home and family," "Discuss pictures about feelings," and "Start a "me" book." The reason for this placement is that children with little experience talking in front of others will usually talk much more openly about self and family in a small group than in a large group. This is why it is important to place personal discussions in small-group time during early time blocks.

A similar reason for placing activity examples in the small-group section is so that the teacher may appropriately introduce them to children. Many skill-based activities, especially those that incorporate new materials or pieces of equipment, should be introduced by adults in small groups before they are fully available for use during free-choice time. A few examples are the use of eye droppers for painting, the use of magnets, the use of dry cell batteries, and the use of musical instruments.

Please notice in Table 8.1, "Perceptual," that instruments were introduced in large group, as "Use instruments," and also inferred as potential suggestions in small group, as "Compare sounds," "Tell direction of sound source," and "Identify simple sounds." In Table 8.2, "Perceptual, Free Choice," you will see the suggestion to "Use some musical instruments in play." Children need to know how to use instruments and other materials safely and in the manner for which they are intended. Notice that some activity examples listed in Table 8.1, "Small Group" in a particular time block or table, and then notice that these activities moved into "Free Choice" in Table 8.2.

An asterisk (*) has been placed next to certain small-group activities. Examples will be found in Table 8.1, "Small Group, Literacy." Whenever an asterisk is placed next to an activity, it indicates that this activity might also be appropriate for large-group discussions. Some teachers might prefer to place these activities into large-group time; I chose to introduce these activities in small group before placing them in large group.

In a final word regarding placement, please remember that some skill-based activities will be found in one category in the earliest time blocks, but in later time blocks, as children use the skill in different ways, the activity may be placed in another category. If you look at the activities on shapes and colors in all seven tables in Appendix A, you will see that these activities begin in the perceptual category; but later (after children conceptualize the shapes or colors and learn their names), they will be found in the memory category.

Individualizing the Use of the System

The main advantage of the Time Block system for lesson planning is that the examples of skill-based activities are already sequenced. This gives the teacher flexibility in controlling the system, the information, and his or her choices.

The teacher can easily move forward or backward in the steps of the sequence for any of the skills in any category to meet the needs of individuals in the group. Teachers can also move forward to the next Time Block in any of the five major categories or move backward to repeat activities. If a teacher finds that certain skills in a particular category have not been "practiced enough" for all children to have been successful, the teacher can repeat those activities before moving on to the next Time Block.

In using small-group time activity examples, the teacher may find that some children in the group are far more skillful than others in a particular activity. This means that those children have moved through the steps in the sequential development of that skill much faster than others. In this case, the teacher can simply move forward in the sequence of that particular skill-based activity example to find activities from the *next* Time Block (in the same category) to suit the children in that group.

Teachers should pay particular attention to children who move through developmental sequences very quickly. Sometimes teachers tend to be less aware of the needs of children who need challenge than they are of those children who are "challenged" and move very slowly through sequences of development. If a child in the small group needs to repeat skill-based activities from a previous time block, the teacher can go back to the previous table and offer those activities as alternatives for that child. These alternatives could be used either during the small-group time itself or whenever the teacher might work with the child individually during another part of the day.

Here's another scenario. Some children in a mixed-level small group might only be able to "match" a color or shape, while others may be able to "find" the color or shape. The teacher could simply pose his or her questions (scaffold) differently to the children in the group, depending on each child's skill level. This is why you will see that in some of the activity examples, the wording is "match OR find" or "recall two OR three objects." You will also often see the word *try* instead of *do* as children begin practicing a new skill.

The Pace of the Teacher or Group

Just as the pace of children within the group differs, the pace of each teacher or classroom group may differ. The system presented here is flexible enough to allow for these differences. At particular times of the year, children seem to have growth spurts where they will practice all the activities in a particular Time Block very quickly and will be eager for new challenges. If so, the teacher can move on to ideas in the next Time Block whenever children are ready. In other groups or at other times of the year, teachers will find that children will need or want more time to finish the activities of a particular Time Block. No problem. The teacher can continue to practice any activities in any categories of his or her choice, going on with the sequence later, when children are ready.

Integrating Themes with Skill-Based Activities

Whenever possible, teachers should integrate skill practice with meaningful and interesting thematic content. When skill-based activities mesh naturally and easily with thematic units, integration enhances interest, motivation, and skill development. This does not mean, however, that every skill-based activity must be done within the context of a theme.

Some teachers live in areas where the seasons change; they often plan thematic units about fall, and the children usually collect leaves from outdoors. Sorting and matching these items from nature; discussing the items; and grouping them by shape, color or size would be an excellent and appropriate way to integrate theme content experiences with perceptual, literacy, or problem-solving skill-focused activities (Table 8.2 "Perceptual, Free Choice").

Many of the skill-based activity examples in Tables 8.1 and 8.2 relate to the primary and recurring themes of the horizontal plan that was shared with you in Chapter 7, "Caring about myself, about others, and about my world." Let's look at some of the ways themes are integrated in Tables 8.1 and 8.2 to nurture children's self-esteem and social-emotional development. First, notice the themes in the titles of the two Time Blocks. Now look at the categories. In the "Motor" category, children practice self-help skills, including health and nutrition skills, and engage in active play and creative movement. In the "Perceptual" category, they enjoy the use of their senses, observe characteristics of self and others, recognize body parts, and help care for the setting. In the "Literacy" category, they talk about themselves; they sign a simple word or phrase; and they talk about their health and safety, their friends and families, their choices, and their feelings. In the "Memory" category, children remember what they enjoyed doing at school, remember each other's names, recall family fun, remember group rules and jobs, and remember safe and healthy habits. In the "Problem-Solving" category, children plan choices and the use of their time; develop group rules; observe nature and changes in the world; weigh, measure, and graph themselves; count body parts; and learn to problem-solve with words.

Using the System in Lesson Planning

To begin using this system for managing skill-based ideas, teachers can look at the appropriate Time Block as they are doing their daily lesson plans. If it is the beginning of a nine-month program, this is Table 8.1, September–October.

Next, teachers would make choices from the examples of skill-based activities listed in each of the five categories, and enter them in their lesson plans in large-group, small-group, or free-choice time, adding detail as necessary. Teachers should remember that these activities are designed to be used over four or five weeks' time. It is best to begin working with each Time Block by choosing ideas for the lesson plan that teachers believe are easiest for all children to accomplish successfully, then proceed to more challenging activities during the later weeks of the time block.

Teachers should keep a simple tally of the activity examples that have been used in lesson plans as they work with each Time Block. Place a check mark or a dot next to each example as it is used. This will help ensure a daily balance in activity choices. Most of the time teachers will use all the activities listed in each time block within the four- or five-week period. Activities not used in a particular Time Block can usually be used at the beginning of the next one.

To sum up, here are the main points for teachers to remember when they use this system in lesson planning:

1. Use the appropriate Time Block for the month. Use time blocks in order as the year progresses.

2. Modify activities to fit one's own program and geographic location when necessary or appropriate.
3. Experiment as desired with new ideas for sequenced activities, and with the placement of activities in the lesson plan.
4. Use activities from previous Time Blocks or from forthcoming Time Blocks, depending on the pace of the group or individual children's needs.
5. Use the Time Blocks with any curriculum methods, modules, or resources, and with any appropriate themes.
6. Head Start teachers may wish to note which Head Start Outcomes domain elements or indicators match learning experiences they choose and to plan ways to use performance-based assessment to collect data that proves the match.

Parent Partnerships: Sharing Information and Time Blocks with Parents

Although my purpose for the detail in this chapter was primarily to introduce the Time Blocks to teachers as a system to use in lesson planning, these Time Blocks have another very important function. They can be extremely useful in the area of parent education and involvement. It is particularly vital for teachers to understand, developmentally, how children learn particular skills in a step-by-step sequence so they can explain to parents how children learn these skills.

When parents give input on skills they want their children to accomplish, sometimes it appears that they are in conflict with what teachers and programs want. But many parents do not know a great deal about the sequences of child growth and development. What seems to be unreasonable expectations may be opportunities to learn more about how children grow and learn.

Parents want the same things for their children that early childhood professionals want. They want their children to have strong self-esteem and skills that will help them be successful when they leave the program. Parents deserve reassurance that the program will teach their children skills that will help them to be more successful in school. The "conflict" is not so much in the skills that should be mastered as in the *ways* they will be mastered.

It is the responsibility of the early childhood professional to explain to parents how children learn to master skills gradually, over time. It is also urgent that teachers show parents the relationships of certain learning activities to future skills in reading and writing.

• Parents need to know that some children may have difficulty following a line on a printed, two-dimensional page if they have not first experienced what a line is, in three dimensions, with their bodies. When parents understand how children learn what a "line" is by gradually learning to follow a line with their bodies and then with their eyes, they will better understand why teachers want children to use balance beams, balls, crayons, paintbrushes, and scissors.

- When parents are made aware of the many steps in the sequence of learning to cut with scissors or to print with a pencil, they are far less likely to demand to know why teachers are not practicing letters and numbers or cutting out squares with scissors at the beginning of the year.
- When parents understand that playing with parquetry and puzzles helps train children's eyes to focus on one point while they continue to see what is in the background, parents will realize that this may help their children later in focusing on one word or one line of print found on a whole page full of print.
- Parents must know that children need to experience books and stories every day, at school and at home, and that children are excited about seeing their own words in print. When children see that adults value their thoughts and ideas enough to put them down as words on paper, children are proud and will become motivated about reading and about communicating with written words.
- Parents need to understand that dramatic play can help children practice language and safety and health habits, and that involvement with meals and snacks not only helps children learn about nutrition but also helps them learn math and science skills.
- Parents need to understand that when teachers help children listen carefully to sounds and play matching sound games, teachers are training children's ears to hear the differences between sounds, and that this can help them later to hear the small differences in the sounds of letters.

Additionally, when *teachers* understand the relationships of skill-based activities to cognitive and psychomotor development, and learn ways to sequence and scaffold these skill-based activities, they will not only do lesson planning that is more beneficial to children but they will also know how to explain to parents what they are doing and why they are doing it!

Sharing copies of the Time Block pages in Appendix A with parents at the beginning of each four- or five-week period will help parents know what their children will experience during the current or coming month. Better still, parents will see, over and over again, that *all* these activities are *learning* activities, and that all of them teach their children self-esteem, social skills, and specific skills in motor, perception, literacy, memory, and problem solving. After I began to use the Time Blocks in this way, I never again heard a parent ask, "Why are they just playing?"

Summary

In this chapter we have discussed the increasingly diverse skill levels of children in today's early childhood classrooms and the corresponding challenge of offering ongoing and appropriate learning experiences that meet children's individual needs. We discussed the need for a management system to organize vertical planning and support consistent scaffolding of children's learning experiences in all skill-based learning domains: motor, perceptual, memory, literacy, and problem solving. It is questionable that early childhood teachers can provide ongoing individualized teaching that leads every child to expected outcomes unless teachers use better systems for managing skill-based curriculum content.

The effective system of managing the vertical curriculum presented in this chapter is based on the concept of the scaffolding of developmentally sequenced skill-based learning activities. The system helps ensure that experiences in all learning domains will occur in the classroom each day, and also gives teachers a practical method of planning meaningful skill-based experiences that match children's developmental needs as they gradually grow, change, and develop throughout the year. Tables 8.1 and 8.2 were used to help you become familiar with the system and the use of the Time Blocks in Appendix A.

Understanding the differences between horizontal, interest-based curriculum and vertical, skill-based curriculum, and using systems to organize curriculum planning more easily and consistently will save teachers time, energy, and paperwork. They'll be able to put their time and energy to use in more valuable ways. They'll have time to pace themselves, observe in all areas of the room, have individualized interactions with children, make notes, help volunteers and parents, and really enjoy their work with young children.

Before we go on to Chapter 9 to see how thematic, emergent, and skill-based curriculum content can be integrated in lesson plans and projects, please look again at the diagram in Figure 8.2. It summarizes the systems of curriculum planning presented in Chapters 7 and 8.

Self-Study Activities

1. If you have thoroughly read and digested all the material in this chapter, you deserve a break! After your break, and in light of your new understanding about vertical curriculum information and the use of the Time Blocks to manage it, read the tables in Appendix A that present all seven Time Bocks for the program year. Choose one activity and follow its sequence through all seven Time Blocks. One example that you might find interesting is temporal ordering, or the gradual introduction and use of time concepts and the calendar with young children.

2. Find some time to reflect on some of the activities you like best to do with your children. List 10 such activities. Then categorize your list by the five major skill categories presented in this chapter. Find out where your ideas fall: motor, perceptual, literacy, memory, or problem solving. Do the activities you chose reflect a balance of all five major areas?

3. Without looking at Table 8.1 or 8.2, choose one skill that you want children to master by the end of the program year. Write a list of all the activities you would use to provide mastery of this skill through hands-on activity. Now list the activities as you would use them in consecutive order, or the order in which you would put them in lesson plans. Check the tables in Appendix A to see if your sequence for each skill meshes with the sequences found there.

Resources and Suggested Readings

For those of you who enjoy a challenge, do some research on the work in the 1970s on the possible connection between perceptual-motor activities and success in reading. The ERIC Clearinghouse on Elementary and Early Childhood Education at the University of Illinois (800-583-4135) can obtain abstracts or articles for you on this topic, based on the research of Bryant Cratty, Marianne Frostig, and N. Kephart, as well as more recent research.

Through college libraries or interloan, look for the book *Growth and Development: The Child and Physical Activity* by Leonard Zaichkowsky, Linda Zaichowsky, and Thomas Martinek, published by C. V. Mosby Company in 1980. Although the book is now out of print, it is worth the effort of a search. The authors summarize the major work of researchers who were proponents of the theory that planned perceptual motor activities are among the factors that are helpful to children in developing prereading and prewriting skills, and that these activities can also help children who have certain reading disabilities.

An ERIC database search indicates that there is no empirical research either proving or disproving the theory that planned practice of perceptual-motor activities helps children develop reading skills. In my interviews with early childhood teachers and disabilities specialists in the field however, I have found ongoing support for practices that support the theories of Marianne Frostig and similar researchers.

$\mathcal{9}$ Putting It All Together

Integrated Curriculum and Integrated Learning

In this chapter we will be "putting it all together," integrating the three types of curriculum content with learning domains in webs and written planning. We will look at both simple and complex planning webs that integrate curriculum, and then we will explore the ways that integrated curriculum is linked with learning domains in actual lesson plans.

Integrated curriculum includes thematic, emergent, and skill-based planning that crosses over several or many learning domains. To understand why integrated curriculum is so important to young children, let's revisit the concept of children as holistic learners. Children learn with their bodies, senses, memories, perceptions, thinking skills, feelings, emotions, and the expressions of their thoughts and ideas. Nothing is turned off in the learning process. Children learn in classrooms, their homes, the outdoors, and the cultural community that is their world.

If children learn as whole, integrated human beings, with all their parts integrated in the process, it follows that the most meaningful learning experiences educators can provide will be integrated, whether they are in planned, written experiences, or in emergent learning projects. Additionally, when teachers provide integrated learning experiences, they can more easily match children's individual learning styles.

The theory of multiple intelligences proposed by Gardner (1993) and supported and expanded on by others in recent years suggests that there are eight ways of learning about the world: verbal-linguistic intelligence, logical mathematical intelligence, visual spatial intelligence, bodily kinesthetic intelligence, musical rhythmic intelligence, naturalist intelligence, intrapersonal intelligence, and interpersonal intelligence. Children actually learn not in just one, but in their own unique combinations of these intelligences. Integrated curriculum experiences give children many different ways to learn, and the elements of all these intelligences or learning styles are already embedded in the early childhood setting, materials, and learning experiences teachers provide.

For example, the science and math areas, the dramatic play areas and the blocks area might particularly appeal to children who learn best through logical mathematic, visual spatial, and naturalist intelligences, but collaboration with others in their work with blocks or their science experiments or dramatic play would also enhance children's verbal linguistic and interpersonal learning styles. Using blocks, art media, or music and movement to create or represent something would particularly help children who learn best through intrapersonal, bodily kinesthetic, visual spatial, or musical rhythmic intelligences.

When educators provide a well-balanced curriculum, offering both interest-based and skill-based learning experiences, when they actively encourage literacy, the arts, and the sciences, and when they make sure children have ample time to use all of the learning centers and the outdoors in the early childhood setting, teachers are opening all the avenues of learning through multiple intelligences. This chapter encourages professional self-assessment and underscores the importance of using practical systems to improve planning and to maintain balanced, integrated curriculum experiences in all learning domains.

Simple Integrated Curriculum and Webs

In Chapter 7 of this book, we talked about teaching and learning webs as a way to illustrate the teacher's plans to use a topic to integrate several curriculum areas, expanding the learning web as new interests emerge from the children. Integrated activities are usually a combination of both horizontal and vertical planning, and can appear in adult-led or child-initiated time on the lesson plan.

We'll get started by examining simple and complex learning webs. A *simple web* is one in which only one experience or one material is used to integrate various curriculum areas. You can likely think of many early childhood materials that have this flexibility, such as unit blocks and water play. Here are three examples of simple integrated activities: playdough, dramatic play, and bean bags.

Playdough

When children play with playdough or other clays such as Silly Putty, they generally use it in the art area to make their own creations. Creativity and creative thinking are primary learning domains that are integrated when children use playdough. Another is physical—practice of small-motor and manipulative skills. If you take your imagination further, you probably know that children often mix colors of playdough to create new colors. This integrates discovery problem solving and cause-and-effect thinking skills.

If children are encouraged to talk about how the playdough feels and smells, and the things they are doing to it, they are practicing both sensory perception and language. If the adult writes down what they say they can do with playdough on a poster or large paper, literacy skills will come into play with a dictation that includes words such as *twist, poke, pinch, stretch, pound, press,* and others. If the adult takes a print with the playdough of some object or texture in the room, and asks children to guess where the print came from, they will be practicing both problem-solving and memory skills.

In addition, when children make "balls" or "snakes" out of playdough, they are beginning to experience conservation skills, even though they usually do not yet fully understand this concept. When they place big, small, and medium "balls" or "snakes" on the table in order by size, they are practicing another thinking skill—that of ordering or seriation (e.g., problem solving).

If children work together to help make the playdough during free-choice time, they will be practicing many math and science skills, as well as literacy, safety, and motor skills. They will estimate, pour, count, measure, observe the ingredients and describe them, and tell what happens to them in cooking, thereby learning about cause and effect. These experiences will also teach children that learning is fun!

TRY THIS NOW

Draw this learning web on a piece of scrap paper or notebook paper. Make playdough the central focus point, and add all the curriculum areas it covers. Although playdough is a simple material, it integrates a great many areas of curriculum, forming a web that looks something like the many petals of a flower or starburst. See what you can add that has not been mentioned. Now see if you can find all five of the categories of learning listed in Chapter 8. Then find all of the eight learning domains listed in the Head Start Outcomes Framework, using the paragraph above for help.

Dramatic Play

Dramatic play and role-play are excellent learning activities that lend themselves to integration with many curriculum areas. Usually, adults facilitate but do not become highly involved or directive in dramatic play. Occasionally, however, a teacher may want to reinforce several curriculum areas at the same time by incor-

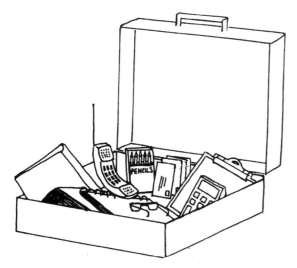

porating them into a pretend situation.

Picture a teacher who has chosen a child or two to help him or her with "pretending" for the audience of the whole group. The teacher wants to reinforce concepts in health and safety and has chosen some dramatic play props for playing "office" in order to do this. The teacher and child or children choose a space in the room for the location of the "office" and pretending.

Next, the teacher might ask, "When you start your day at the office, you don't wake up there, do you? Where do we really wake up?" The teacher and child can go to a different area of the room to pretend "waking up," stretching, doing a few knee bends, or bending to touch their toes.

"What is the next thing you do when you wake up? Do you get dressed first or eat breakfast?" The child and teacher can pretend to look outside to check the weather, decide what clothes to wear, and pretend to dress. Then the teacher and child can pretend to wash hands before eating a pretend breakfast.

The teacher could ask, "What foods should we eat for breakfast?" The child can talk about good breakfast foods and why it's important to eat breakfast. After the pretend meal, the teacher could ask, "What do we always try to do after we eat?" and lead the child to decide to brush his or her teeth. Usually, the child and teacher would return to the "bathroom" area and pretend to brush (gently, round and round, way in back too); then look in the mirror to see their clean teeth; and then, perhaps, brush, pick, or pretend to braid their hair.

Now it may be time to go to the office. "Who shall we say goodbye to and hug? Do they have the office phone number? Where are the car and the keys?" The child and teacher can now use two chairs, side by side, for a car, unless the child chooses to travel to work in some other manner. In the car, the teacher should give the keys to the child, who will drive, and ask, "What is the first thing we always have to do before we start?" Usually, the child will know that they must put on their seat belts. Perhaps the child will check the mirror and the gas when starting the car. Maybe the car would be warmed up.

During the drive, the teacher could say, "Oh, I see a red sign up ahead with white letters that say 'Stop.' It is a circle . . . no, it is an octagon shape. What does that mean?" The child will say it is a stop sign, and the teacher can ask what they should do. "When we stop, we have to look both ways" (more pretending). Next, the teacher should "see" a traffic light and ask the child what to do if the light is red, green, or yellow. (Be prepared for any answer!)

A few moments later, the teacher might "see" some litter along the road. Perhaps the teacher and child can discuss what can be done about litter. Later, the teacher can say they have arrived at the office. The child parks the car, they get out, lock the car, and go into the "office," where the child begins to examine and use the contents of the briefcase.

During the seven or eight minutes of this dramatic play episode, the teacher will have integrated and reinforced many health and fitness concepts (sleep, exercise, appropriate outerwear, handwashing, toothbrushing, grooming, and hygiene) as well as good nutrition. In addition, the child has acted out and internalized many safety concepts. The adult and child were also engaged in conversation throughout the scenario, some of which focused on the environment. The simple learning web would look like Figure 9.1.

Dramatic play is a wonderful vehicle for integrating curriculum elements, not only in this scenario, but in many others, such as playing "camping," or going to the "beach" or the "river." In the dramatic play example shown here, thematic content (safety, health, nutrition, ecology, social studies) as well as all five learning domain categories listed in this book would have been integrated; so would all eight of the Head Start Outcomes learning domains.

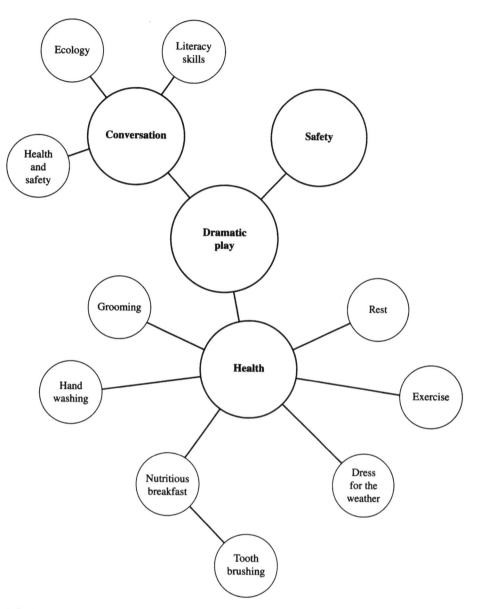

FIGURE 9.1   Learning Web for Dramatic Play

Bean Bags

Sometimes simple classroom materials lend themselves to opportunities for integration, if teachers use their own divergent thinking skills to use them in new ways. Bean bags are usually square or rectangular and are made from scrap material. Why not try making them in other shapes and of other materials? Why not make some of these shapes big and some of them small? Why not make them in different colors and with different textures—real or fake fur, velvet, burlap, scrap leather, and so on? At the same time, why not stuff them with something other than beans or rice? Small bags could be stuffed with many fragrant things, including potpourri, fragrant dried grasses, cinnamon sticks, cloves, or cotton scented with peppermint extract.

With bean bags like this, the teacher is offering a multisensory learning experience and an opportunity to describe and talk about colors, sizes, shapes, smells, and textures. In addition, the bags can be used in many ways to promote motor development, practice the use of prepositions, and name body parts.

A few shapes could be made on the floor or carpet with masking tape. Children could use these as targets and toss bags of particular shapes, colors, or sizes into them. They could put the bean bags on their heads and walk around the circle or stand next to the square on the floor, or even jump into a shape. They could hop, run, or gallop with the bean bag on their heads, inside their elbows, or under their chins. They could walk with a bean bag between their knees. Many areas of curriculum can be integrated when we use old materials in new ways.

Figure 9.2 shows a simple teaching and learning web describing the integration of learning experiences around the simple focal point of bean bags. Can

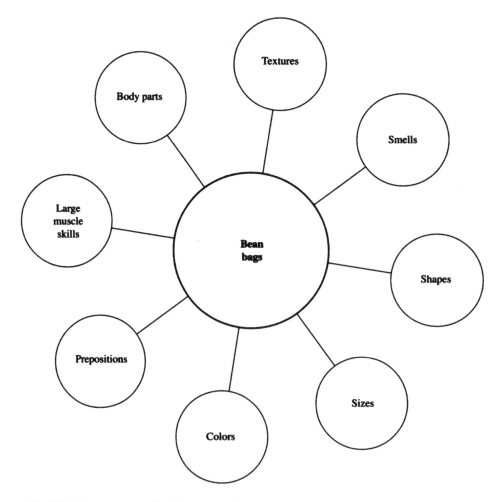

FIGURE 9.2 *Learning Web for Bean Bags*

you think of ways to integrate thematic and skill-based content and all of the learning domains?

Complex Integrated Curriculum and Webs

Now let's look at more complex learning webs. The first two examples in this part of the chapter, an apple and old newspapers, will be presented first as simple webs. Then we will see what a more complex web would look like if children's emergent interests were expanded in the planning web and the teacher's lesson plans.

An Apple Snack

Teachers know that activities with foods unite many parts of the curriculum, but sometimes they don't capitalize on the opportunity to expand the integration of these simple activities. Most teachers comment and ask open questions as children prepare a snack so that children will practice skills in nutrition, math (measuring, estimating, counting), science (changes, cause and effect), colors, shapes, and the names of foods and ingredients.

Let's look at the example of preparing just one apple for a group of four people (one adult and three 4-year-olds) in a small-group situation. First, the teacher should ask the children what they need to do (always) before they handle foods. Expanding on the children's answers, as the teacher and children wash their hands with soap and water, the teacher might ask children why it is important to wash hands before "cooking." When teachers ask about health rules and routines, children need to think about and explain the reasons, which gives them more practice in both thinking and language skills. In this example, the children are learning and practicing a health concept as well as thinking and telling.

Next, the teacher might show the children the apple, ask them to describe it (size, shape, color, bumpy or smooth, smell, stem or no stem), ask about other apples they have seen, and if their colors were different or the same as this one. The teacher's use of open questions could expand the children's language, memory, and literacy skills. Have the children ever seen or climbed an apple tree? Were there flowers on the tree and bees buzzing, or bare branches, or were there apples on the tree? What time of the year would that be? Next, the children should wash and dry the apple, and talk about the reasons for doing this. (Apples are sprayed with pesticides.)

The teacher should ask the children what they think should be done. Here are four people, and only one apple. The children will suggest that the apple be cut up, which gives the teacher the opportunity to discuss ways to use such tools as knives safely, and only when an adult is present.

The teacher should take time to show children how the knife is made, helping them observe the handle, and both the sharp and dull sides of the knife. He or she should help the child cut the apple in half, holding the apple and placing one hand over the child's for necessary pressure and safety. When round objects are cut, they wobble, and adults should help with the first cut so that the next cuts, if any, can be made with the flat side of the fruit or vegetable down on the cutting board. If parents are observing, the teacher may want to comment that showing a child the parts of the knife and how to use it safely can be a good problem-prevention technique.

At this point, the teacher has a chance to ask the children what to do when there are four people and only two pieces. Have the children count the people and the pieces. They will say that the apple must again be cut, and can figure out the best way to do so. If children have not directed that there be two more cuts, the teacher will repeat the question and problem-solving process until there are four ("Let's count them") pieces of apple, all of the same size. It is interesting for children to see at this point that all four pieces can be put back together and held to form the whole apple again. They have just had a concrete, meaningful experience in using fractions.

Other things should have been going on simultaneously during this entire cutting process. As the apple is cut, the children can describe the inside of the apple, how it is wet, how good it smells, and how the inside differs from the outside. Do the children notice and comment that, even when apples have different colors outside, the color inside is the same? (Just like people!)

When the apple is cut, seeds will be observed, and children can describe them, count them, and decide whether to save them to put on the science table, plant them, or use them in a collage or in other ways. The core of the apple can be examined, and the children can decide if the core should be discarded, given to one of the classroom pets, or put into the compost pile outside.

When all the work is completed, children can pass and serve themselves the pieces of apple, perhaps using "Please" and "Thank you." When they eat the apple (chewing it well and talking about why this is safer than gobbling), they can describe (when their mouths are not full) the apple's taste and how the taste compares with other apple foods (pie, apple butter, apple sauce, apple juice). They can discuss their preferences and what they know about the ways other apple foods are made. If they use the apple pieces with a dip, it can open new avenues of language.

The process of using an apple snack as a simple integrated experience takes about 15 minutes, depending on the children and their spontaneous verbalization. In that 15 minutes a teacher would have combined, united, and *integrated* the following parts of the curriculum: safety, health, nutrition, memory, language, perception, motor skills, sensory learning, problem-solving skills, antibias, environmental awareness, and social skills. Literacy, math, science, antibias, and environmental awareness would have been integrated. More specifically, children experienced integrated learning about colors, shapes, smells, textures, counting, fractions, comparing, apples, tools, and focused observation (science). All of the Head Start Outcomes Framework learning domains would have been incorporated. There is much more to having an apple as a snack than one would suspect!

A simple web, starting from the interest point of the apple snack itself and integrating it with all the curriculum areas just mentioned, could be drawn, as in Figure 9.3. But a more complex web could describe the ways that the emerging interests of the children could lead the teacher to expand the teaching and learning web, integrating many other topics and learning domains. At some point, the apple web might even look like Figure 9.4.

TIP

This and other simple foods experiences are excellent home visitor activities. The home visitor can easily involve the parent or have the parent lead the activity throughout the process. The activity takes very little time but includes all the elements that home visitors are encouraged or required to cover on a home visit. All the examples presented in this chapter could be suitable for either the classroom teacher or the home visitor.

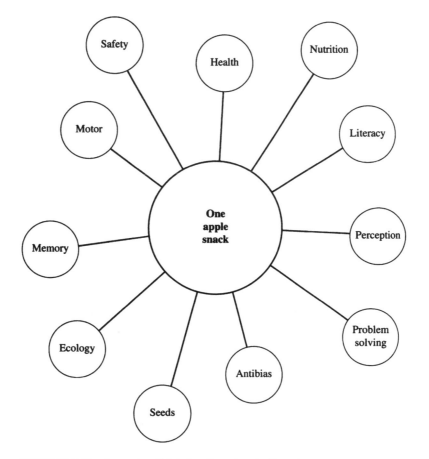

FIGURE 9.3   *Learning Web for One-Apple Snack*

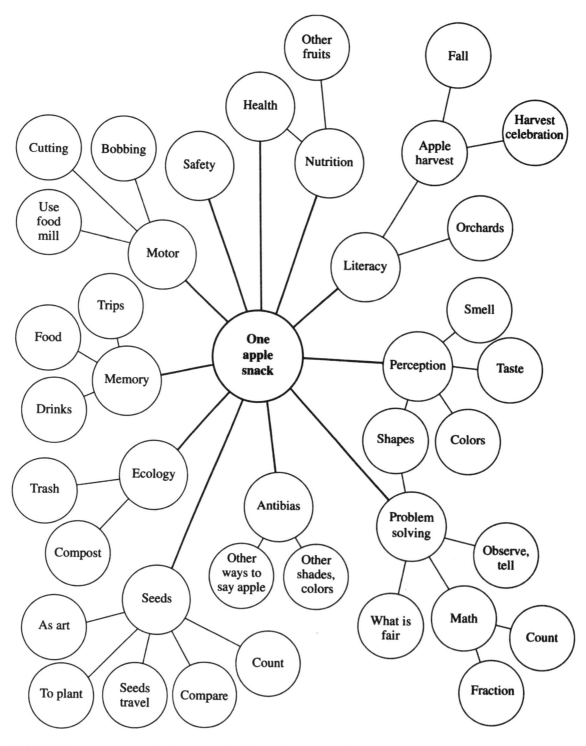

FIGURE 9.4   An Expanded Learning Web for a One-Apple Snack

Newspapers

Old newspapers are easy to obtain and can be used to integrate such curriculum content as large- and small-motor skills, literacy, creativity, the use of prepositions, the naming of shapes and body parts, recycling concepts, safety concepts, cause and effect, and dramatic play. If there is enough space inside the center, or outside on a pleasant, calm day, the teacher and staff could do the following activities with several small groups of children, simultaneously. But the first time these ideas are introduced, and most of the time thereafter, the teacher could probably choose seven or eight children to be involved and would repeat the activity to be sure all children would have a turn.

Start by putting sections of old newspaper, folded once, on the floor in a circle, just as you would place carpet squares on the floor as sit-upons. Ask, "Who would like to come play this game?" It is wonderful to include parents in this game when they are visiting in the classroom. "What are some things we could do with this paper?" The teacher could start by leading the choices to walk around the paper, stand next to it, jump over it, hop around it, or sit under it. This could be followed by putting your toe on the paper, your knee, your elbow, your nose, or your chin.

After this active movement incorporating prepositions and body part names, the teacher and children could sit on the floor and talk about some of the many ways people use old paper. Children may tell how paper is used to train puppies, clean fish, or start campfires. They will talk about how people read papers, color on them, put them on the easel, or protect the floor with them when the walls of a house are being painted. They may talk about recycling paper.

The teacher could ask children to close their eyes and then tear or crumple paper, and then ask what the sound was, and ask them to point to the direction of the sound source. The teacher could go on to say that it is lots of fun to tear paper, too, and everyone could enjoy tearing strips of paper or even shapes like rectangles, squares, or circles.

With the addition of an old sheet, the teacher, parents, and children could crumple paper balls and toss them into the sheet, which has become a pretend skillet in which to make popcorn. They could pretend to add the oil and turn on the heat, taking time to comment on never cooking or using the stove at home unless a grown-up is helping. When everyone grabs the edges of the sheet, the pretend popcorn can sizzle and get hotter and hotter until it pops—all over the area, of course—as children and adults use hands and arms to shake the sheet.

Young children need to be brought down to a calmer state after all this excitement. The teacher can ask each of them to gather up the crumpled paper balls in small piles in front of themselves. Now the group could pretend that the popcorn has changed into snow, and talk about snowball safety. ("What do we do with snow?" "Where are safe places to throw snow?" "Why?") The group could also discuss icicle safety. Big icicles fascinate children, but they can be deadly.

After this brief quiet period, have the group divide into two teams, and have a grand and glorious, safe snowball fight. This is great exercise and fun. The teacher can declare the contest a draw and bring out an old, clean empty pillowcase. "Let's make a big, giant snowball by putting all the small ones inside the pillowcase."

Children will happily clean up the crumpled paper and can then play toss and catch with this giant stuffed ball. Even 2- or 3-year-olds, who might normally be unable to catch a big ball, will successfully catch a stuffed, lightweight, squishy pillow. Pillows feel familiar and safe. This ending circle game employs active movement but is structured so that it brings children down to a calm state after the excitement of the snowball fight.

The children will notice that their hands are dirty. Help them think about and discover where the newsprint ink on their hands came from, and take time to wash hands with soap and water. As they return to the group or circle, a discussion could occur about how paper is made from the wood pulp of trees. Children might be interested in knowing that three feet of stacked old newspapers equal one tree.

As you see, old newspaper, in a time frame of about 15 minutes, can give teachers the opportunity to integrate and incorporate many curriculum areas and to expand the learning web to new areas. A complex web about newspapers could look like Figure 9.5 and offer many opportunities to do online searches of topics on the Internet.

Earth

Earth and water provide excellent opportunities for planning integrated activities. In Chapter 7, a narrative example of a simple integrated activity on soil or earth was presented, followed by an illustration of what would happen if more interests emerged and more curriculum areas were covered (see Chapter 7, Figure 7.5, an illustration of a complex learning web about soil).

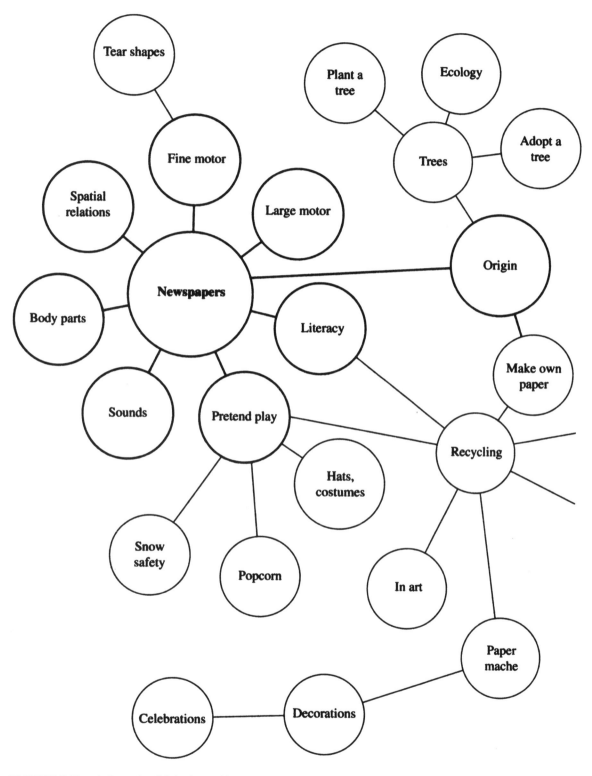

FIGURE 9.5   A Complex Web about Newspapers

TRY THIS NOW

On scrap or notebook paper, make or trace a rough copy of that complex web. Now let's explore ways the web could change and grow, depending on the emerging interests of the children.

Suppose your children have already gone outside to collect and sort different kinds of soil, examined it carefully, talked about it, smelled it, weighed and measured it, and tried to dissolve it in water, while telling what happens at each step. They have already practiced many skills in literacy, mathematics, and science.

To expand on the "Experiments" part of the web and to do an activity relating to ecology and the environment, children might do an experiment to see what happens when they fill a large glass jar with moist earth and put different items into the jar, between the dirt and the glass, so that they can see what happens overtime. Try some of these items: a piece of Styrofoam, an aluminum ring from a flip-top can, a small piece of bread, a small piece of carrot or other vegetable, a piece of an apple core, and a piece of a leaf that has fallen from a tree.

When children watch the jar for a few weeks, they will see that the bread, vegetable, fruit, and leaf all disappear into the earth, but the other items do not. This is an excellent way for children to become aware of the use of compost, the need to control littering, and the purpose of sanitary landfills. Your web has grown from experiments to the use of earth as compost, and from compost to thematic content, landfills and litter.

In your rough drawing, look at the area of the original web that grew from "Soil" to "Different kinds," then to "Topsoil," and then to "Plants." Here is a way to extend the "Plants" part of the web to new thematic content, "Terrariums."

Children might want to use some of the topsoil for plants to make a terrarium for the classroom and put small plants or animals inside it to observe. Some teachers find they can keep small hermit crabs, lizards, or toads successfully in terrariums, and in some classrooms I have seen small snakes, and even a tarantula spider, in a terrarium. Most often, mealworms are used to feed snakes, toads, and lizards. Some of these animals try to hibernate during part of the year.

TIP

In some cultures, such as Hopi, Navajo, and others, having animals in the classroom (especially reptiles or amphibians) is taboo and not permitted.

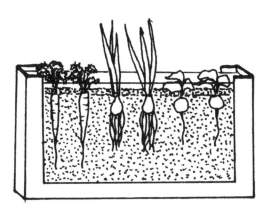

Look again at the "Plants" part of your sketch of the soil web. Children might add to the "plants" part of the web by doing experiments with seeds or bulbs and tubers planted in soil, and examine or compare the roots that grew from them. They might want to know more about crops planted in topsoil. Now the "Plants" part of the web would have grown new curriculum connections to seeds, bulbs, tubers, and crops. Children may notice that some plants grow in sand. If you plan activities about this, you will be adding a new connection to the "Sand" part of the web.

Look back at the original focus of the web, soil itself. Here is another way to extend the learning web and its illustration. Most children are interested in tracks. First of all, they do a lot of "tracking in," and adults comment on this. In addition, finding tracks outside is exciting for children. Both animal and human tracks can often be found outside in earth or in snow.

Children can look at tracks with their eyes or with magnifying glasses, talk about and compare them, try to figure out what person or animal made them and why. Where was the person or animal going? Children can look at the bottoms of their own shoes and compare the different kinds of tracks made by their shoes or boots. With careful supervision, they can look at vehicle tracks and compare differences in those of cars, trucks, or the school bus (science/math, literacy, problem solving).

Now you see that you have been able to add a new part to the web. It has grown from "Soil" to "Tracks," and from "Tracks" it has grown to include "Human tracks," "Animal tracks," and "Vehicle tracks." This is an especially good curriculum activity in areas of the country where trackers have long been considered as important people.

Let's think about one more way this web could change and grow. All children will be interested in the fact that some animals live underground, in the dirt. If they want to learn more about what animals live in soil or make their homes in it, the illustration of your web would grow from the center, soil itself, to a new connection, "Animals." From "Animals," many more new connections could be added. For example, children could study worms or ants, and the teacher could purchase or create an ant farm for the classroom. Children might want to do Internet searches about moles or other animals that live underground.

Water

Water, one of the basic necessities of life, is another good medium for many types of integrated activities. Use some scrap paper to design a rough sketch of a learning web containing some of your ideas for activities about water. Your ideas might include any on the following list and many more. Some of your ideas will change, depending on the interests of your group.

- Water for drinking and cooking
- Water for cleaning
- Water for plants and animals
- Water for enjoyment and relaxation
- Water for experiments with sounds and music, dissolving, blowing bubbles, floating and sinking, estimating, weighing, boiling, freezing, melting, and painting
- Animals and plants that live in water
- Jobs—people who work with water
- Transportation on the water
- Water safety
- Conservation and water pollution

Integrating Web Information with Horizontal and Vertical Planning

This is a good time to mention that drawings of teaching and learning webs are excellent brainstorming and preplanning devices. But the ideas in webs will still need to find their way to the paper of a long-range plan, or monthly plans, and daily-weekly plans. The systems in this book for organizing horizontal and vertical plans can help teachers accomplish this.

Look at the web about earth to see which parts of it are designed to give children a greater body of knowledge, or factual content. These are the thematic and emergent parts that fit the interest-based horizontal plan. The parts of the web that give children practice in actual skills fit the skill-based vertical curriculum plan. For example, in the web you drew about soil or earth, here are the parts of the web that fit into the long-range horizontal plan:

- Children learn facts about different kinds of earth.
- They learn different uses for soil.
- They learn about animals that live in the earth.
- They learn that they can do experiments with soil.
- They learn that they can plant things in soil.

But when children actually *do* the experiments, or *do* the planting, or *do* the telling and dictating about what they observe, they are practicing skills. All of the problem-solving skills they practice will be related to skills in planning, language, process thinking, and science and mathematics. Their "telling" will be a literacy skill. These are the parts of the web that fit your vertical planning:

- Create pots from clay and compare different pottery (motor, creative problem solving, and literacy).
- Make a terrarium for small plants and animals to observe (motor, problem solving, literacy).
- Plant seeds, bulbs, and tubers to observe (motor, problem solving, literacy).
- Do experience posters about uses for gravel (motor, problem solving, literacy).
- Make sand paintings (motor, creative problem solving).
- Observe and graph changes and comparisons of roots growing from seeds, tubers, and bulbs (literacy, problem solving).
- Do experiments to see what plants can grow in sand (literacy and problem solving).
- Try to dissolve earth or sand (literacy and problem solving).
- Examine earth; discuss and compare (problem solving and literacy).
- Weigh and measure earth (problem solving, motor).
- Do compost experiments (literacy, problem solving).

Linking Web Information with Curriculum Objectives

Now you can see that what is drawn on your web about earth or soil can be sorted into the interest-based horizontal and skill-based vertical parts of your curriculum. Let's use another example to take this management process to the next step. Suppose you have decided to use water as the basis for many integrated curriculum activities, and you have drawn your initial planning in a rough sketch of a learning web about water. You already know what parts of that web are content-focused (horizontal) and what parts are skill-focused (vertical). You have already planned for activities in your web that promote children's self-esteem, activities that support their abilities to work with others, and activities that promote their awareness about our world and the living things in it.

Now you need to put your entries into daily lesson plans. You need to decide whether they fit best in "large group," "free choice or planned activity time," "small group," or maybe even "outdoor" time or "meal and snack" time. Some may even fit into the lesson plan in "ecology/environment" or "health and nutrition." Let's take specific examples of some of the integrated curriculum activities, and see how they could be entered in a daily lesson plan and linked to learning domain objectives.

Large Group

- Show a large see-through container or pitcher of water to the group, and pass small paper cups of water to drink. Ask the children to tell you what they observe or know about water and its uses. Write an experience chart or poster, listing their comments as they talk *(horizontal curriculum:* facts about water, *vertical curriculum:* memory and literacy).
- Show pictures of water in many forms to the group and let them comment. Do an experience poster, listing what they say about different forms of water, such as lakes, oceans, rivers, falls, and ponds *(horizontal:* facts about forms of water; *vertical:* memory and literacy).
- Show globes, maps, and pictures of the world, explaining that the earth has more water than land and that lands are surrounded by water *(horizontal:* facts about water and our earth; *vertical:* literacy and memory).

If it is the beginning of the year with a group of 3- and 4-year-olds, these activities could also be done in small groups, and might elicit more language in small groups than large. Notice that these activities follow the *sequence of showing a concrete example of actual water, then pictures of water, and then more abstract illustrations of water.*

Small Group

- Use small cups of water, a small paper plate, and eye droppers to let children learn how to use the eye droppers. Ask them to drip and count the drops they make on the plate. At another time, paint or food coloring can be added to the water *(horizontal:* facts about water; *vertical:* motor, literacy, problem solving).
- Use water with small cups, individual straws, and several pieces of paper towel at each place. Let the children blow bubbles in plain water; ask how to make more bubbles that last longer. Add liquid soap and blow bubbles to see the difference. At another time, add small drops of food color to the surface of the bubbles to see geometric patterns formed at the base of each connection. Try different colors to see what happens. Capture and save paper towel designs with a plain paper "print" *(horizontal:* facts about water, water bubbles, and colors with water; *vertical:* motor, problem solving, perception, literacy, and creativity).
- Let the children see and discuss how musical sounds can be made with water in glasses, and compare the sounds made in glasses filled in differing amounts.

Make music *(horizontal:* facts about water; *vertical:* motor, literacy, problem solving, and creativity).

- Have the children experiment by dissolving salt in water, and discuss and compare the results. Try other substances as well *(horizontal:* facts about water and dissolving; *vertical:* motor, problem solving, literacy).
- Let the children talk about and make their own drawings of some things that live in the water; write their dictation next to the drawings *(horizontal:* facts about life in the water; *vertical:* motor, perceptual, literacy, memory, creativity).

If further discussion included facts and problem solving on clean water or water pollution, this could also be entered in the ecology section of the lesson plan format. (One can easily see the possibilities for investigative projects with older children.)

- Talk about what happens when there is no rain for gardens and crops. What can be done about this? Follow up in free choice with an experiment comparing a marigold plant that is watered with one that is not *(horizontal:* facts about plants and water; *vertical:* literacy, memory, and problem solving).

This is sometimes appropriate for large-group time, and if discussion and problem solving were included, it could be entered in the ecology section of the lesson plan form.

- Talk about the ways animals drink and how these are different from how people drink. Discuss where animals go to drink water. What happens if the water is dried up or dirty? What can be done? *(horizontal:* facts about animals and water; *vertical:* literacy, memory, problem solving).

This is sometimes appropriate for large-groups time and could also fit under ecology in the lesson plan format.

- Talk about and draw things that could "go" or float on top of the water or underwater. Add dictation to drawings *(horizontal:* facts about water; *vertical:* literacy, motor, memory, creativity).

This is sometimes appropriate for large groups, in which dictation could be done as a group poster. Follow up with free-choice group art mural and dramatic play.

- During small-group snack or meal, let the children pour and serve themselves water in addition to whole milk or juice. Talk about the ways water is good for people *(horizontal:* facts about water and health; *vertical:* motor, memory, literacy).

If discussion includes health, this can also be entered in the health and nutrition part of the lesson plan.

- During foods experiences at meals and snacks, possibly prepared ahead during free-choice/activity time, let the children make drinks from water and powdered mixes, discuss what happens when water is added, and compare these drinks (*horizontal:* facts about water; *vertical:* motor, literacy, perceptual, problem solving).

If discussion includes comparisons of the nutritional values of drinks, this can also be listed in the nutrition and health part of the lesson plan.

- During health routines such as handwashing, talk about dirt, germs, and the importance of using soap. You can also talk about skin color and that dirt can be washed off but skin color in each person is different (even in all Caucasian children) and does not come off. Skin color is unique to every person and comes naturally from one's parents (*horizontal:* facts about water and soap; *vertical:* motor, literacy, perception, memory).

This can also be entered on the lesson plan format under health and, if discussion of skin color was included, under antibias or multicultural awareness in the lesson plan, if the format includes it.

Free Choice—Planned Activity Time

- In the foods experiences area during children's activity time, let the children help make foods from mixes and water. Some can be mix-and-eat activities; some can be mix-and-cook (or bake) activities. Talk about changes that occurred and make comparisons. Try instant versus cooked pudding and compare the taste and the preparation time (*horizontal:* facts about water and foods; *vertical:* motor, literacy, perceptual, memory, problem solving).

If nutrition was discussed, this can also be listed in the health part of the lesson plan format.

- Let the children help prepare vegetable soup to eat the same day or the next. Talk about the tastes and how cooking in water changes the taste, smell, and look of the vegetables. Talk about the changes that occurred during cooking, and recall the steps in the process of making the soup (*horizontal:* facts about water and foods; *vertical:* motor, perceptual, literacy, memory, problem solving).

Nutrition will be discussed, so this activity can be entered in the health and nutrition part of the lesson plan format.

- Have the children help wash and dry chairs and tables or dolls and housekeeping dishes with small buckets or tubs of soapy water, small brushes, and towels. Put towels under the tubs or buckets for splashes. Talk about why it is important to keep things clean (*horizontal:* facts about water and soap in controlling dirt or germs; *vertical:* motor, perceptual, literacy, memory, problem solving).

This can also be entered in the health part of the lesson plan format.

- Have the children estimate and discover how many cups of water at the water table can fill a large container or small bucket. Discuss "more" and "less, "as well as counting the cups as they are poured (*horizontal:* facts about water and mass; *vertical:* motor, perception, literacy, problem solving).

Depending on the skill levels in the group, try similar guessing, discovery, and cause-and-effect experiments with water wheels, basters, and siphons (same skills).

- Freeze some water in ice cubes and set them out to be observed and discussed as they melt. Snow, if available, can also be used in this way. Graphs can be made to compare the speed at which snow and ice melt in the classroom, or even in different areas of the building. A variation is to make ice and compare the time it takes to freeze outside in cold weather versus inside in the refrigerator (*horizontal:* facts about water and changes from liquid to solid; *vertical:* motor, perceptual, literacy, problem solving).
- Do sink-and-float activities at the water table or in tubs. Have children experiment, observe, tell, and graph what happens. See what happens when a toy boat is filled with heavy, small pebbles. Another variation is to use real clay and experiment to discover and compare how clay balls sink, but clay pancakes float (*horizontal:* facts about water and buoyancy; *vertical:* motor, literacy, memory, problem solving).
- Put a variety of objects found underwater, such as pebbles and shells, into the water table. Add toy boats if desired. Discuss how rocks, shells, and pebbles look different when wet or dry (*horizontal:* facts about water; *vertical:* motor, memory, literacy, perceptual, problem solving).
- In a dramatic play area add "fishing" props, either for fishing from boats or docks, or for ice fishing. Include props such as appropriate clothing and life jackets, and discuss safety. On another day, try "beach" props, including empty sun block containers, sunglasses, hats, life preservers, and sandals. Consider snorkeling props and paper underwater creatures (*horizontal:* facts about water; *vertical:* motor, literacy, memory, problem solving, creativity).

This is also a health and safety activity.

- Do follow-up activities from group discussions. For example, do experiments with watering versus not watering a plant, or do a group art mural of things that live in the water. Sand could be glued to the bottom of blue/green paper, and children's own designs of colored or painted fish, creatures, and plants can be cut out and pasted to the mural *(horizontal:* facts about marine life; *vertical:* motor, perceptual, memory, literacy, problem solving, creativity).
- In the sandbox or sand table, create an island surrounded by water. See pictures and maps of islands for comparison and discussion *(horizontal:* facts about water and land; *vertical:* motor, literacy, memory, problem solving, creativity).

This learning can be extended to discussions of what is in the water around islands, what foods island dwellers often eat, and what sorts of art and jewelry they make. If learning about island cultures is included, this can be entered in the antibias/multicultural awareness section of the lesson plan format. This would also make a great investigative project for children ages 4 through 8.

Outdoor Time

- Have the children collect and measure rain water in a bucket or rain barrel. Tell, dictate, and/or graph observations *(horizontal:* facts about water; *vertical:* motor, perceptual, memory, literacy, problem solving).
- With safe supervision, get samples of water from a nearby pond, stream, or beach. Observe, compare, and discuss. Is the water clean or polluted? Fresh or salty? *(horizontal:* facts about water; *vertical:* motor, perception, literacy, problem solving).

If the discussion includes clean water and pollution, this can also be entered in the ecology part of the lesson plan format.

- If there is snow, consider spraying it with pink or red tempera mixed with water, from big spray bottles, as in the Dr. Seuss story *The Cat in the Hat Returns. (horizontal:* facts about water and paint; *vertical:* motor, literacy, perceptual, memory). Children can also have opportunities to help mix tempera powder paint with water for use in the art area
- Where ice is available, "adopt" an icicle to observe and study (even photograph) from a *safe* distance. Watch changes in the growth of the icicle. Discuss and graph *(horizontal:* facts about water and its changes from liquid to solid; *vertical:* literacy, problem solving, perception, memory).

This is also a safety activity.

- See what happens in cold climates when soapy water bubbles are blown outdoors in below freezing conditions *(horizontal:* facts about water and temperatures; *vertical:* motor, literacy, problem solving).

- With small buckets of water, wet the pavement or sidewalk and draw on it with colored chalk. Find out and note how long the pavement takes to dry or the water to evaporate. Another variation is to use wallpaper or big brushes and plain water in small buckets to "paint" the sidewalk, or the side of the building; watch the change caused by evaporation *(horizontal:* facts about water and evaporation; *vertical:* motor, literacy, perception, problem solving, creativity).

Now you know how to take ideas from your preplanning webs, sort them into vertical and horizontal planning, and organize them for inclusion in your daily lesson plans. Integrated activities demonstrate multiple links between planning and outcomes.

Summary

In this chapter, we have talked about integrated activities as a logical and meaningful way to teach young children, who are always learning and who learn in an integrated manner. Integrated learning experiences also mesh with many learning styles. Since children learn best through their own unique combinations of learning styles, providing daily integrated experiences helps teachers more effectively reach and teach every child.

We have looked at both simple and complex integrated activities and seen examples (dramatic play, beanbags, playdough, apples, newspapers, soil, and water). The teacher's mental planning for integrated activities can be drawn as teaching and learning webs, and these webs, whether they are simple or complex, can continually change, depending on the emerging interests of children.

Pictures of learning webs are wonderful aids in thinking and planning. They open the mind to the possibilities for children's emergent interests in the curriculum. When you look at a complex web, you can see activities that are both knowledge-based and skill-based, or *horizontal* and *vertical.* However, a teacher would not he carrying around a batch of pictures of learning webs to use as a year-long horizontal plan.

To do daily lesson planning, you will still need a *system* to put your ideas on paper in a long-range horizontal plan for the year. An outline format, such as seen in Chapter 7, makes it easy for you to adjust to emerging curriculum interests. To do good *daily* lesson plans, you will also need a system to manage your skill-based ideas. Be sure you are planning a balance of all skill areas, and that you are linking curriculum activities to specific learning domain objectives, meeting the needs of each child in your group. Chapter 8 and Appendix A will give you that system. This chapter shows the system in action.

Using integrated activities, supporting children's emergent curriculum interests, and facilitating children's learning by implementing hands-on activities in the classroom are some of the most exciting and challenging aspects of teaching young children. Teachers of young children need to be flexible, creative, full of energy, able to think on their feet, and able to do several things at a time. This is a demanding, but exhilarating and fulfilling career. If this is what teaching means to you, there is no better choice than to teach young children.

Self-Study Activities

1. Go back over some of your old lesson plans and find two materials or experiences that you expanded, during one day in the classroom, to integrate other areas of the curriculum. Now draw the two simple learning webs that would illustrate your teaching. Are there ways you could have added to your webs?

2. Review old lesson plans or your horizontal long-range plan of themes for the year.

Could some of these theme activities have been expanded to integrate other emergent interests of the children? What could you have done to encourage this? Draw complex webs for two such thematic units, imagining and including other topics that might have emerged and been integrated.

3. Draw a learning web about one of your own personal interests or hobbies. Might other interests emerge that could be added?

Resources and Suggested Readings

Armstrong, Thomas. *In Their Own Way: Discovering and Encouraging Your Child's Multiiple Intelligences* (rev. ed.). New York: Jeremy P. Tarcher/Putnam; Penguin Putman, 2000.

Campbell, Linda; Campbell, Bruce; & Dickinson, Dee. *Teaching and Learning through Multiple Intelligences* (2nd ed.). Boston: Allyn and Bacon, 1999.

Carlisle, Ashby. "Using the Multiple Intelligences Theory to Assess Early Childhood Curricula." *Young Children,* 56, no. 6 (2001): 77–83.

Chen, J. (Ed.), Gardner, H.; Feldman, D. H.; & Krechevsky, M. (Series Eds.). *Project Spectrum: Early Learning Activities.* New York: Teachers College Press, 2000.

Gardner, H. *Multiple Intelligences: The Theory in Practice.* New York: Basic/HarperCollins, 1993.

Karges-Bone, Linda. *Lesson Planning: Long-Range and Short-Range Models for Grades K–6.* Boston: Allyn and Bacon, 2000.

10 Classroom Management

Social-Emotional Outcomes

Experienced teachers know that no matter how comprehensive one's planning has been, and no matter how many fascinating learning experiences are provided in a well-equipped, perfectly arranged setting, if a teacher has poor classroom management, chaos is more likely to occur than is in-depth learning. When a teacher is inexperienced in using management and guidance techniques, a few children can disrupt the teaching/learning process so much that none of the children benefit from what may have been excellent curriculum planning.

The goal is to have children enjoy learning and to have teachers enjoy teaching. When teachers use effective classroom management and guidance techniques, they are more able to scaffold positive social emotional outcomes for children and also accomplish their other curriculum goals.

In this chapter we'll start with a brief list of what to avoid, and then we'll cover the kinds of management strategies that prevent most management and behavior problems. Many things can be done to prevent problems before children even enter the classroom. Next, we'll discuss what kinds of management techniques to use when children are actually present (e.g., how to respond "on the spot"). Finally, we'll cover some special challenges in classroom management, such as working with children who have special needs or behavior problems.

What to Avoid

Humiliating, shaming, frightening, threatening, or hurting children
Comparing children to others or bringing up past mistakes
Giving children too many rules or stating expectations that are not clear
Giving choices when there are none or making promises you cannot keep
Creating consequences that don't relate to the behavior or that are postponed
Overusing or misusing time-out, which should be used *rarely* and correctly if at all

Preventive Management and Guidance

Schedule

Plan ample time in the schedule to do routines and transitions without rushing. And for the children, be sure there is ample time for uninterrupted work and play during free time to avoid frustration or stress. Just like adults, children are upset when they cannot finish a focused activity; they need to know ahead of time when free time will be ending. Plan the way you will give them this information with visual or auditory cues (lights, tiny bell, special music, special puppet), or by having a "helper" child move about the room to let others know that "cleanup time is coming in five minutes."

An age-appropriate and predictable routine should work for you, not against you, and that routine should include a flow of both active and quiet experiences. Plan ample time for transitions and ways to make them easy and reassuring. Designate a meeting place (perhaps on the rug to read books) where children can go to wait for others until the next activity.

Your curriculum should be developmentally appropriate and provide both success and challenge to children. When children are busy doing things that interest them, they rarely exhibit behavior problems. Include movement, experimentation, exploration, and manipulation of materials.

Materials

Be sure materials and equipment are age appropriate, and that they provide both success and challenge to children. Provide enough materials so that sharing won't be a problem. (Have duplicates of more popular favorites if possible.) Plan to offer concrete, hands-on, open-ended, sensory materials and time to fully explore them. Arrange logical use of materials that must be shared. For example, you might indicate with floor footprints that only four can play at one time at a small water table. A sign could be posted that shows that only five can play in blocks at one time. Most teachers post these signs in each learning center, using photos, symbols, stick figures, silhouettes, or drawings to show how many can play. Other materials that are to be shared should be accessible on low open shelves near the tables and chairs where they will be used. A visual cue such as a red Stop sign should mark storage areas where children cannot go.

Room Arrangement

Plan for a good traffic flow with no long open areas that invite running. Be sure to use low, open shelves and learning centers to break up large spaces. No high cupboards should block the adult supervisors' view of the areas of the room. Learning centers should be well defined so that children can see the choices available to them. Label each learning center and also post a list of *what children learn* in each center (see Chapter 3) in addition to the signs about how many children can normally play in each area. Signs should be clear, attractive, and posted at children's eye level.

Play Slots or Play Spaces

Open all learning centers during free-choice time. Plan many spaces where children can work in groups of two or three, and sometimes in groups of four. Some areas, such as blocks, can accommodate five if there is enough space. Create some areas where children can work individually. Count play slots or spaces to ensure that there are 2½ times as many as children (see Chapter 3). Where there are enough interesting play spaces, there are far less behavior problems. Children are busy, happy, and learning; they are not bored, restless, or wandering.

Here's an example: If the teacher plans to allow only the use of three or four learning centers during free-choice time, all the children will want to engage in activity in those areas. If the four open centers are a climber, a small housekeeping area, an easel with space for two, and some crayons and paper on one table and puzzles and beads on another table, where will we find most of the children? Perhaps two or three will be in the art area, and two in the manipulatives area, and perhaps three will be in housekeeping, but you are likely to see eight or nine children trying to use the climber at once. This can lead to safety and guidance problems. More work/play slots always means more learning for children and fewer management problems for teachers.

Balance of Stimulation

When planning to offer activities that are the children's favorites, or that are very stimulating and inviting to use, be sure these materials are not placed in just one area of the room; this will invite overcrowding and frustration, as many children will try to be in that area. Plan stimulating and favorite activities in *several* areas to draw children into all the spaces of the room. If one of your learning centers is not being used, plan to put something inviting there, like water play in a dishtub on top of a beach towel on a table or on the rug. Other possibilities are making playdough, doing a foods-tasting activity, or using shaving cream as fingerpaint on a table.

Stress Reducers

Plan activities with yielding media—such as playdough, clay, paint, water, and sand—to relieve tension, and offer these *every* day. These stress relievers can reduce behavior and management problems. (If a child comes into the classroom looking tense and under stress, plan to have the child sit and use playdough for about five minutes or play at the water table for five minutes before starting the day.)

Accessibility

Ensure that materials are in the areas in which they will be used, and that they are on low, open shelves so children can get them out to use and put them away (see Chapter 3). Be sure to label shelves, bins, and boxes with words and pictures to convey to the children the contents and to make putting away easy and fun. The labels also help children practice perception and literacy skills.

Ratio

There should be enough adults to provide safe supervision and adequate attention to the children in the group. Many states require specific adult-to-child ratios for each age level. Staff should also be qualified and trained before children start attending school so that they are comfortable with setting clear expectations and giving children positive guidance. All adults should be prepared to use the same guidance strategies and be consistent in their use.

Whenever possible, enlist volunteers and student teachers or community workers to supplement the ongoing staff so that children will have more individualized attention and scaffolded dialogues. Plan effective placement of adults in various learning centers during free-choice time indoors and outside and in group time (supporting the adult leading the group). Training in classroom management should be given regularly to all staff and to all volunteers.

Parents as Staff

Many teachers are lucky to have parent volunteers who can be an important supplement to the team teaching staff. In order to feel comfortable in setting limits and using positive guidance techniques, parents need to have training, direction, and encouragement. When they work with teachers in the classroom they will continue to need direction and *plenty of praise*. Training should include child development; parents need to know what kinds of behavior to expect. It should also include information about how children learn and about what they are learning in each discovery center in the room. Until they are completely at ease in their roles, volunteer parents should be placed in learning areas where they feel most comfortable. Some parents prefer the art area, others prefer blocks, woodworking, or manipulatives.

Management and Guidance in Action

Rules

During the first days of school, the children, in large- or small-group discussions with the adults, should discuss the need for some simple rules for the safety and comfort of group members. With adult guidance, children can be led to make a few simple rules for the group, such as, "We walk indoors; we can run outdoors." "We use quiet voices indoors." "Sand stays in the sand table; water stays in the water table." "We do not bring action toys, play guns, or knives to school." "We respect our friends and their personal space." (Each child should have a cubby or personal space for his or her own belongings.)

Children's rules should be stated positively, printed clearly, and posted in the room where they can be seen. Rules will be modified as needs arise, but beginning group rules are an important step in problem prevention. Especially at the beginning of the year, rules should be few and should emphasize safety. One rule of thumb is to have only one rule per each year of the child's age (e.g., many teachers start the year with only four rules for a group of 3- to 5-year-olds).

Some teachers develop and post rules for safety that are separate from rules for the use of materials or for the ways children will interact with each other. This prevents the problem of having one very long list of unrelated rules. Safety rules could be developed with the children first, and posted separately from other rules. A few rules for outdoor safety could be posted near the exit door to the outdoor area, such as, "We climb up the slide safely; we slide *down* the slide." A few rules for bus safety could be posted on the bus; for example, "We get on the bus one at a time, and we buckle up."

Add rules as necessary when situations come up that require them. For example, if toys are allowed to be brought to school, the issue of what can be brought and who can play with them can present problems. Play guns and weapons should not be allowed. The children and teacher could discuss and develop a rule regarding whether or not (or when) to bring toys to school, or a rule to tell the group about a cherished possession at circle time and then put it in the cubby for the rest of the day.

Ask the Rules Rather Than Tell the Rules.   When adults tell children rules, sometimes repeatedly, young children simply stop hearing them. They "turn off the adult" and certainly don't spend a second thinking about the rule they helped make or the reasons for it. By a couple of weeks into the program year, most children will know the rules. Instead of telling, *ask* the rule: "What was that rule we made about running indoors?" The child will now have to think, remember, and tell the rule. He or she will think about how the rule applies to the situation at hand.

Then ask the reasons for the rule: "Why did we make that rule, do you remember?" The adult can then problem solve with the child about ways to help him or her remember that rule. For example, perhaps a secret signal can be used, or perhaps the child could help make a visual cue, such as a "Stop" or "Slow—School Zone" sign. These techniques are much more logical and effective than telling children rules over and over again.

Positive Guidance

Teachers and the support staff guide children best when they are aware that their verbal and nonverbal communication has great impact on children. When the staff states expectations or reminds children of rules, the statements must be positive. Children are confused when teachers say, "Don't do ..." because they hear the behavior teachers do *not* want, prefaced by the word *don't*. Children understand much better when they are told what the teachers *do* want from them. Children also learn as much or more from facial expression and body language than the words. The way the adult *says* his or her words is more important to them than the actual words. Verbal guidance should be positive, calm, and firm but soft-spoken.

Guidance should include questions that make children think about their behavior and their responsibilities, and should help children accept the consequences of their behaviors. It should include clear, simple expectations and an attitude of trust in the children to follow through. Guidance should also include praise and reinforcement that tells children the ways adults want them to behave, and what behaviors adults approve.

Teachers should also be aware that their guidance and interactions are actually teaching children life skills—the skills of positive communication and interaction, positive social skills, and self-control. Parents who are in the classroom observing the staff's modeling are also learning; they will pick up on new ways to teach these life skills to their children at home. Most parents will learn much more from modeling than from a parent meeting or workshop on guidance and discipline.

Positive Modeling

Teachers must model the behaviors and language they want from children. They cannot run after a child who is running, shouting, "Don't run!" They cannot sit on the tables or edges of the sand table instead of on chairs. They need to use pleasant voices as they speak to both children and other adults. They need to continually model positive social language and positive statements of rules or expectations. When stating important expectations for behavior, they need to maintain eye contact (if this is culturally appropriate) or get down on the child's level and speak quietly, positively, and firmly. When teachers remain calm and take the time to communicate clearly in this manner, children understand what is expected and are likely to cooperate.

Teachers will find that if they try to control situations by turning up the volume of their voices, children's voices will also be louder; if they speak quietly, the noise level will go down. Some teachers actually use whispering as a technique; children start to whisper too. Others very effectively use body language and some simple signing as they speak. Because young children pay more attention to the teacher's facial expressions and body language than words, they are confused when verbal and nonverbal communication doesn't match. (In other words, don't laugh or smile when you are stating a safety rule to prevent a problem.)

Diffusion and Redirection

Sometimes the simple placement of an adult in an area is enough to prevent a potential problem from escalating. Teachers and adult assistants have an effective nonverbal impact on children's behaviors by their very presence, facial expression, and body language. This impact can often be enhanced when the adult sits down nearby or enters the play situation; children are likely to try harder to use self-control and appropriate behaviors.

Another way to defuse potential problems is by taking props into the potential problem area; this interests the children and redirects their attention. A cloth drawstring "guessing bag" with an object hidden inside is an easy prop to have handy in these situations. A ukelele is another great diffusion/redirection aid; striking up a familiar song releases tension immediately. Asking a child for help with a task is another redirection strategy.

Transitions

Teachers can also use transitions for redirection, so it's wise to have a few of them in mind and on hand at all times. Fingerplays or funny rhymes are the easiest kinds of transitions to use "on the spot" in diffusion or redirection. Planned transitions, however, have an important place in the teacher's classroom management. Transitions are the glue that holds the children together in the 5 minutes or so between the events or activities in the schedule. Without planned transitions, the children wander off or begin to play again and need to be gathered. The 5 minutes can become 10 or more minutes of chaos. Planning the transitions that can be instantly used in between events is vital, especially for inexperienced teachers who have not yet developed a repertoire of them.

There are basically four types of transitions, and it's wise to know and use a variety of each type. *Musical transitions* are self-explanatory—they are songs, the use of instruments, or recorded music that can be used to move children from one place to another or to gather children together in between events. Many transitions can easily be tied in with the current themes in which children are involved.

Creative transitions involve pretending and imagining, and are often effectively used in circle time, such as, "Let's pretend that we are standing on a cloud high in the sky. What else can we see up here?" or "Let's pretend to be snowmen. What happens to us when the sun shines and we start to melt?"

Physical transitions usually involve gathering the children together and having them use their bodies in some way as they move from one activity to another. This type of transition is usually combined with imagination or pretending. For example, making a "train" that can "choo choo" to the door and down the hall to the bathrooms is both a creative and a physical transition. Walking like little mice, or butterflies, or like kings and queens are both physical and creative transitions. Resting on the rug and listening to quiet music is a purely physical transition.

The fourth general type of transition is *cognitive*. These transitions include things such as having children identify their names as seen printed on cards as they leave the circle one at a time, or having them identify shapes, colors, and so on. Another cognitive transition is having children who are wearing green (or whatever color) go to wash their hands first. Still another cognitive transition is having children meet on the rug and read books independently after finishing breakfast.

Circle Time

Student teachers and inexperienced teachers often have management problems during large-group time until they have more confidence in leading the group and learning to use visuals, props, facial expression, and vocal expression to keep the children's attention. Two important things teachers can do is to be well prepared (knowing generally what will be said and done and in what order) and to have another adult be in the circle for support and assistance. It is often helpful to inexperienced teachers if the large group is split in half, having each teacher take seven or eight children in the circle instead of leading the entire group.

Teachers must be aware of the needs of children in the circle and be ready to respond appropriately. For example, if children seem bored or restless, that's the teacher's cue to shorten the discussion or change the activity and do something active. Children could stand in the circle and stretch out and breathe deeply or do some "Do what I do" exercises; they could sing "Head, Shoulders, Knees and Toes," do the "Hokey Pokey," or toss and catch a big pillow stuffed with newspapers. After this type of active movement, however, children need a teacher-led transition to be "brought down" from their excitement to a calmer state. A good transition is to act out a melting snowman, ice cream cone, or ice cube, which calms children and gets them back to position on the floor.

Another circle time management technique is to use carpet squares as spaces for children's seating. This gives each child a clear location for his or her personal space on the rug. Carpet squares are also useful for gathering children into the circle and focusing their attention on the adult leader. For example, as children are coming into the group and taking their places, the teacher can play a game in which children put various body parts on the square (e.g., their toes, elbows, knees, noses, and so on), ending with children sitting on top of the square.

The use of props, such as a "talking stick" or "talking feather" or a similar object, can help children take turns and talk one at a time in the circle. The prop is passed around the circle and each child who wants to share something holds it as he or she talks.

Positive Expectations—Positive Reinforcement

If teachers or parents expect the worst from children, they will usually get it. Always expect the best from children, and you'll usually get it. When teachers let children know through words or facial expression that they trust them to follow through on an expected behavior, they are passing the responsibility to the child. This tells the children that the adult has positive expectations and trusts them to demonstrate the positive behavior. This technique gives many children the pride and self-respect they need to change their negative actions into positive behavior.

Whenever children make any effort to change behaviors from negative to positive, they should receive positive reinforcement from adults. This could include a smile, a hug or other positive touch, a reward that is meaningful to the child, and, most of all, descriptive praise. Nothing will help a child to achieve positive self-discipline better than praise. Children repeat behaviors for which they are praised by adults or by peers.

Descriptive praise, like constructive criticism, should always describe the child's behavior and how it makes the adult feel: "I noticed that you helped rebuild the block tower that fell when you got too close; that was the right thing to do. It made your friends feel better and it made me proud of you." "I am noticing that your voice is getting very loud, and it hurts our ears. What can you do to help us out?"

To reinforce positive learning experiences or positive social-emotional growth, descriptive praise should always be used. Saying "Good job" is not enough. After hearing it a few times, "Good job" (which is highly overused) is not meaningful to children; it doesn't tell them what the adult actually likes or why it's important. Compare "Good job" to these comments that are meaningful to children: "I see that you mixed some yellow and blue paint and got a new color—green. You made an exciting discovery!" "I was really proud of you today when you remembered to keep the sand in the sand box. Thank you." Children need to know what the teacher considers appropriate behavior approve and why. Giving children descriptive praise for behaviors the teacher wants them to repeat is very effective.

Like praise, rewards (when given) should also be meaningful to the child. Some children will appreciate the reward of being a "helper" or first in line; others just appreciate a smile and hug; and some like to be praised in front of their peers. Match the reward or reinforcement to the child.

In addition, teachers should enhance the "family" feeling of the group by giving praise to any child who helps another child. Any time a child is asked to help someone else, or do something that benefits the group, praise and thanks are in order. Group praise can also be given to the entire group, enhancing the feelings of responsibility to the group in all of the children, such as, "You all did a very careful job of cleaning up today and you finished the job quickly. I am proud. Hooray! Let's give ourselves a cheer and a big round of applause." These strategies foster a feeling of community among the group.

Choices

Giving children choices allows them to feel a sense of self-control and experience in self-discipline and self-reliance. But never give children choices when there is no choice. For example, at cleanup time one would not say, "Would you like to help clean up the blocks now?" If the children were prepared for cleanup time, and a child is not helping, a teacher might say, "It's cleanup time now. Would you like to pick up those small square blocks or the long ones?" Or, "Would you like to carry the blocks over, or be the one who puts them on the shelf in the right places?" If a child is resistant about cooperating, giving the child two alternative choices helps the child feel in control and not boxed into a corner. When presenting these two alternatives, the adult should exhibit (face and body language) a positive attitude of trust in the child to cooperate.

Problem Solving

If two children are having a conflict, try to let them solve it themselves if possible. Be supportive by asking questions to get the problem solving started. Ask both children to tell their side of the story and how they feel about it. Then ask them to identify the problem. Next, ask them to try to think of different ways to solve the problem. Help them negotiate and compromise to choose one way to resolve it. Try it, and if it isn't satisfactory, try again until a compromise is reached. This kind of problem solving is a life skill that is often practiced in early childhood programs.

Consequences

Teach responsibility by letting children experience the consequences of their choices. Children do understand cause and effect; take advantage of this. If children don't keep the sand in the sand box, they cannot play with the sand. If they don't keep the playdough on the table, they cannot play with the playdough. If they make a mess on purpose, they have to clean up the mess. During work and play time, when children accept responsibility for their actions and learn to follow the rules for using materials, they are learning important life skills. They are also learning that privileges come hand in hand with responsibilities.

Contracts

Another way to help children learn to accept the consequences of their choices and learn responsibility is to use contracting. Contracts can be helpful to children who have difficulties in managing self-control. It makes them feel important and competent, and they also feel that the adult trusts them to try to fulfill the task in the contract. Tell the child the desired behavior, such as being able to use the climber and wheel toys outside without pushing and shoving. Agree on a reward that is meaningful to that child. Explain that if he or she can accomplish the task, the reward will follow. Depending on the seriousness of the behavior and how hard the child must work at self-control, the reward might be being a special helper or being recognized and applauded during circle time by peers. If the child follows through on the contract, the reward is given.

Contracts are completely different from bribes. When an adult gives a child who is already misbehaving a reward to stop misbehaving, it's bribery and it will backfire. The child who is bribed will simply repeat the bad behavior to get the reward again. Contracts, on the other hand, help children accept responsibility and learn to repeat good behavior.

Be Consistent

Sometimes children have a hard time following the rules. This often happens with children who have special needs. Since they really want to be just like the other children, not different, be sure to use the same rules and limits for them as for other children. Expect their best; don't make excuses for them and be very generous with praise for good behavior. Special education support staff or resource persons can also give teachers advice and individualized tips to use with these children to help them learn self-control.

Say No and Say Why

It is perfectly acceptable to say no to children and to let them know the behavior or language that is unacceptable. Children need the security of limits. They need to know that adults, not they, are responsible for making final decisions, and they need to see adults model ways that they take on this responsibility. When adults are clear about limits, children feel safe. Sometimes children act out or have tantrums instead of using words to test their limits. The adult should ignore the tantrum behavior and stay calm and in control of the situation. The child still needs to know that the adult is in charge.

Do More and Say Less

A child having a tantrum cannot hear the adult, and when an adult "talks at" or lectures young children who are misbehaving, what the adult is saying is usually "turned off." Instead, the adult should try using the face and the eyes to talk to children, and use fewer words. For example, instead of an entire paragraph about why Josh should hang up his jacket, the adult should get eye contact, point to the jacket, and say, "Josh . . . jacket," or simply, "Josh." In many guidance situations and with many types of children, doing more and saying less is very effective.

Help Children Calm Down

In most cases when children get too loud or rowdy, it's because they really have not yet learned how to calm themselves down. This is not a skill that children are born with; it must be learned and adults need to help teach it. Develop special, individualized strategies to help children learn to calm down. The real goal is to teach children to eventually recognize their own "out of control" feelings and take independent action to calm themselves.

Some children will have the control to slow down or lower their voices if you have arranged a secret signal to give them when they need to calm down. Others will need specific help, such as being invited to rest a while, "take a break," and hear a story. Other children need help in slowing down their physical movements gradually—for instance, "Now let's try to move as slowly as you can; do 'moon walking' with slow giant steps." Or, "Now let's take deep breaths and listen to our breathing."

Time-Out

Time-out should be used only as a guidance technique when the goal is for the child to calm down and regain control of himself or herself. It should not be used as punishment or for isolation. Sometimes the best way to do this is to suggest to the child that he or she needs to sit down for a time to regain self-control. Many children would prefer or actually need to be held on an adult's lap for a short time instead of sitting alone on a chair. The adult can gauge the child's responses best by placing both arms around the child in a hug. The child should know and be able to express why he or she is taking some time-out. When the adult feels the child relax and breathe normally, the child can be asked if he or she is calm now and ready to go back and play.

The last seven items discussed—consequences, contracts, being consistent, saying no, doing more and saying less, calming down, and time-out used appropriately—are especially effective techniques for children with behavior problems. Often, special needs consultants can give teachers other, more specific techniques that will help these children learn self-control. One of the most important elements in working with challenging behaviors is the inner response of the adult.

The most common error of adults in interacting or responding to challenging behaviors is to move too quickly into the "What shall I do?" mode; this often creates a hurried, "putting out fires" approach. Instead, it's more effective for the teacher to observe and assess the situation silently and quickly and mentally ask, "What does this child need?" If you will look again at the seven tips above, you will see that in each case, *the teacher is responding to the child's needs.*

When children act out, they are telling the adult they are losing control and need help in regaining it. By meeting the child's needs for assistance in ways that work for each child, children with challenging behaviors are better able to learn self-control and self-discipline techniques. When adults or students in the classroom rush about, especially during free time, thinking, "What should I do?" instead of "What does that child need?" techniques that are not helpful to the child are likely to be used.

Attitude is another obstacle that hinders the adult's ability to help children with challenging behaviors make changes and improvements. Unfortunately, children with challenging behaviors are often labeled as "bad, hyper, or uncontrollable" in the adult's mind. Children are very insightful and sensitive to adults' true feelings; when adults mentally label children and expect the worst from them, children perceive themselves as bad, hyper, and uncontrollable and they act that way.

Teachers and staff must get to know children with challenging behaviors personally, one on one. Try to understand the reasons for the child's behavior and build rapport and trust with the child. The goal is to make the child feel that someone really cares—that the child is not really bad and uncontrollable, and might be able to actually "fit in."

Peer Reinforcement and Challenging Behaviors: A Case Study

Here is a case study that proves this point and that will give you insight on another excellent strategy for guidance: peer reinforcement.

Harry, a child with special needs, was in our cooperative preschool program; we met three mornings a week. In addition, he was in a child guidance clinic preschool program two days a week. Harry wore very thick glasses and was cross-eyed. He had a hearing loss, which affected his learning of language, so his speech was very difficult to understand. He was also a healthy, active, and strong 4-year-old.

Within two weeks of entering the cooperative preschool program, Harry had been successful in terrorizing both the children and their parents, who were the adult staff persons working with the teacher-director. Harry threw sand, knocked over block constructions, and hit and pushed children down both outdoors and in the classroom. He also regularly kicked adults who tried to restrain him, and acted out his anger one day by spitting in the juice pitcher. (The teacher said, "No. This is not allowed; you cannot spit in the juice at our school," and had Harry dump out the juice, wash the pitcher, and return it to the snack table.)

Since this was a cooperative preschool, anxious and angry parents called for a special meeting. Most parents wanted Harry removed from the program. Harry's mother begged to be allowed to speak to the group. She explained that Harry had been born with the hearing loss and crossed eyes, and that the thick glasses that allowed him to see, along with his vision problem, gave him terrible daily headaches. Three surgeries were planned to correct Harry's crossed eyes, but these would take place over several years. Harry's mom told the other parents that Harry loved going to the coop preschool more than anything in his life, talked about the children there, and asked daily if they could go every day instead of three days. Parents were very surprised to hear this, because it didn't seem to fit with Harry's behavior at school.

It did "fit," however, when the teacher and parents stopped saying to themselves, "What should we do? What can we do about terrible Harry?" His behavior made sense when the teacher and parents discussed the situation and asked themselves, "What does Harry need? What does he want more than anything else?" What Harry needed was to feel that he fit in and was just like everyone else. He needed friends who liked him; he simply had no idea of how to get them. When the teacher and parents realized this, they came up with a plan based on what Harry needed. Each one of them, as rotating staff, promised to follow this plan to the letter and see if it worked. If the plan worked, Harry would stay with the group.

The plan was to focus on two of Harry's needs: the need for Harry to feel he was just like everyone else, and the need for Harry to have friends. Other elements of the plan were focused on Harry's physical needs to cope with stress, and to be able to calm himself down.

When Harry came to school the next day, the teacher greeted him and held him on her lap and said, "Harry, I think you will have a better day and be happier if you play with the playdough first, before you go to the blocks area. Can you do that?" From that day on, Harry started his day with 5 to 10 minutes at the playdough or clay table or at the water table, instead of rushing over to the large-muscle toys and blocks area. This calmed him down and gave him a transition to move from overexcitement to normal eagerness.

Whenever the adults or teacher saw Harry doing something inappropriate, they put their hands on his shoulders, got down to look him in the eyes, and said slowly and clearly, "Harry, in our school children cannot hit other children or push them" (or kick, or knock down the blocks, or throw sand, depending on what he was doing) "Harry, *you are just like everyone else,* and so you cannot do those things either." Each adult said the same words, emphasizing that Harry was just like the other children.

If Harry looked as if he were starting to lose control, the teacher would take him on her lap and hold him, saying, "Harry, it looks like you are losing control. You are not feeling good about what you are doing right now. Sit here with me for a few minutes until you feel OK." When Harry relaxed and started to breathe deeply and normally, the teacher would ask Harry if he felt OK and if he thought he could go play now and remember the rule about keeping the sand in the sandbox (or walking carefully around block towers, or whatever). If he agreed, he went back to play; if he started losing control, the process was repeated.

But by far the most effective strategy in changing Harry's behavior was the praise by the other children. As most adults know, young children love to observe and tell. Observing and telling is actually a science skill, but most children use this skill for tattling. We knew that the children were already beginning to label Harry as a "bad" child, and we had to turn that label around with "positive tattling." Whenever an adult noticed Harry doing even a tiny thing right, the adult quickly asked one of the children nearby, "John, did you notice that Harry is trying hard to keep the sand in the sandbox? Can you please tell him you noticed?" "Betsy, did you notice that Harry remembered to push in his chair when he was done with the playdough? Can you please tell him you noticed?" "Susie, did you see that Harry took his turn on the slide without pushing? Please tell him you saw that." We knew it was much more important for Harry to get praise from his peers than from adults; this is true of any child who wants to have friends and fit in.

We started by asking a few children to help us "notice" good things and tell Harry, but within three days, all the children were trying to do positive tattling about Harry. Children intuitively knew that Harry needed help. Their praise began to work a miracle. Within two weeks, Harry was beginning to succeed in controlling his impulsive and aggressive behaviors. The label "bad child" was disappearing from the minds of adults and children. Within a month, Harry could demonstrate cooperation and self-control for the entire day; he would calm himself down by sitting on someone's lap occasionally. He continued to use water or playdough as he started the day. He was talking to the children (who understood his speech better than the adults did) and would say he was sorry if he accidentally knocked something down.

At the end of the preschool day, the children gathered on the floor in a circle, and as each car pool of children were picked up, all the others smiled, waved, and said goodbye. We knew Harry had found what he needed when he smiled and waved back at all the children who were smiling at him and saying, "Bye, Harry. See you next time."

Summary

In this chapter we have covered the basics of positive classroom management, starting with prevention strategies that can be planned by the teacher before children start school, and moving on to strategies of all kinds to use with children in the classroom. Positive guidance and communication, clear expectations, rules developed with children, logical consequences, descriptive praise, circle-time strategies, transitions, and peer reinforcement were among the many management tips that were discussed.

The chapter emphasized that adults can work best with challenging behaviors if they develop trust and rapport with the children and concentrate on learning what the child needs before rushing in with things adults could do. Concluding the chapter was a case study of a child with challenging behaviors and the ways adults and children worked together to turn his behavior around. Using stress relievers, clear expectations, calming techniques, and, especially, peer reinforcement gave the child what he needed and helped him learn self-control and positive social behavior.

Self-Study Activities

1. Think about a child with whom you have worked who has difficulties getting along with others. List his or her possible needs. Now look at the lists in the chapter for prevention and on-the-job strategies to see if the techniques you have used match the child's needs. Are there some techniques that you haven't tried?

2. Think about a child who has great difficulty with self-control. Are there some strategies in the chapter that might help him or her? List them and come up with a plan of action.

3. Read some of the resources in the suggested reading list and share what you learn with others. Outline a plan for a workshop on guidance and discipline for parents in your program, using this chapter and some of the books listed.

Resources and Suggested Readings

Bakley, Sue. "Through the Lens of Sensory Integration: A Different Way of Analyzing Challenging Behavior." *Young Children*, 56, no. 6 (2001): 70–76.

Essa, Eva. *A Practical Guide to Solving Preschool Behavior Problems* (4th ed.). Albany, NY: Delmar, 1999.

Faber, Adele, & Mazlish, Elaine. *How to Talk So Kids Will Listen and Listen So Kids Will Talk*. New York: Avon Books, 1982 (20th ed. 1999).

Feldman, Jean. *Transition Tips and Tricks for Teachers*. Beltsville, MD: Gryphon House, 2000.

Gartrell, Dan. "Replacing Time Out: Using Guidance to Build an Encouraging Classroom." *Young Children*, 56, no. 6 (2001): 8–16.

Ginott, Haim, G. *Teacher and Child: A Book for Parents and Teachers*. New York: Collier, 1995.

Head Start Bureau, Administration for Children and Families, U.S. Department of Health and Human Services. *Supporting Children with Challenging Behaviors: Relationships Are Key* (Training Guide). Washington, DC: Head Start Bureau, 1997.

Henthorne, Mary; Larson, Nola; & Chvojicek, Ruth. *Transition Magician 2: More Strategies for Guiding Young Children in Early Childhood Programs*. St. Paul, MN: Redleaf Press, 2000.

Hewitt, Deborah, & Heidemann, Sandra. *The Optimistic Classroom: Creative Ways to Give Children Hope*. St. Paul, MN: Redleaf Press, 1998.

Katz, Lillian, & McClellan, D. E. *Fostering Children's Social Competence: The Teacher's Role*. Washington, DC: National Association for the Education of Young Children, 1997.

Miller, Karen. *The Crisis Manual for Early Childhood Teachers: How to Handle the Really Difficult Problems*. Beltsville, MD: Gryphon House, 1995.

Mitchell, Grace. *A Very Practical Guide to Discipline with Young Children* (rev. ed.). West Palm Beach, FL: Telshare, 1998.

Petersen, Evelyn. *Growing Responsible Kids: The Seeds of Success Series*. Grand Rapids, MI: Totline Imprint/McGraw-Hill Children's Publishing, 1997.

Stone, Jeannette. *Building Classroom Community: The Early Childhood Teacher's Role*. Washington, DC: National Association for the Education of Young Children, 2001.

11 Trends and Priorities in Early Childhood Education

One of the most satisfying things about being an early childhood teacher is knowing that you are part of a field of professionals who have expanded public awareness about the importance of the early years, and that you have had a positive impact on public and private education for young children.

For many years, early childhood professionals have shared information about the ways children learn and develop. We teachers have shared the work of Jean Piaget, Lev Vygotsky, Maria Montessori, and others who have given us insight on the ways young children grow and learn. We have shared our child-centered curriculum planning and assessment methods, the rationale for our learning environments, and our beliefs that parents need to be full partners in the teaching and learning process. Our voices are being heard.

This chapter will highlight the trend to achieve developmental continuity in education from birth to age 8, the trend to serve children under age 3 in child care or early education programs, the trend to develop and maintain parent partnerships, and the trend to assess and report children's progress. Discussion will focus on the movement to plan curriculum that helps children value cultural diversity and inclusion, and the early childhood curriculum priorities of literacy, math, and science; some of the ways in which technology is playing an increasingly important role in these areas will be highlighted. Many examples of learning experiences in literacy, problem solving, math, and science will be shared.

Current Trends

Developmental Continuity

For at least 20 to 30 years, many preschool, kindergarten, and primary teachers have been working to achieve the goal of developmental continuity across the preschool years and the primary grades. Developmental continuity is a way to design curriculum so that it is linked to children's knowledge and to appropriate experiences. It flows naturally from simple to more complex learning content so that children progress successfully within a spiral of knowledge, skills, and experiences across the preschool and primary years.

In accomplishing this, teachers, administrators, and parents are working together to plan and provide developmentally appropriate learning experiences for children that not only help children meet expected outcomes but that also meet individual needs and learning styles. Integral to this trend are efforts to eliminate grades or placement based on achievement tests, and to provide smooth transitions for children as they move from preschool to kindergarten and to each of the primary grades. Language and literacy play a leading role in the process of developmental continuity, as do opportunities for children to work together to do discovery learning, construct their own knowledge, communicate what they've learned to others, apply what they've learned, and evaluate their own work.

Even though the goal of developmental continuity in all schools has not been realized, many positive changes have occurred that affirm that the goal is reachable. Growing numbers of kindergarten and primary grade teachers are working toward continuity and developmentally appropriate practices. Preschool, kindergarten, and primary teachers have developed better systems of communication and collaboration and have created smoother transitions for children between preschool and public school. Also, there are growing numbers of child-centered learning environments and more flexible daily schedules both in full- and half-day kindergartens and in the primary grades.

In a majority of classrooms for 5- to 8-year-olds, teachers are now using observation and performance-based assessment, portfolios, and children's investigative project journals to record and share the children's progress. Teachers in preschools, kindergartens, and primary grades are increasingly using discovery teaching and the project approach in an emotional climate that supports all aspects of child development. The movement toward developmental continuity is by no means complete, but it is sure and steady; the catalyst for change will continue to be active involvement and advocacy by early childhood teachers and the parents of the children with whom they work.

Programs for Children under Age Three

The movements to provide both early childhood education and quality child care for children under age 3 have grown simultaneously and rapidly since the 1980s. The increase of single mothers, the growing numbers of women in the work force, the loss of the extended family, and the welfare-to-work legislation have all contributed to the cry for more child-care programs for infants and toddlers. In addition, the escalating need for both parents to work to pay for their increasing health care and insurance costs, as well as their wants and needs, has created a bigger demand for child care.

In the late 1990s, new brain research about the amazing capacities of infants and toddler for learning flooded the media, resulting in increased public awareness and great impetus to the already burgeoning waves of "0–3" or "Early" infant and toddler programs that had been funded by Head Start earlier in the decade. To Head Start and other early childhood educators, the importance of the infant and toddler years in child development, parent-child bonding, and the formation of children's learning patterns and attitudes was not news.

The Early programs are not just for infants and toddlers; they are based on partnerships with children's parents. Parents learn to observe and interpret their children's behavior, share information with the program, and respond to their infants and toddlers in appropriate ways to foster children's total development and learning. In addition, parents learn their own importance as the child's most important teacher, and are encouraged to perceive their homes as valid learning environments. They learn about their children's physical development and health and nutrition needs, and about their needs for a secure, positive environment in which positive feelings about self and others can be fostered.

Some Early programs are center based and many others are home based. In either case, teachers or home visitors work with individual families as well as encourage networking and mutual support among parents. In addition, parents learn to access and use available community resources. Annual educational institutes provide training, share new research, and help programs share successful techniques with others. Just as the Head Start program for 3- to 5-year-olds had a positive effect on preschools in this country, the Early movement is beginning to have a positive influence on the quality of family day care and child-care centers. More staff persons in these centers are beginning to take advantage of child development training and Internet college courses.

Due to increased costs of services in both infant-toddler and preschool programs, there is an escalating trend in Head Start to develop community partnerships so that resources for all preschoolers can be shared more effectively. These partnerships vary because they are unique to the needs of the community and its families. In some cases, a resource in the community might provide the space and equipment for child care, and Head Start might provide renovations, the staff, and increased enrollment in the child-care program. In other cases, Head Start might contract with a child-care program and pay the cost of child care for eligible children whose parents have gone from welfare to work. In these cases, the child-care programs would agree to follow Head Start standards of quality and have staff attend all Head Start training sessions.

Due to the increased numbers of preschool, child-care, and infant-toddler programs and the impact of a better informed media, the public is more aware than ever before of the importance of child development and early childhood programs. A better-informed public has precipitated advocacy for parent education, quality child-care, and better training for teachers. Although the salaries of early childhood teachers have improved somewhat as teachers have earned credentials and degrees, the disparities between qualifications, competency, and salaries has not yet been resolved. It is hoped that removing these disparities will also become a trend.

Partnerships

Early childhood educators have known for many years that working with parents as partners is important and that when parents are involved, students try harder and do better work in school. In the past, early childhood professionals always tried to reinforce and support parents for efforts they made to be involved in their children's education. Teachers welcomed parents in classrooms and centers, introduced them proudly and thanked them personally and in print for whatever help they provided. Teachers wrote short positive notes about children's progress, talked to parents at conferences and on home visits, and set up special meetings with them when problems arose.

Today's trend to include parents as partners means much more than the kinds of positive reinforcement just mentioned, most of which was only one-way communication. Just as there are growing numbers of community partnerships to implement services and education for young children, the trend today is to develop and maintain real partnerships with parents and practice ongoing two-way communication and collaboration.

In today's programs, parents are taking on the roles of joint planners in their child's education. Although they respect the roles of teachers and their specific training and curriculum expertise, most of today's parents are more confident in their interactions with teachers than were parents of past generations. They ask more questions, and they want to have more say in what goes on in the classroom. They want to give input to the program's curriculum planning. (This is required in Head Start.) They want to know why children do certain activities, and how they learn from engaging in various learning experiences or by using particular materials. It is not only their right to know these things, but it is the responsibility of professionals to be able to answer their questions.

When parents ask why preschool teachers schedule free-choice time, teachers should be able to say much more than "so that children can learn through play," which is meaningless to parents without specific examples. (See Chapter 8, "Sharing Information and Time Blocks with Parents" for examples.) In addition, teachers should explain that free-choice time, which may look like play time to the casual observer, is largely preplanned. The materials and experiences offered fit the themes and emergent interests of the children so that the factual content about topics being studied is meaningful. Skills in all learning domains are also practiced during free-choice time. Parents also need to know that the experiences of free-choice time (or "project time" in kindergarten and primary grades) give children the chance to practice life skills they will continue to use as they grow to adulthood. They practice time management, prioritizing, choice making, self-discipline, and self-regulation in ways that match their ages and abilities.

The children's time for accomplishing their plans is usually restricted to about one hour. Within the classroom's rules and parameters, children learn to plan and prioritize their time, deciding where (what learning centers) they will work and play, with whom they will play, and how long they will engage in activities there. As they work and play, they also learn skills in concentration, creative thinking, and problem solving. In the give and take of cooperative play, they are involved in communicating, decision making, negotiating, and compromising. Children must use the materials and equipment in the classroom in safe and responsible ways and respect the personal property of others. These are all life skills that parents and teachers agree children should have.

But today's partnerships between parents and early childhood teachers mean even more than fully understanding what children in classrooms are learning. Parents are partners in goal setting and joint planning for their own children, based on their children's particular needs and learning styles. In the past, parents shared ideas, helped children with skills at home, and were casually involved with the program or school. Now, parents collaborate with teachers in planning educational and social-emotional goals, and learning experiences are planned for both school and home settings. (Joint collaborative planning is required in Head Start.)

Partnerships with working parents has been made much easier by the technology of the Internet, email, and cell phones. After an initial face-to-face meeting on a day or evening that is convenient, parents and teachers can stay in touch regularly with electronic media. Teachers can send home ideas and learning activities by email attachments. Technology has enhanced the trend of partnerships, just as it has made teachers' written curriculum planning and record keeping about children's progress much easier.

Assessment: Reporting Children's Progress

Chapter 6 discussed the escalating trend of funding sources, policymakers, and administrators to gather more "hard" data on the progress of children and groups of children. This trend is likely to continue, and with it will probably come increasing pressure for teachers and programs to prove that the performance-based assessment and authentic assessment methods now being used in early childhood programs actually provide valid data.

A position statement was developed in 1992 by the National Association of Early Childhood Specialists in State Departments of Education and the National Association for the Education of Young Children called "Guidelines for Appropriate Curriculum Content and Assessment in Programs Serving Children Ages 3 Through 8." The following definition of *assessment* appears on page 10:

> Assessment is the process of observing, recording, and otherwise documenting the work children do and how they do it, as a basis for a variety of educational decisions that affect the child, including planning for groups and individual children, and communicating with parents. Assessment encompasses the many forms of evaluation available to educational decision-making.

The most common strategies of performance-based assessment currently used in early education include work samples, interviews, games, and portfolios. *Work samples* are commonly thought of as portfolio collections or samples of children's work. In work samples, however, the samples collected should show a purpose; that is, they are linked with specific outcomes and curriculum objectives or goals. As stated in Chapter 6, developmental assessment tools such as the Work Sampling System, the Children's Observation Record (COR), and the Creative Curriculum Developmental Continuum Assessment all incorporate observations, work samplings and portfolio materials, record-keeping systems, checklists, and summary reports.

Interviews can be conducted informally by the teacher when the child is working in a learning center or on a project. When the teacher sees behavior that is relevant to a curriculum goal or objective and wants to record what the child says to show an understanding of a particular concept, an interview can be done with a tape recorder or with written notes. Preplanned, structured interviews can also be done in which specific questions are asked to elicit the child's thoughts.

Teachers can design *games* for specific learning objectives. When children play the game, they demonstrate their thought processes and game strategies. *Portfolios* are familiar to early educators, and have been used to collect samples of the child's work over time. These can be organized in many ways, including organization by learning domains. Again, the goals and objectives of the curriculum should be linked to the contents of the portfolios.

These methods are accepted and commonly used, but teachers and programs, as well as funding sources, are somewhat concerned about their validity. The trend is to give these performance-based methods and other authentic assessment methods, such as checklists, more reliability by linking them to curriculum goals and objectives and by making sure that the teacher makes connections between these methods and instructional planning. Teachers can also boost the validity of their observations with photographs, videos, and audio tapes that prove children are working toward specific outcomes by engaging in learning experiences that match learning domain elements and indicators.

Since the trend is to gather more hard data, many teachers and programs are concerned that the data will someday be used to create standardized tests for children from ages 3 to 8; early educators think this would be quite inappropriate. It is hoped that longitudinal studies of performance-based assessment will prove its reliability and effectiveness in documenting children's progress. The trend to gather data and records outcomes about children's progress will continue to impact early childhood education. The job of early childhood professionals is to continue to demonstrate that outcomes are the natural and gradual result of developmentally sequenced curriculum (see Chapter 8) and that outcomes are linked both to curriculum and to child development.

Cultural Diversity and Inclusion as Curriculum Priorities

In the past 20 years, there have been great strides in legislation and policy making to make all aspects of U.S. society more inclusive and more "barrier free." The positive effects of this trend can be seen in public places, schools, businesses, buildings, transportation, designs of cities, job applications, and the language of funding sources. Along with the movement to include physically challenged children and adults fully in all aspects of society and to give them access to new opportunities came the logical movement for inclusion.

Inclusion, in the narrow sense of the word, means to include fully those children who are physically, emotionally, or educationally challenged in the classroom instead of removing them to resource rooms or other programs. Inclusion policies of some kind are part of every school system, and the debate over whether inclusion is completely successful or good for every child has not been concluded. Most early childhood teachers believe inclusion can be a good thing if teachers are given ongoing specific training on working with children who have special needs, and if classroom aides can provide the one-on-one interactions and support that these children often need. Head Start has been practicing inclusion for 20 years, requiring that 10 per cent of the total enrollment in each funded program or grantee must include children who are challenged or have special needs.

What is most important to early childhood teachers and their ongoing curriculum, however, is not the laws and policies that happen on the periphery of children's lives, but the ways children treat each other in day-to-day living. Because so many attitudes about life, learning, and other people are formed in the early years, the curriculum must be designed to help young children recognize and appreciate each other's sameness and differences. A classroom might include children with special needs, but if *other children* don't include those individuals, policies about inclusion are meaningless. When minority children are ignored by others, or when the cultures or heritages of some children are not included in curriculum activities, educators' words about best practices, cultural relevance, and helping each child reach full potential are also meaningless.

In early childhood education, a culturally relevant curriculum discards stereotypes, celebrates diversity, and is inclusive of all children. These goals are both necessary and appropriate in early education, and become more necessary each year. An appreciation of diversity and individual differences is crucial in today's world; it will help prepare children to grow, live, and work together in today's global village. The issue, then, is how to achieve those goals.

In *Teaching Young Children to Resist Bias: What Teachers and Parents Can Do* by Louise Derman-Sparks, Maria Gutierrez, and Carol Phillips (NAEYC, 1989), the authors say that because today's society is racist and biased, adults actively need to foster children's antibias development. When children are exposed to messages that subtly reinforce bias, and educators do nothing to counteract them, then teachers are giving their silent or tacit approval to bias.

Teachers must try to help young children understand that doing things differently or looking different or speaking differently from the majority in the group does not make either the majority or the minority "superior." Different is just different, and different is often very interesting. Another way to say this is that in early childhood programs, educators try to teach "I'm okay, you're okay" attitudes; they integrate this concept and other aspects of antibias, inclusion, and cultural diversity into the curriculum.

Cultural diversity and antibias curriculum experiences have changed dramatically in recent years. In the past, early childhood teachers believed that teaching children to value diversity meant to schedule "multicultural activities" each month in which children would learn about geography, foods, clothing, and customs in other cultures. But this did not ensure that children would respect, value, or appreciate people who were different from themselves. The goal should have been not facts about another culture, but the concept that many things about people are the same and many things may also be different, not "better" or "worse."

Today's early childhood teachers can successfully implement antibias and culturally relevant curriculum when they genuinely understand *why* antibias and diversity are important to everyone as human beings. When teachers understand the *whys* personally and emotionally, as well as intellectually, their spontaneous responses and the activities they plan will come naturally. To understand the whys and to take appropriate action, teachers need to take the steps of awareness and understanding. Part of the problem in getting to the first step, awareness, is that the pressure to "teach" children to value cultural diversity and inclusion or antibias has made teachers take action to teach something too quickly, before they have had time to think, feel, and reflect. The other part of the problem is that most adults are too steeped in their own cultures to understand the thinking or feelings of people in other cultures.

Culture is simply a collection of beliefs that a group of people hold. If teachers want children to learn that it's okay and natural for people to have different beliefs, then teachers need to believe it too. When adults are having trouble understanding or accepting this concept, it helps to look at culture in a simple, understandable way. For example, the culture of preschool teachers has a collection of beliefs. They save everything (and I do mean everything), recycle, we carry lots of "junk" in their cars, own numerous tote bags, and often use masking tape loops to affix things. Even people living in the same state may have different cultures, because they believe and think differently about the weather, manners, foods, leisure activities, whether cars or trucks are the best vehicles, and how many miles over the speed limit is legal.

Thinking of culture in this sense, one realizes that all the individual heritages and cultures that exist in classrooms also exist within the broader cultures of geographic locations and the culture of being American. Where should one begin teaching children to recognize and cherish people's sameness as well as differences? Awareness and understanding should not begin with themes or units about far away places, but in one's own classroom.

Thinking, feeling, and reflecting about why people need to value diversity is awareness. It is a step taken within one's consciousness that is almost immediately followed by a leap of understanding of what it is really like to walk in another's moccasins. But when awareness and understanding take place, teachers will find that their observations, responses, and interactions with adults and children are more open and genuine. Many teachers will find that they are able to work with each other, with parents, and with challenging children more easily, because they are seeing and hearing with more than their eyes and ears. They will be able to respond more unconditionally, meeting parents and children where they are instead of where they "should" be.

Aware teachers will use spontaneous teachable moments to celebrate differences every day, not just on special days. They will no longer be speechless or ignore a child's racist remark to another child; they'll know what to say. They will be more likely to use brown, pink, and white paint at the easel, and know how to explain to children why skin color will not wash off. They will not plan activities or have discussions based on generalizations about Native Americans, because they will understand that there are hundreds of Tribal Nations, clans, and bands, each with unique histories and customs.

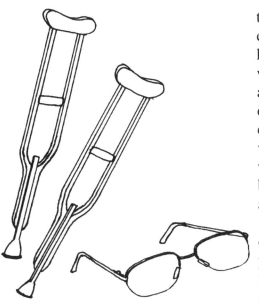

Teachers who are aware will continue expanding the trend to teach children an appreciation of differences by adding eyeglasses without lenses in the housekeeping area, or adding a child-sized crutch or wheelchair in the classroom. They will try to find appropriate dolls and puppets to teach children about disabilities and how people with who are physically challenged can still do great things. They will invite visitors with disabilities to come and talk and play with the children. Antibias and inclusion will become an ongoing part of the curriculum, not just an item relegated to themes or units.

Understanding and aware teachers will invite parents to share traditions, will try new foods and recipes, and will dance to new music. They will use some themes in the curriculum that are universal and that can teach the children about doing things differently in natural ways, such as making and eating different kinds of bread from many cultures. They will find ways to bring music, dance, pottery, sculptures, masks, and artifacts to the classroom that are relevant to the children's current interests and to their heritages. These teachers will also put decorations, play foods, cooking utensils, and serving pieces into the housekeeping area that are commonly

found in the homes of the children in the classroom. They will be able to comfortably and confidently lead children in group-time conversations about individual and family traditions, likenesses and differences.

The curriculum priority to help children learn about and appreciate diversity and accept differences without feelings of superiority or inferiority will continue to grow stronger. Early childhood teachers will persist in using both planned activities and spontaneous learning experiences that help children in small, natural, and genuine ways to appreciate each other's likenesses and differences.

Curriculum Challenges

Student performances in literacy, math, and science in the United States are long-standing concerns. Educators, state departments of education, and the U.S. Department of Education agree that, in spite of ongoing efforts to emphasize math, literacy, and science in education, U.S. students are still not at the same level of achievement in these areas as are students in other developed countries. The trend for literacy, math, and science to be high-priority curriculum areas in early childhood education has been prevalent for nearly two decades and continues to grow.

Early educators know that the most formative years for learning are from birth to age 8. Most of a child's attitudes about learning, reading, and problem solving are formed in this period. Child development knowledge and ongoing observations of children reveal that the best ways to develop literacy, math, and science skills are to encourage curiosity and enthusiasm, reinforce discovery learning and problem solving, and promote meaningful learning activities in these areas.

When young children are excited and motivated, and when they are praised for their language, literacy, and problem solving with math and science materials, their skills in these areas improve. If early childhood educators are committed to addressing national educational concerns in these learning areas, the challenge is to continue to do what they know works. Teachers must include in their curriculum planning even more discovery-learning activities in math, literacy, and science, enhancing children's learning with technology in ways that are appropriate.

Language and Literacy

Language and literacy are important learning domains for many reasons. Not only do they make it possible for children to communicate their needs, wants, feelings, and ideas to others but they are also an integral part of the ways children relate to others in the home, classroom, and the larger community. Language and literacy are the foundation for social-emotional interactions and behaviors.

In addition, language is critically tied to learning. Learning is dependent on the child's experiences, and experiences lead to the formation of concepts. Concepts are mental constructions or representations about objects, activities, people, places, events, and the way things work or change. As the child learns, old concepts are changed and new concepts are added. Language is a vehicle for making sense of concepts, at first in the child's mind, and later, in spoken language. Language is critical in labeling all types of concepts and their elements. Language, then, unspoken or spoken, is vital to the formation of math and science concepts, and makes divergent thinking and problem solving possible. This is why it is so important for teachers to link and integrate literacy with math and science whenever possible.

Language and Literacy with Infants and Toddlers

Although much is known about how to nurture language and literacy in children, the miracle of how humans learn language has never been fully known or explained. One knows that an infant communicates different wants and needs with body language, sounds, and facial expression. An infant's language can be nurtured by a caring adult's body language and facial expressions, and by imitating the many sounds the infant makes. One also knows that it is important to describe in speech the things that the infant does, and to reinforce with words, touch, and smiles all the efforts of the infant to copy the adult's words or to communicate. It is also known that it's important to provide and read appropriate books containing pictures of familiar objects in the infant's environment.

In toddler programs, early childhood teachers use all of these strategies, but on the toddler's level. In addition, adults "extend" the toddler's language by repeating what the child says and adding appropriate words. For example, a toddler might say, "I hungry" and the adult would repeat, "You are hungry." Or the child might say, "Ball," and the adult would extend by saying, "You want the ball."

A toddler's setting is rich with appropriate things for him or her to see, hear, handle, and manipulate; it is rich with pictures, photos, and picture books. Teachers tell and read stories to individuals and small groups, sing simple songs, and do nursery rhymes and fingerplays that incorporate language. When they describe what children are doing, adults give children words and language to use in their mental processes. Many new words are learned as children label objects and communicate with each other and adults. Toddlers learn language rapidly and can understand and use as many as 200 to 700 words.

It is important to continue to read books and talk about pictures with toddlers, and to sing songs, say rhymes, and do fingerplays. Toddlers love rhythm, rhymes, and chants, and they like to hear adults describe what they are doing and what they will do next. They also like playing guessing games with objects hidden in a sock or bag.

Additionally, it is an important prewriting skill to have toddlers strengthen their fingers by using playdough, sand, water, fingerpaint, and manipulatives that help them learn to control their hands in tasks such as using tongs, pulling scarves from a tissue box, ripping paper, and squeezing playdough. Toddlers need opportunities to use markers and crayons for scribble drawings, and they need materials with which to experiment in invented writing. When children volunteer information about their paint or crayon creations, adults should write the child's dictated words on the paper, along with the child's name and the date.

Also, a language-rich toddler setting should include a simple "talking time" for toddlers. Since the only time toddlers really sit down together as a group for 10 to 15 minutes is at meal or snack time, this is the perfect time to nurture language development and communicative interactions. Parameters for this semi-structured event should be simple. Each child should have a turn to talk, one person talks at a time, and the others listen; after one person talks, if another child has a question or response, that's fine. When everyone has had a turn, the activity ends.

Teachers of infants and toddlers find that giving toddlers a few subjects to talk about is helpful. Subjects that interest toddlers most, and that they like to talk about are "Mommy or Daddy," "Shopping," "Food," "Things I Can Do by Myself," "What I Did Today," and pretend or silly talk. Silly talk demonstrates how advanced toddlers really are in using their sense of humor and imaginations. If an adult starts them off on a silly subject, toddlers can pick up on a silly talk game easily and quickly. For instance, the adult might say, "Well, I really like eating these green graham crackers today, don't you?" Toddlers will usually chime in and tell about the strange crackers they are eating, or the unusual colors of other foods.

Language and Literacy in Preschool Programs

The Teacher's Role

The teacher's role in fostering language and literacy is very comprehensive:

Share books, including purchased or child-made "Big Books."
Model reading behaviors.
Model positive communication, including active, focused listening.
Talk about letters by name and sounds.
Create a print-rich environment.
Read and reread favorite stories, rhymes, and poems.
Provide props and flannelboard pieces for retelling or acting out stories.
Encourage creative language and new vocabulary in play.
Provide opportunities for children to write their names (on work and to "sign in").
Write children's dictated words on their work, on their summaries and conclusions, and on experience stories.
Provide print materials that enhance dramatic play with props.
Encourage children to experiment with invented writing.
Encourage children to experiment with the computer to express themselves.

Plan daily times for conversations, talking, sharing, and listening, and encourage conversation during play and meals.

Read or tell stories every day and involve the children in the process.

The Setting

All the learning centers in the setting—including the computer area, project display areas, and science areas—should show written evidence of children's thinking, questions, observations, experiments, and conclusions. The more that children represent their ideas and thinking through writing, invented writing, or dictation, the more knowledge they will construct about concepts and about how written language works. Here are some ways that the setting itself plays a part in the emergence of literacy:

- The setting should promote a print-rich environment that is stimulating without being distracting, containing displays of children's words about their observations and work as well as both printed and perceptual labels for materials and storage. Labeling can be done in short words or sentences, and should be printed in both English and other languages if appropriate.
- Learning centers should be set up to encourage small-group interaction and conversations.
- The schedule should allow time for children to converse with peers and adults during meals and planned play activities.
- Dramatic play props should be used to encourage both the retelling of events and stories and the acting out of children's own dialogues in creative role-play.
- Displays of children's art and work containing their own dictation should be seen at their eye level.
- The use of the computer, play telephones, tape recorders, and listening stations should be observable.
- Both the reading and the writing learning centers should be inviting, should contain materials appropriate to children's skill levels and current interests; and should contain children's own big books, rebus recipes, and journals.

Open Questions

In their interactions with children, teachers need to ask open questions that encourage children to observe, to tell or describe, to imagine, to think of the possibilities of various answers, and to explain their reasons for their answers. Open questions are those that have endless possibilities for answers, rather than only one answer. The kinds of open questions that prompt children to experiment, estimate, explore, or discover are the best to promote learning: These are usually "What do you think might happen if..." questions.

The simplest open questions are those that ask children, "What do you think about such and such?" or "Why do you think that happened?" or "What are some things you could tell us about this table?" Children's answers to the open question about a table would vary, covering the table's shape, size, color, and possible uses.

A more sophisticated open question about a table would be, "If you could take this table to your house, what would you do with it?" In this case, the children need to move the table mentally to a new physical environment and use their imaginations in their thinking. This level of open question opens up an entirely new set of possible answers. With 3-year-olds, teachers will probably focus on "observe and tell what you think" types of questions; with 4- and 5-year-olds, more sophisticated open questions, incorporating the child's imagination, can be used.

Active Listening

Active listening is listening intently to the meanings behind a child's words and responding to them. The teacher's focus in active listening should be like attentive focus during child observations. The teacher is listening to the child's inner thoughts and feelings about what is being said and responds with a comment to elicit more language. Teachers should wait as long as it takes for the child to say what he or she needs to say. Active listening is an excellent strategy for eliciting more language from the child; more language means more opportunities for developing literacy skills.

Related to active listening is the ability of giving very young children the words they need to describe their feelings or what they are doing. The teacher can describe what is happening as a child enjoys a material or practices a skill: "You look like you are enjoying using that yellow paint. You are smiling . . . maybe yellow is a color that makes you happy," or "You put one foot on that step, and the other foot on the next step . . . you are learning to be a very good climber," or "Do you see the salt we put into the water? When we can't see it anymore, it has disappeared into the water. We say it has dissolved." When children hear words that describe what they are doing, and hear new descriptive words such as *scrumptious* and *tantalizing aroma,* they pick up on the use of new descriptive words and the skill of communicating to others what they are doing and why they are doing it.

Some children need adult encouragement to communicate to other children how they feel or what they need or want. Teachers sometimes need to say, "Alica, use words to tell Conner what it is you need," or "Tell Ramon how you felt when he said that you could not play." Using words to communicate needs and feelings to others is a lifelong skill, which, when used effectively, can reduce much of the stress in people's lives.

Dictation and Experience Stories

The importance of writing down the child's own words about his or her art or constructions, math and science observations, computer discoveries, block structures, feelings, made-up songs and stories—anything the child thinks about and wants to relate in words—cannot be overemphasized! These pieces of dic-

tation should be posted where the child can see and "read" and reflect on them, and examples should be placed periodically in the child's file or portfolios. Nothing seems to please a child more than having a teacher show that he or she values the child's ideas and words enough to take the time to write them down on paper.

After visitors have come to share knowledge or talents, and after outdoor walks or field trips, the children's words about the experience should be written down on poster paper as an "experience story" or a thank-you letter.

Sometimes, when children develop rules for the room and the group, the rules they thought of and the names of the children who developed each rule can be posted as an experience story.

Other types of experience stories are "I Am Special" or "My Family Is Special" posters, including the child's own words about likes, dislikes, pets, family members, and interests. A related kind of experience story used to promote self-esteem and friendships in the group is "Jack Is Special Because. . . ." In this case, the children tell all the things they think are special about a certain child. To promote family relationships, a similar poster could be titled "What I Like Best about My Mother's Hands." If the child wants his or her words to be written in both English and another language, every effort should be made to do so.

Step-by-step picture or rebus recipes including the children's words in the directions are still another form of dictation or experience story. More recipes can be added as the children try new ones and can be kept in an oversized card file, in a scrapbook, or as posters. Collections of recipes could make a children's big book, and the children's words about their own parents' recipes in a collection of family recipes for the group will make delightful and original reading.

Journals

Related to dictation and experience stories are the personal journals of children, done in individual scrapbooks, in blank books, or in notebooks. Older children can keep their journals in electronic folders on the computer. Children should be encouraged to write down their thoughts or feelings about the day or about any other topics in their journals. They may use their own methods of writing and spelling, or give dictation to an assisting adult. In this way, children can begin to write their own books on topics of their choice.

Traveling journals to expand family literacy can also be developed. These blank books or scrapbooks could go home on weekends with a stuffed animal or puppet from the center, and the parents and child could write about the toy's "experiences" at their house in the journal. As the journal travels to each home, parents will read, write, and share stories. At the end of the year, the group could make a "Big Book" or keep the completed journal in the classroom library.

Reading and Writing Centers

These centers were discussed in Chapter 3 on the early childhood setting. The space teachers create for reading and writing centers is not as important as what teachers put into these centers and how they encourage children to use them. Writing center materials can be simple and should be appropriate to children's interest and skill levels. Recycled envelopes, stickers, trading stamps, stamp pads, and greeting cards with big pencils or markers and paper will fill the bill, especially if adults praise and encourage children for using the materials frequently and for creating messages for family members or peers. If space is a problem, small baskets can sort and hold these materials.

In the reading center, books and pictures to create or reinforce interest in a thematic unit can be added to the picture books and stories for young children. Books should be nonsexist and should often reflect the cultural interests of those in the group and other cultures. Often, puppets for acting out stories, flannel-board stories, photo albums of the children and their experiences, or children's own books can be added.

Children should be encouraged to read independently or in small groups, with or without an adult during the day; they should always hear a daily book or story in large group. If the center has few or no books of its own, funding should be developed to purchase them each year; poor-quality books in disrepair do not do much to encourage literacy.

Libraries can be used regularly to supplement the center's library with books for children and families. Books and stories can be extended with props and dramatic play, with child- or teacher-made flannel stories, and with tape recordings of children's own stones or their conversations with each other and adults. Programs should also consider Reading Is Fun (RIF) as a resource. The RIF program can provide funding for free children's books and family literacy initiatives.

Dramatic Play and Props

The dramatic play areas of the classroom always abound with children's conversations. In the housekeeping area or in places where adults have helped children set up a "store," a "campsite," or a "vet clinic," teachers can hear children using their own words and many new words to describe what they are doing or pretending to do. Adding props such as magazines to a "hospital waiting room" or a "barber shop," adding part of a daily newspaper, a calendar, an appointment book, a phone book, or magazines to the housekeeping area, adding sale or price signs in a "store," and adding recycled restaurant menus and note pads to "restaurant" play are good ways to add to a print-rich environment and enhance literacy skills.

Props can also be used to encourage children's discussions about special things that are used in their own homes and are pertinent to their own cultures, traditions, or even special disabilities or needs. Putting out several pairs of children's eyeglasses (frames only, no lenses), scavenged from out-of-date models at a store, is helpful in making a child who wears glasses more comfortable about wearing glasses. Most of the other children will enjoy trying on or wearing the glasses!

Using prop boxes for dramatic play to vary the housekeeping area is a frequent strategy of teachers, but with a classroom of mixed 3- to 5-year-olds, it may be best to set up extra dramatic play in another area so that the younger children can use the "house" and its dolls and dishes to their hearts' content while the older children do pretending that reflects their greater knowledge of the world and adults. Dramatic play prop boxes should be labeled clearly without stereotypes, stored accessibly for frequent use, and include hats, briefcases, old computer keyboards, and clothes for boys and girls.

Teachers often use props to enhance their storytelling literacy activities, especially in circle or large-group time. Some teachers keep props for characters in the stories in a special apron pocket and bring them out in their order of appearance in the story. Props can enhance stories such as *Caps for Sale* and *Stone Soup*, too. Hats or felt squares representing hats can be used to act out *Caps for Sale*. A large pot or kettle, a spoon, play foods, and a washed rock can help children act out *Stone Soup*. Teachers can also make real stone soup in the classroom, although some children in my own group could never be convinced that I had not made the soup entirely from the stone.

Puppets

Child-made puppets are useful as "buddies" to talk with or use in storytelling or "reading" by children. Different kinds of puppets can also be used to reinforce other concepts. A special puppet can be used to signal cleanup time; to ask the outdoor play rules; or to ask children about taking care of their teeth, eating healthful foods, being kind to each other, or using appropriate touch. As mentioned earlier, teacher-made or purchased persona dolls (or puppets) can be used to increase children's awareness and discussion of children who may look different than they do or who have special needs or disabilities. Excellent reading material on these strategies can be found in *Anti-Bias Curriculum* by Louise Derman-Sparks (1989).

A literacy activity related to puppets and dolls is to have children make "pet rocks" out of hand-sized stones, glue, and odds and ends of material, pipe cleaners, fake fur scraps, and the like. Children can make up and dictate stories about these "pets" on tape, on paper, or on the computer.

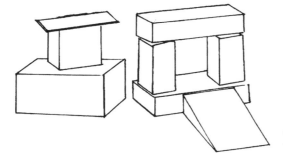

Blocks

Literacy can also be enhanced in the blocks area, not only by having children name the blocks or use descriptive words to tell about block creations but also to extend and act out familiar stories.

The big hollow blocks and the unit blocks have different purposes (see Chapter 3). Big hollow blocks are used to build a "set" in which children, as actors, play out a role. They might be going fishing from a boat, riding on a train, or playing in an office or a fire station. If they are going fishing in a boat, be sure to include life jackets as props with the big blocks.

The computer can be useful in enhancing literacy in all types of dramatic play. Tickets and travel schedules can be created, lists of what to pack for camping or fishing can be made, as well as signs children need.

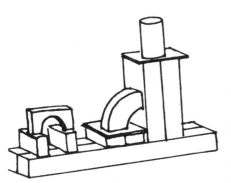

When they use unit blocks, children are like giants, manipulating the story emerging from the block play. Here, teachers can add small people, trucks, cars, road signs, and stone mountains and boulders. They can create a suspension bridge with tape, string, and towers, or a lighthouse surrounded by rocks and small boats. Adding these props to the use of the unit blocks enhances all sorts of language and storytelling by children.

Another way to add literacy to the block area is to take instant or digital photographs of the construction or creation that a group of children have produced with unit blocks or with combinations of unit blocks and other types of blocks. As the children tell about their construction, what it does, and who built it, teachers can write down the children's words and post them in the blocks area with the photograph.

Putting paper or drawn representations of the various kinds of unit blocks on the shelves that hold them is another way to represent concrete objects with symbols, so this is a good link with literacy. Keeping pads of paper and pencils in a small basket in the block area to encourage children to make labels and signs for their creations is another way to promote literacy.

It is important to give children large cardboard boxes occasionally (or as needed) to use in place of or in combination with the large hollow blocks. Sometimes children need to use these cardboard boxes to represent something they have studied in a project. Sometimes the boxes come in handy when children are acting out a play they have written, and they need to construct items or furniture for the "set" of their play.

Sharing Conversations in Groups

Early childhood teachers almost always schedule large-group circle time to give children opportunities to share in conversations. Usually, these conversations are about what is going on in the children's lives, but they might also include teacher-guided discussions relating to the current themes of the curriculum.

Mealtimes are another group time where children can converse with each other and with adults. These sociable, relaxed conversations include what the children want to discuss (themselves, their families, their likes and dislikes, new skills, etc.), but they can also be guided discussions in which the teacher asks open-ended questions related to his or her own goals (plans for the day, evaluations of the day, plans for field trips, theme-related topics, and health and nutrition).

Large-group circle time for sharing conversation is sometimes misused. It is not appropriate to the skill levels and attention span of 3- to 5-year-olds to sit for 20 or more minutes for "show and tell" about toys brought from home. It is questionable whether children really need to have show-and-tell time at all, since there are so many other rich opportunities for literacy and language activities in the center. If show and tell is an absolute must for the teacher, there are ways to manage it that are more age appropriate and that will effectively promote literacy, learning, and family involvement.

For example, children can do show and tell in two or three groups at the same time, guided by three adults. Another method is to stagger the times for children's show-and-tell days, so that only four or five would share on any given day. Teachers can also suggest to parents in a simple flyer or newsletter, "We are studying the color red and the concept of round. On your child's show and tell day, explore your house to find something 'red' and 'round' to talk about." Teachers could even provide parents with a flyer about upcoming themes, and ask that on their child's show and tell day that the child bring *only* something related to the current theme.

Nonverbal Communication

Teachers can help children learn about and have empathy for children who are hearing impaired, and also learn some of the elements of a new language, by using simple signing with the children. The phrases *I love you, work, play, come,* and *time* are easy to sign, and young children respond very well to this sort of communication. Children are great observers and users of body language. (They can always tell when adults' words do not match their real feelings.) They can also be encouraged to discover and act out gestures that convey meaning to others without using words. They all know how to tell you without words when they like or dislike something, or "I don't know," or "goodbye." Books without words are helpful in trying out nonverbal communication, and the book *Talking Without Words* by Marie Hall Ets provides many good ideas as a starting point.

The Art, Sensory, and Woodworking Areas

Remember that when children create anything with art media, just as when they construct with woodworking or blocks, they are making representations of their thoughts and ideas—things they have conceived in their minds. Representation is therefore linked to literacy, in which symbols, letters, and words represent thoughts and ideas. Enhance literacy in the art area with language, comments, descriptive praise, and ways to integrate the use of print.

Earlier in this book an example was given that described a way to use play-dough as a literacy event. When a list of what the children say about the play-dough or what they can do with it is made and posted in the area, literacy is being integrated. When children bring their woodworking constructions to the art area and paint them, and when adults make signs or posters using the child's words to describe the wooden creation and what it might do, literacy is being integrated. When adults write the words children say about their drawings, they are integrating literacy, and when children combine invented writing with their art, they are practicing literacy.

When children examine, explore, sort out, or use sensory materials to create art, they usually have very interesting things to say about the rice, seeds, beans, popcorn, dried flowers, pebbles, shells, and other items. An adult at the table can record lists or children's descriptive comments and post them. When the children make cornstarch clay that looks "just like mashed potatoes," or silly putty that is "weird, funny, and gooey," these words can be written out and posted to show the children in print what they are feeling and saying.

Adults often use language to give children input or descriptive praise in the art area. When they use the basic elements of art in their comments, teachers do better describing and give children many new words and concepts. Here are some examples:

- *Colors:* "Your lake looks mysterious and misty and murky." "I see crimson red and lavender violet in your rainbow." "Your blue water makes me feel icy."
- *Line:* "You've made lots of zig-zag lines here, and you put stripes over there." "You made thick lines with the paint that drip downward." "You have lots of criss-cross lines here."
- *Shape or Form:* "You made a pattern with little boxes." "Your dragon has a row of triangles on his tail." "You made one tree for each house." "You enclosed this space and opened that space."
- *Design:* "You made an X after every heart." "You used many rows of circles to make your design." "Your red, wavy lines make patterns that hold all your other colors."
- *Space:* "Your clouds are all floating across the top." "Your birds are all clustered together in this tree." "Some of your people are inside and some are outside."

The Computer Center

The computer center has come into its own as a tool for learning in the early childhood classroom. Computers in the classroom can enrich curriculum content in many ways by giving children access to more information about any topic of interest. Hands-on and exploratory software can help children discover many wonders of nature and the world and help them play with words, numbers, sounds, and math concepts. Discussion of the computer is in this section because the use of computers in literacy development is being emphasized, but computers and computer software actually provide early childhood programs with integrated curriculum. They can expand literacy and factual content and also extend math and science concepts in many meaningful ways.

Teachers want children to learn the habit of using computer technology as a tool to solve problems and accomplish tasks. For example, if children are going to have a restaurant in the dramatic play area, the computer can help them make signs and menus. If a classmate is ill and has missed school, and if that child has a computer at home, the other children can write email notes or send free greeting cards to cheer up their absent friend. If children need to share information with another group about the project they are working on, the computer can print their words, and even send it to another classroom by email. If older children in the primary grades do research about pioneer times and want to write a play about it to act out, they can use the computer to write the script. Computer literacy is not so much about knowing all the ways to operate the machine, but knowing how to approach a learning situation.

Computers have some specific advantages in language and literacy for preschoolers and older children. When children are investigating a topic, they can print out pages showing facts, pictures, and games—whatever they discover. They can also make lists of what they have observed in the study of an object on the science table and post it in the science area. For example, children might list that the outside of a fall pumpkin is round, orange, big, smooth, and cool, and has ridges and a stem. The list could be done on the computer in large letters, printed out, and posted next to the pumpkin.

Children might use the computer to summarize what they want to find out about a topic, or make a list to show what they have discovered about a topic. Their lists can be shared with others on a bulletin board by the computer or in the appropriate learning center. Well-planned display areas for children to post and share their work nurtures literacy. Children can compose original stories and illustrate them, or play with design and color to make representations or unique creations. Teachers can even create a personal folder for each child in which they can save their work or write ongoing personal journals.

When young children use the computer to access information on the Internet or with software, they become excited about learning and motivated to learn more. Software such as "Mixed Up Mother Goose" (Sierra On-Line) reinforces familiar stories and roles and gives children ways to play them out cooperatively. "The City" (Kidware) enhances children's thematic learning about neighborhoods, vehicles, occupations, and community helpers. "Millies' Math House" (Edmark) helps children explore shapes and blueprints that represent homes. "Imagination Express" (Edmark) can take children to the ocean to see what lives there (or almost anywhere else) and can help children create picture books about the things they learned.

Software programs often spark new interests in children, such as the study of pollution or advocacy about animals, leading them to search for more information on the Internet. In these ways the Internet and the computer integrate curriculum and fit in perfectly with the concepts of emerging interests, scaffolding, and investigative projects. Through the use of learning specific software and with information they have accessed about their themes or projects, children will practice many skills in problem solving, particularly in the literacy, creative, math, and science learning domains.

There is so much excellent computer software now available for young children, but this book can list only a few examples. It is important to remember, however, that the software chosen for young children should be open ended, exploratory, easy to use, and free of bias. Children should be able to control the learning process; represent ideas in pictures, sounds, words, and music; try out things as individuals or part of a group; and do creative, divergent thinking as they proceed. The book *Young Children and Technology* by Susan Haugland and June Wright (see Chapter 3) and the Haugland/Shade Software Scale included in the book is an excellent resource for teachers.

In closing this section, teachers should also perceive computer technology as another way to teach children to value cultural diversity and antibias. When teachers evaluate software, they should check for these characteristics: mixed gender and role equity, diverse cultures, diverse family styles, and diverse ages and abilities. In addition, teachers should take advantage of the computer's adaptive potential for children with special needs and for children who are visually or physically challenged. Now let's look at the other long-standing priority areas in early childhood education: math and science.

Discovery Learning: Math and Science

Divergent Thinking

When children think of more than one way to answer a question or find a solution, they are using divergent thinking skills—the same thinking skills used by scientists and mathematicians. Materials in the setting itself abound with opportunities to nurture divergent thinking, and math and science activities can take place in all learning centers, as well as outdoors.

Divergent thinking and problem solving can be prompted by questions: "How can we find some good ways to store our scrap wood for the workbench?" "Is there another way to use these blocks to build a ramp?" "We are out of orange tempera, but we need orange paint. Is there a way we could make some?" "We don't have a yardstick. Is there some other way we could measure how tall you are?" "Does a bucket of sand weigh the same as a bucket of water?" Let's look first at some of the learning centers where a great deal of divergent thinking and problem solving takes place: the art, sensory, and woodworking centers; the manipulatives center, blocks, and the foods experience center. Some of the problem solving in these centers will include specific math and science activities; others will focus more on divergent thinking and discovery.

Art, Sensory, and Woodworking

The art, sensory, and woodworking centers are full of daily opportunities for

discovery learning. At woodworking or at the sand or water table, and in exploring materials such as recyclables, clays, and rice, children are encouraged to pour, fill, dig, mold, sort, categorize, and see likenesses and differences. In these areas, adults should encourage children to make guesses to estimate how much or how many and to experiment to find out the answers. In this process, children can talk about "more" and "less"; they can compare and they can count. Children should also examine intently, with all their senses if possible, and tell what they see. These are the things that mathematicians and scientists do. Children are practicing the same kinds of thinking, as adults in these fields, but at a concrete and sensorimotor level, not an abstract level. This is exactly where math, science, and discovery learning skills begin, which is why it is important for children to practice them.

It is vital that sand, water, art and/or sensory materials be available to children every day, and that they be a part of the ongoing curriculum. Three-year-olds and young four-year-olds are particularly sensitive to learning through their senses, but all children will improve their thinking skills through the daily use of open-ended, sensory materials and art media.

When children explore music, dance, and dramatic play, they are learning that there are countless ways to create. When they use open-ended art media such as paint, clays, collage materials, crayons, and computer art software, they are learning that there are not only countless ways to create but also countless ways to solve problems and find answers. Here are some examples of ways that the use of art media can promote divergent thinking and problem solving.

When children are given fingerpaint or at the easel, adults can provide two primary colors of paint (and white if desired). Children will mix these colors as they experiment with the paint and discover they have made new colors. Nearby adults can facilitate these discoveries and use dialogues and open questions to help children use words to describe what happened. Then they can ask the children if they can make it happen again, perhaps in a new way.

Another way to expand divergent thinking with paint is to let the children experiment with tempera painting on different types of paper or surfaces. Children will find that some surfaces absorb the paint quickly and some reject the paint, not allowing it to adhere. To do this project, adults can collect corrugated paper, aluminum foil, clear plastic sheets, sandpaper of different grades, wood, bark burlap, and other materials. Children will see that painting on different surfaces creates interesting textures. They will have many comments and questions, and will make many conclusions that can be printed out and posted.

If the current curriculum theme is the color green, the teacher could enable the discovery of making green from yellow and blue paint even more meaningful by integrating this discovery with other curriculum. Torn blue and yellow tissue paper, when used with glue, is another way to create green. Children could make their own green Silly Putty or playdough, and the teacher could read the story of *Little Blue and Little Yellow,* which is illustrated with torn paper representations of two children. Green can also be discovered when children in small-group time are given a clear plastic cup of water and asked what might happen if they drop in a piece of yellow crepe paper. (Children will find that it eventually sinks and the color bleeds into the water.) If children add a tiny bit of blue crepe paper, they will see the water turn to emerald green. With these meaningful discoveries, children will learn the concept of "what green is" very naturally and quickly.

Children should make their own modeling materials—playdough, cornstarch clay, and Silly Putty—whenever possible, because they will measure, mix, and see changes in the materials in the process. Modeling materials are also very helpful in learning about the concepts of ordering (smallest to largest), conservation, and quantification of number. Young children need many experiences in seeing that the quantity of a material stays the same, whether it is kept in a big piece or made into small pieces. If children see two equally large balls of playdough, and then see one of these balls made into many small balls, they may not believe that the amounts are still equal until all the small balls are put back together to form the original sized ball.

It's easy to demonstrate the concept of conservation with modeling materials, and experiences of this kind will also help the child understand reversibility—to know that they can cut a whole into parts and then reunite them again. When children "count" by rote, they do not understand the meaning of numbers or the representation of numerals to mean certain quantities. When children count balls of clay and touch each ball as they count, it helps them learn that number represents quantity. One is just one object but two is one more object added to the first, or a set of two balls of clay. Children also find it easier to count a group of objects that are the same, instead of a group of different things.

The more children use and explore all the things they can do with clays and other modeling materials (without the addition of cookie cutters or commercial gadgets), the better they will understand the science and math concepts of ordering, conservation, reversibility, and the structure and meaning of number.

Clays, paint, and other art materials are media children use to represent objects, people, plants, animals, fantasy creatures, and events. Whenever they represent their thinking in a concrete way, they are constructing knowledge and reinforcing the concepts they are learning. In much the same way, woodworking materials also give children a medium for representation and problem solving. In mixed groups of 3- to 5-year-olds, as well as in kindergartens and primary classrooms, offering art materials, clays, and woodworking is important because these media offer opportunities to create representations of children's learning. This is especially useful in investigative projects.

Woodworking materials require children to estimate, measure, count, compare, and use tools to accomplish a task. Children may have to figure out how to put together two pieces of wood with a hammer and nails; they may want to make the "roof" of the house they are making slanted instead of flat; they may want to saw a piece of wood or Styrofoam a certain length to fit into the boat they are making; or they may want to know how to attach the wall of the birdhouse they are building to its floor. A great deal of creative, divergent thinking and problem solving is going on in the art, sensory, and woodworking centers of the setting!

Manipulatives

Anyone who has watched a child intently try to solve a puzzle or make something with manipulatives such as snap beads or bristle blocks knows that these materials promote problem-solving skills. It is important for adults to provide manipulatives every day that encourage both success and challenge. Help should be given to the child only as is really necessary to solve the problem with which he or she is working. Breaking down the skill into its smaller parts is helpful. For example, doing a puzzle has several logical steps:

- Look at the complete and intact puzzle picture first; see what it's about and what its parts and colors are.
- Turn over the puzzle, and then turn over each piece so that the colors and design show.
- Begin with the easiest parts of the picture, usually the corners.
- Watch for clues from what is remembered about the picture until all the pieces are found.

Teachers need to carefully plan, choose, and rotate the manipulatives that will be offered in this learning center to meet the skill-level needs of the children in the group.

When children have created something original with a manipulative material, or successfully mastered a challenge, praise from adults and peers is important. Original creations made with manipulatives also give teachers excellent opportunities to discuss what the creation is or what it can do, and write down the child's words. Colors, patterns, shapes, and number or quantity can also be discussed.

Blocks

The problem-solving opportunities presented by blocks have already been

emphasized, but let's summarize a few of them. Blocks help children practice many skills—not only thinking skills but also social, creative, language, memory, perception, and motor skills. Blocks should be a part of every daily lesson plan. When space is a problem, big hollow blocks and unit blocks can be rotated with other equipment; table blocks can also be used to give children opportunities to practice thinking skills. With blocks, children problem solve to construct things, dealing with design and balance. They learn about shapes, sizes, space, patterns, colors; they learn the concepts of *wide, narrow, tall, light, heavy, short, long, equal, more,* and *less.* This is certainly math and science at the child's level!

More than any other early childhood material, blocks lend themselves to integration of all the curriculum areas of early childhood education. Many teachers, however, do not take full advantage of the use of blocks in integrating curriculum. The book *1,2,3 Blocks: Building Block Activities for Young Children* by Evelyn Petersen shows how to integrate unit blocks, hollow blocks, table blocks, and child-made blocks with all of the curriculum areas of early childhood education. In each of the four sections of the book, teachers will find ways to use each type of block to build language and literacy skills and to enhance themes, dramatic play, perceptual skills, math, science, music, motor skills, and social-emotional skills.

Learning games with unit blocks are provided, such as shape games, letter games, and math games. Vocabulary building and literacy with blocks, and many math and science activities are provided, including ways to experiment with the concepts of ordering, reversibility and quantification, and ways to explore the properties of blocks such as weight, shapes, color, and texture. When teachers use early childhood resources such as the *1,2,3 Blocks* book with children, they can more easily incorporate appropriate dialogues and questions about blocks to help scaffold learning that leads to outcomes in many learning domain areas. Here are some examples of questions teachers can ask themselves and ask children as they play with blocks:

Things to Ask Yourself as Children Play with Unit Blocks

To help you be a better observer . . .

• Which children are building bridges? Are they ready to repeat the bridge pattern, or place one bridge on top of another?

- Which children like to sort and match the blocks?
- Which children are leaving spaces for doors or windows?
- Which children need spools or small blocks for decorations?
- Is a child getting frustrated because his tower won't stand up on the carpet? What can I give him to make the base flatter?
- Which children are combining shapes into one structure (towers, bridges, enclosures)?
- Which child has found ways to use arches, ramps, and pillars?

To help you be a better manager . . .

- Have I encouraged block play by "starting" a building lately?
- Are there pictures or books I should add here this week?
- Have we been using the words posted in the block area?
- Do we need to take a photo of this and tell a story?
- Do the children need some string and tapes to measure that?
- Have we counted the blocks in someone's tower lately?
- Have I used descriptive praise in the block area today?
- Are there more accessories we should make this week?
- Have we told a story with blocks lately?

Things to Ask Children as They Play with Unit Blocks

To scaffold learning…

- Which block is heavier? Do you think these two weigh the same? How could we find out? What if we get the scale?
- Which of these blocks do you think is bigger?
- Which tower do you think is taller? How could we find out?
- Could we build a house with just the square blocks?
- How will your people get out of the castle?
- How will you get the sheep into the corral?
- Will you make the road go over the bridge or under it?
- Is your road to the house as long as the one to the barn?
- What is the shortest way to the space ship?
- What will you do if this road is closed? Can we make a detour road? How could you do it?
- Will it fall if you put that big one on top?
- I see you are balancing it on each side. Can you balance one more on top of that one?
- How could you make a way for the cars to get over that river?
- How can you make a way for people to park upstairs in this parking garage?
- I see you have boats at this dock, but what if they float away? What can you do? What will you load on these boats?
- I see that your truck is taking away these logs. Will you plant more new trees in the forest where you cut these down?

In the block area, teachers can help staff and parents remember to ask questions like those listed above if they post a list of "cue" words in the block area. *Using these words help children think, discover, and use math and science concepts.*

Wide   *Narrow*
Short   *Tall*
More   *Less*
Heavy   *Light*
Long   *Short*
Many   *Few*
Big   *Small*
Open Space   *Enclosed Space*
Shapes (name and talk about shapes)
Count (count and touch the blocks being used)
Patterns (see and name patterns)
Towers
Bridges
Arches
Windows
Fences/Walls

Food Experiences

There may be no better way to teach math and science skills than through children's involvement in food preparation or meal and snacktime experiences. Not only do children estimate, measure, count, compare, sort, and discuss what they see but they also see changes in matter that occur when foods are mixed, combined, baked, or cooked. For example, they can see an egg change from liquid to solid form; they can see that some liquids, such as water, can change from liquid to solid and back to liquid. As a bonus, they practice literacy and social skills during food preparation as they read picture recipes, talk about what they are doing, and take turns doing it.

Teachers who want to encourage math and science skills in children, as well as literacy, health, and nutrition, should include food experiences in the daily lesson plan whenever possible, even if these are very simple experiences. Food experiences should be planned at least once a week. These experiences are best implemented with small groups of children during small-group time or free-choice time.

Math Activities

Opportunities for mathematical manipulating and thinking, counting, sorting or tubbing, measuring, weighing, graphing, and learning about the concepts of time and money are available in all learning centers. However, teachers often need to note actual reminders and strategies in the lesson plan in order to take advantage of these opportunities. Some examples of math learning activities for the lesson plan have already been mentioned, but here are a few more math ideas:

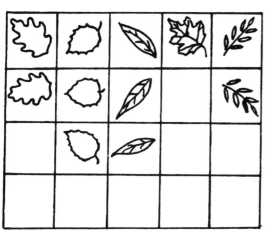

- In small group, help the children notice how many of them there are. Count the body parts of one person or of two people. Count the number of shoes in the group.
- Weigh and measure the children regularly, and mount this information on the wall so they can see changes in their growth.
- Graph the children by size or other characteristics.
- Graph what sinks or floats.
- Graph the different kinds of crackers or cereals in a snack before eating it.
- Make a graph to show identical sets of two when the children match pairs of sound cans (film containers with items inside).
- Use math props in dramatic play such as play money, calculators, scales, and measuring tools of all kinds.
- Sort and compare many different recyclables—keys, bottle caps, plastic bread tags, stones, leaves, and plastic numerals. Sort purchased materials too, such as cubes, teddy bears, poker chips, and so on.
- Graph objects from nature, such as different kinds of leaves, twigs, pebbles, and shells.

Many everyday activities incorporate math. For example, as children help set the table for meals, they can count children and settings for each table, doing one-to-one correspondence. When the children estimate how much food to serve themselves, the adults can scaffold the experience by using praise with the words *guess* and *estimate*. Rebus picture recipes may be used to count and measure ingredients for dips, snacks, and modeling materials.

During free-choice time, adults can encourage children to count how many are playing in a center, and check the sign posted about how many can play, to see if there is room for them to enter at that time. Outdoors, children can count how many times a child rode around the track with the wheel toy, to see if it is someone else's turn. In the sand pile or the garden, children can compare the sizes of sand castles, or estimate how many buckets of top soil are needed.

In the music area or at music/movement time, children can do call-and-response games with rhythms, copy clapped rhythms with an adult leader, march to music while keeping the beat, and create their own music on a synthesizer, using a beat generator or "drum machine."

To help the children understand the passage of time (temporal understanding), they can put flannelboard or picture card representations of the daily events in order by sequence. They can gradually learn to use a grid to show the passing of days and weeks, and can put up special stickers on the grid to represent "special" days, such as holidays, and see the sequence of these days over time. (Sequenced activities regarding calendars and temporal understanding are seen in Appendix A.)

Children can also enjoy learning about numbers in literature that incorporates math concepts, from rhymes such as "Over in the Meadow," "One, Two, Buckle My Shoe," "This Old Man," "Five Little Monkeys," "Here Is Thumbkin," and "One Potato, Two Potatoes" to books such as *So Many Cats; Goldilocks and the Three Bears; The Hungry Caterpillar; More, Fewer, Less; Shapes, Shapes, Shapes; The Doorbell Rang;* and *Just Enough Carrots.*

In investigative projects, children will learn about math by using it to measure, to problem solve, to explain an idea, and to plan their collaborative work and their representations. When children are engaged in dramatic play, they will learn math concepts by making and using play money, and by buying and selling things in play stores. In small-group experiences, adults can help children identify, sort, and match real coins. In the math center, children may count, sort, and match many items and put them in tubs or containers. The early childhood setting is full of opportunities to learn about math and science in concrete ways.

Science and Nature

Many science activities have already been mentioned in Chapter 9 and in other sections of this chapter. More activities will be found in this chapter's suggested readings. Science does not have to stay in a corner. Children can observe, tell, and practice learning about science concepts indoors, outdoors, and in most learning centers. Children begin to learn about physical science by using such things as balance scales, measuring tools, and dry cell batteries; they begin to learn about natural science by observing living and growing things including themselves, plants, and animals.

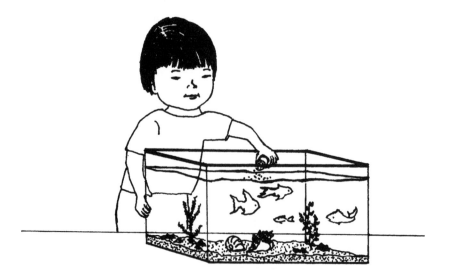

Perhaps the most important thing teachers should remember about science with young children is to allow it to be simple. Children are excited about every small discovery—discoveries that adults often ignore or take for granted. Teachers should focus on the fact that the scientific method, at its core, simply means observing something very carefully, and telling what is seen. Sometimes an experiment might be done to see "what will happen if. . . . " Again, the scientist observes and tells what is seen and why it might have happened.

Children are natural scientists; they follow these steps of the scientific method very easily. Teachers can help them observe more carefully, help them tell more about what is seen, experiment (safely) to see what might happened, and make conclusions about what did happen that can be written and posted.

TRY THIS NOW

To understand how simple science can be, take some time to discover in the ways that children do. Get a few friends together and find some potatoes in your kitchen. Each of you should take one potato and study it carefully. Get to know your potato well—as well as you know your best friend's face. After a few minutes, put the potatoes down and mix them up. Then, one a time, find your potato and explain to your friends how you knew it was yours. This is the kind of science we can do with young children to help them learn to observe and tell, and it is the kind of discovering that children love.

If teachers have science tables, the same old Indian corn, rocks, and magnifying glass should not stay there all year collecting dust. Science displays should be changed often, not only to encourage interest but also to mesh items with current thematic plans. If the children are studying rocks, a great variety of rocks, including minerals and crystals, could be examined, as well as stone utensils and tools of the past. If they are studying shells, shells and books on shells, shell buttons, and shell jewelry could also be explored.

Adults should always point out what new items are on the science table and should encourage the use of these materials with adult presence and open questions. It is an excellent idea to provide children with small flashlights and magnifying glasses for focusing on and examining the items displayed. Lighting up an item is particularly helpful in eliciting more detailed observing, comparing, and telling.

Early childhood teachers should make strong efforts to include plants and animals in the classroom so that children can observe and discuss what plants and animals need in order to live and grow. Plants and animals add warmth and life to the setting. Children can learn much from observing how animals breathe, how they eat, and what skin coverings or other adaptations (such as mouths, beaks, webbed feet, and claws) they have. Teachers should help children research and learn about the reasons for these adaptations.

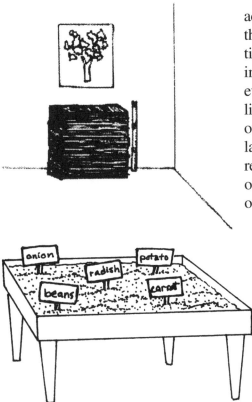

Whenever possible, teachers should include activities in the horizontal plan and daily lesson plans that concern nature, the environment, and ecology. Any time children are outdoors, teachers can point out important things about caring for our environment, even if these are small but important things like controlling litter. If possible, a garden should be planted, either outdoors or inside the classroom. This can be done in a large recycled tire outside, or indoors in a toddler's recycled sandbox. Sometimes the climate or geography of a program will prohibit a growing and harvest season outdoors, but efforts to grow and harvest can be made indoors.

When teachers point out that recycled newspapers, if stacked up to a height of three feet, equal one tree, children may think more about taking care of trees or planting them. Perhaps they will go outdoors and look at trees, compare their heights, their branch patterns, and their bark, and talk about what they like about trees in their journals or on an experience poster. They may want to plant or "adopt" a tree to study.

Physical Science

It is important for young children to have experiences with physical science as well as natural science. Here are three ideas that can be done either in the classroom or shared with parents to try at home. All three promote discovery learning and problem solving:

- Give the children an old VCR and a short Phillips head screwdriver and let discovery take its course. When the children take the VCR apart, they will find many magnets with which to do experiments.
- Give the children a dry cell battery, some copper wire, a switch, and a job for the electricity to do, such as a small bell to ring or a tiny lightbulb to turn on. Help the children hook up the wires, and let them discover that the electricity will not do any work for us unless it can complete its path back to its "home" (dry cell battery storage). If the circuit is broken, electricity won't do the work. Children can safely try many ways to break or connect the circuit.

- Give the children some "junk" odds and ends such as paper plates and cups, plastic lids, paper tubes, golf tees, pipe cleaners, straws, bits of Christmas tree garland, and so on. Using masking tape and a sturdy paper plate as a base, encourage them to build upward and outward, inventing as they go. The three-dimensional construction will take fantasy forms and may resemble something from a Dr. Seuss book. After it is admired, the creation can be taken apart, and the junk items can be put in a bag and recycled as a new and different construction another day. A great deal of problem solving and fine motor skills are practiced with this activity. If the children tell a story about their creations, take dictation and post it.

Summary

In this chapter, we have explored some of the current trends in early childhood education—developmental continuity, zero-to-three programs, parent partnerships, and assessment of children's progress. The chapter also covered curriculum priorities in early education and provided you with learning experiences and teaching strategies for antibias, literacy, problem solving, and math and science activities, in all areas of the setting.

In addressing these curriculum areas, the early childhood teacher has both a wonderful opportunity and a challenging responsibility. The early childhood field has traditionally worked to improve the quality of life for children and families. These efforts must be both continued and improved in order for an impact to be made. Early childhood teachers, working with young children in their formative years and with their families, have the best chance to address national educational priorities in ways that can make positive changes in this country's future.

Self-Study Activities

1. Choose two trends, issues, or curriculum areas about which you want to learn more. In the periodical section of your library, look up and read articles on these topics. Many excellent articles on these subjects can be found in the three major professional journals of the early childhood field: *Young Children*, the journal of the National Association for the Education of Young Children (NAEYC); *Childhood Education*, the journal of the Association for Childhood Education International (ACEI); and *Children and Families*, the journal of the National Head Start Association (NHSA).

2. Go back in this chapter to the priority area or areas that are most important to you as a student or teacher. List the activities in these areas that gave you new ideas for teaching. Now list those activities that fit your horizontal or thematic planning, and list those that are skill-focused ideas that fit in with your vertical planning. Try to add them to your long-range horizontal plan or to your monthly skill-focused goals.

Resources and Suggested Readings

Avery, Charles. *Everybody Has Feelings: The Moods of Children.* English and Spanish. Beltsville, MD: Gryphon House, 1997.

Barbour, Nita, & Seefeldt, Carol. *Developmental Continuity across Preschool and Primary Grades: Implications for Teachers.* Wheaton, MD: Association for Childhood Education International, 1993.

Berger, Eugenia Hepworth. *Parents as Partners in Education: The School and Home Working Together.* New York: Macmillan, 1991.

Brown, Sam (Ed.). *Bubbles, Rainbows and Worms: Science Activities for Young Children.* Beltsville, MD: Gryphon House, 1991.

Cohen, Richard, & Tunick, Betty. *Snail Trails and Tadpole Tails: Nature Education for Young Children.* St. Paul, MN: Redleaf Press, 1993.

Davidson, Jane. *Emergent Literacy and Dramatic Play in Early Education.* Albany, NY: Delmar, 1995.

Derman-Sparks, Louise, and the ABC Task Force. *Anti-Bias Curriculum: Tools for Empowering Children.* Washington, DC: National Association for the Education of Young Children, 1989.

Derman-Sparks, Louise; Gutierrez, Maria; & Phillips, Carol. *Teaching Young Children to Resist Bias: What Teachers and Parents Can Do.* Washington, DC: National Association for the Education of Young Children, 1989.

Dodge, Diane Trister, & Phinney, Joanna. *A Parents' Guide to Early Childhood Education.* English and Spanish. Washington, DC: Teaching Strategies, 1990.

Edwards, Sharon, & Maloy, Robert. *Kids Have All the Write Stuff: Inspiring Your Children to Put Pencil to Paper.* New York: Penguin Books, 1992.

Estess, Patricia, & Barocas, Irving. *Kids, Money & Values: Creative Ways to Teach Your Kids About Money.* Cincinnati OH: Betterway Books, 1994.

Glazer, Susan, & Burke, Eileen. *An Integrated Approach to Early Literacy: Literature to Language.* Boston: Allyn and Bacon, 1994.

Goffin, Stacie G., & Stegelin, Dolores (Eds.). *Changing Kindergartens: Four Success Stories.* Washington, DC: National Association for the Education of Young Children, 1992.

Gould, Patti, & Sullivan, Joyce. *The Inclusive Early Childhood Classroom: Easy Ways to Adapt Learning Centers for All Children.* Beltsville, MD: Gryphon House, 1999.

Greenberg, Polly. "Ideas That Work with Young Children: How and Why to Teach All Aspects of Preschool and Kindergarten Math." *Young Children*, 49, no. 2 (1994): 12–18.

Haugland, Susan, & Wright, June. *Young Children and Technology: A World of Discovery.* Boston: Allyn and Bacon, 1997.

Hoffman, Stevie, & Lamme, Linda (Eds.). *Learning from the Inside Out: The Expressive Arts.* Wheaton, MD: Association for Childhood Education International, 1989.

Holt, Bess Gene. *Science with Young Children* (rev. ed.). Washington, DC: National Association for the Education of Young Children, 1982, 1991.

Isenberg, Joan, & Jalongo, Mary R. (Eds.). *Major Trends and Issues in Early Childhood Education: Challenges, Controversies and Insights.* New York: Teachers College Press, 1997.

Kamii, Constance. *Number in Preschool and Kindergarten: Implications of Piaget's Theory.* Washington, DC: National Association for the Education of Young Children, 1982.

Kamii, Constance (Ed.). *Achievement Testing in the Early Grades: The Games Grownups Play.* Washington, DC: National Association for the Education of Young Children, 1990.

Kasting, Arlene. "Respect, Responsibility and Reciprocity: The 3 R's of Parent Involvement." *Childhood Education*, 70, no. 3 (1994): 146–150.

Katz, Lillian; Evangelou, Demetra; & Hartman, Jeanette. *The Case for Mixed-Age Grouping in Early Education.* Washington, DC: National Association for the Education of Young Children, 1990.

Kerr, Judy, & Swim, Terri. *Creative Resources for Infants and Toddlers.* Albany, NY: Delmar, 1999.

Kolh, Mary Ann. *Preschool Art: It's the Process, Not Product.* Beltsville, MD: Gryphon House, 1994.

Kohl, Mary Ann. *Math Arts: Exploring Math Through Art for 3 to 6 Year Olds.* Beltsville, MD: Gryphon House, 1996.

Kohl, Mary Ann. *Making Make Believe.* Beltsville, MD: Gryphon House, 1999.

Kohl, Mary Ann. *Big Messy Art.* Beltsville, MD: Gryphon House, 2000.

Koralek, Derry; Colker, Laura; & Dodge, Diane Trister. *The What, Why and How of High Quality Early Childhood Education: A Guide for On-Site Supervision.* Washington, DC: Teaching Strategies, 1993.

Marshall, Hermine. "Cultural Influences on the Development of Self Concept: Updating Our Thinking." *Young Children*, 56, no. 6 (2001): 19–25.

McCracken, Janet Brown. *More Than 1,2,3 . . . The Real Basics of Mathematics*. Washington, DC: National Association for the Education of Young Children.1990.

McGee, Lea M., & Richgels, Donald J. *Literacy's Beginnings: Supporting Young Readers and Writers*. Boston: Allyn and Bacon, 2000.

Moomaw, Sally, & Hieronymus, Brenda. *Much More Than Counting: More Math Activities for Preschool and Kindergarten*. St. Paul, MN: Redleaf Press, 1999.

Moomaw, Sally, & Hieronymus, Brenda. *More Than Letters: Literacy Activities for Preschool, Kindergarten and First Grade*. St. Paul, MN: Redleaf Press, 2001.

National Education Goals Panel. *A Nation of Learners: National Education Goals Report*. Washington, DC: U.S. Department of Education, 1993.

Ollila, Lloyd O., & Mayfield, Margie (Eds.). *Emerging Literacy: Preschool, Kindergarten and the Primary Grades*. Boston: Allyn and Bacon, 1992.

Owocki, G. *Make Way for Literacy: Teaching the Way Young Children Learn*. Washington, DC: Heinemann/National Association for the Education of Young Children, 2001.

Petersen, Evelyn. *Growing Creative Kids: The Seeds of Success Series*. Grand Rapids, MI: Totline Imprint/McGraw-Hill Children's Publishing, 1997.

Petersen, Evelyn. *Growing Thinking Kids: The Seeds of Success Series*. Grand Rapids, MI: Totline Imprint/McGraw-Hill Children's Publishing, 1997.

Petersen, Evelyn. *1, 2, 3, Blocks: Block Activities for Young Children*. Grand Rapids, MI: Totline Imprint/ McGraw-Hill Children's Publishing, 1998.

Petersen, Evelyn. "Finding Purpose in Paint Puddles," *Children and Families*, 17, no. 3 (1998): 28–35.

Petersen, Evelyn, & Petersen, Karin. *Sams Teach Yourself e-Parenting Today: Using the Internet and Computers*. Indianapolis, IN: Macmillan, 2000. (Available on amazon.com.)

Petrash, Carol. *Earthways: Simple Environmental Activities for Young Children*. Beltsville, MD: Gryphon House, 1992.

Pica, Rae. *Moving and Learning across the Curriculum: Activities and Games to Make Learning Fun*. Albany, NY: Delmar, 1998.

Raines, Shirley C., & Canady, Robert. *More Story Stretchers: More Activities to Expand Children's Favorite Books*. Beltsville, MD: Gryphon House, 1991.

Rockwell, Robert. *The Wonders of Water*. Beltsville, MD: Gryphon House, 1997.

Rockwell, Robert; Page, Debra; & Searcy, Bill. *Linking Language: Simple Language and Literacy Activities Throughout the Curriculum*. Beltsville, MD: Gryphon House, 1999.

Rockwell, Robert; Sherwood, Elizabeth; & Williams, Robert. *Hug a Tree and Other Things to Do Outdoors with Young Children*. Beltsville, MD: Gryphon House, 1990.

Rockwell, Robert; Williams, Robert; & Sherwood, Elizabeth. *Everybody Has a Body: Science from Head to Toe*. Beltsville, MD: Gryphon House, 1992.

Schiller, Pam, & Hieronymus, Brenda. *Count on Math: Activities for Small Hands and Lively Minds*. Beltsville, MD: Gryphon House, 1997.

Striker, Susan. *Young at Art: Teaching Toddlers Self-Expression, Problem Solving Skills and Art Appreciation*. New York: Owl Books/Henry Holt & Company, 2001.

Weikart, Phyllis. *Round the Circle: Key Experiences in Movement for Young Children* (2nd ed.). Ypsilanti, MI: High Scope Press, 2000.

West, Sherrie, & Cox, Amy. *Sand and Water Play: Simple, Creative Activities for Young* Children. Beltsville, MD: Gryphon House, 2001.

York, Stacey. *Roots and Wings: Affirming Culture in Early Childhood Programs*. St. Paul, MN: Redleaf Press, 1991.

Websites

www.edmark.com   Edmark Publishing

www.gryphonhouse.com   Gryphon House Publishing

www.nhsa.org   National Head Start Association

www.beritsbest.com   Berit's Safe learning sites for children

www.sln.org   Science Learning Network

www.ala.org   American Library Association

www.2edc.org/NCIP   National Center to Improve Practice in Special Education Through Technology

www.wheelock.edu   Wheelock College, Boston

Skill-Based Learning Experiences: September to May

You have permission to copy and enlarge the seven Time Block tables in this appendix. With this appendix as a guide, it will be possible to use the time blocks as a guide in daily lesson planning from the beginning to the end of the program year. The appendix will make it possible to plan developmentally sequenced, skill-based activities for various times of the day in all areas of the setting. The format of each of the seven time blocks in this appendix will also remind teachers to provide a consistent balance of learning experiences in all five skill-based areas (motor, perceptual, literacy, memory, and problem solving).

Many teachers who use this book are in Head Start programs. They will be planning experiences that lead to outcomes, and doing performance based data collection to prove this. The following tips for Head Start teachers will help them use the Time Blocks effectively to link their planning to outcomes in all learning domains.

1. When you choose experiences from the Time Blocks for lesson plans, check your choices (particularly for small group and individualizing) to see which activities match with specific indicators or elements in the eight Head Start Outcomes Framework domains. Remember that the Outcomes Framework indicators are developmentally sequenced, as are these Time Blocks. (You are not expected to work on *all* the outcomes of a particular domain at the same time—only those that match with children's current but ongoing development.)
2. Remember that the *Problem Solving* category of this appendix includes many activities that will lead children to **Math, Science, and Creative Arts** outcomes.
3. All of the experiences found in the *Literacy* category will match domain elements and Outcomes Framework indicators in both the **Language and Literacy** domains.
4. Often, experiences in the *Motor* and *Perceptual* categories will also match outcomes indicators in **Language and Literacy.** (Examples: Auditory Perceptual activities will lead to outcomes indicators in Phonological Awareness. Visual perception activities will lead to outcomes indicators in Print Awareness and Early Writing. Use of art media tools will lead to outcomes in Early Writing.)
5. Most experiences/activities leading to **Physical Health and Development** outcomes will be found in *Motor* category; many can also be found in the *Problem Solving* category.

6. Activities leading to **Creative Arts** outcomes will most frequently be found in the "Free-Choice Time" section of the *Motor* and *Literacy* categories, and in the *Problem Solving,* category. (See "Body Movement," "Art Media," "Body Language," "Talk, Listen, Do," "Writing Center," "Blocks," and "Dramatic Play.")
7. Learning experiences leading to **Social-Emotional Development** outcomes are integrated throughout the seven time blocks and found in all categories.
8. Activities that lead to outcomes in **Approaches to Learning** are integrated throughout the time blocks in all categories; many will be found in the *Problem Solving* category.

In closing, remember that this appendix has been developed to present *a system* of organizing and using information. Information that the teacher brings to the lesson planning experience is crucially important, as it reflects not only the teacher's ideas but also the values of his or her culture, community, and parents. The examples that follow should serve as a springboard for your own skill-based activity ideas. Remember to review Chapter 8 for help in using the Time Block system of developmental sequencing. Answers to most questions will be found there.

TABLE A.1   *Skill-Based Activities—Me and My World*
Time Block 1 (September–October)

MOTOR	PERCEPTUAL
LARGE GROUP **Body Movement:** Copy and/or create to music, songs, chants, rhymes. Act out prepositions. **FREE CHOICE** **Using Blocks:** Use unit and large hollow blocks. Stack, lay, carry, build. **Active Play Inside/Outside:** Use all types of locomotion, including wheel toys. Follow line or path with body or toy. Practice climbing and rolling. Jump with both feet. Toss, catch, and pass with big, soft beanbags, or paper-stuffed pillowcase. Use hammer with pegs or *soft* wood or Styrofoam. **Clays and Playdough/Sand and Water:** Use freely; fill, pour, float, sink, mold and dig. **Dressing and Undressing:** Practice with outer wear, dress-up, and zipper/button toys. **Art Media:** Use crayons, markers, chalk, paper. Use easel paint and fingerpaint. Paint at tables. Use varied collage materials. **Manipulatives, Table Toys, Floor Toys:** Use large, easy puzzles. Use large pegs/pegboards. Use large lego blocks. String large beads. Use stack and nest toys. Use shape box toys. Use snap and bristle blocks. **SMALL GROUP** **Games:** Follow object with eyes. Tear paper at random. Use tongs and pinch clothespins. Trace simple templates with fingers; free form, one line. Practice pouring water. Practice any manipulatives. **Meals and Snacks:** Pour, pass, serve, spread. Clean up, brush teeth.	**LARGE GROUP** **Music and Circle:** Use instruments. Recognize body parts. Listen to sounds and identify some. Notice what we are wearing. **FREE CHOICE** **Blocks:** Use all types. Handle and match types. **Exploring with Senses:** Use clays, playdough, water, sand, earth. Explore and match textures. Handle and match recycled items. Handle collage items. Match familiar objects. Use various paints. Compare colors used in art media. Notice smells, tastes. **Manipulatives, Table Toys, Floor Toys:** Use simple, large puzzles/parquetry. Use face–body parts activities. Match textures. Match familiar silhouette shapes. **Cleanup:** Use pictures and perceptual labels. Recognize sound cues. **SMALL GROUP** **Games:** Compare sounds: high, low, loud, soft. Tell direction of sound source.* Compare ourselves regarding sizes, hair, eyes. Guess a hidden object by touch alone. Match some primary colors. Compare objects: big, small, like, unlike. Match like objects. Examine/match circles and ovals. Identify simple sounds.* Recognize familiar shape silhouettes. **Meals and Snacks:** Perceive colors, textures, tastes, smells, temperatures.

LITERACY

LARGE GROUP
Literature:
Hear stories and books.
Do fingerplays and rhymes.
Do songs and chants.
See flannelboard stories.
Use/talk with puppets.

Conversations:
About work and play choices.
About plans and routines.
On simple rules for safety.
About friends and names.
On things that make us happy or sad.

Body Language:
Move to music.
Imitate animals and nature.
Act out prepositions with music, rug squares.

FREE CHOICE
Talk/Listen/Do:
Use books and pictures.
Use people's names.
Name items and equipment.
Talk about healthful ways.
Use friendly words.
Use, talk about safe ways and rules.
Play with puppets.
Talk about art and creations.
Use picture recipe to make playdough.
Use tape recorder.
Use listen station.
Use play telephones.
Examine computer.

Dramatic Play:
Converse spontaneously.
Use materials creatively.

Writing Center:
Do creative "writing" and communicating.

SMALL GROUP
Games:
Discuss me, my home and family.
Start a "me" book.
Discuss pictures about feelings.
Discuss work and play choices.
Use puppets together.
Discuss health and safety.*
Read a picture book.*
Discuss visitors/helpers. *
Discuss outdoor walks.*

Meals and Snacks:
Discuss and name foods. Tell preferences.

MEMORY

LARGE GROUP
Learning Together:
Copy adult modeling.
Imitate in simple games of "Do What I Do."
Hear and talk about stories.
Sing songs in unison and call and response.
Enjoy and learn fingerplays.
Try counting by rote up to 5 in songs, rhymes, birthdays.
Learn daily schedule, routines, limits.
See picture sequence of daily schedule.
Use names of friends in songs, rhymes, and games.
See own name in print.

FREE CHOICE
All Area Learning:
Learn names of areas, materials, and equipment.
Learn how we use materials and equipment.
Learn names of friends.
Learn limits, expectations, and routines with practice and helpful visual cues.
Learn helpers' jobs with practice and helpful visual cues.
Use healthful habits at snacks and meals, when toileting, and in cleaning to prevent spread of germs.
Use safety habits with materials, movements, fire drills.

Cleanup:
Learn adult cue to start.
Learn where things go.

SMALL GROUP
Games:
Talk about fire and tornado drills.
See sequenced pictures of the daily schedule.
Recall today and what I liked best.
Repeat own and each other's names in rhythmic chant.
Remember summer and family fun.*
Recall one or two objects when these are removed from a group and hidden.
Guess names of areas from adult clues.
Sometimes recognize own printed name.
Recall some friend's names.

Meals and Snacks:
Learn the routine.
Copy positive social language.

PROBLEM SOLVING

LARGE GROUP
Conversations:
On work/play choices from day's options.
On the schedule of the day.
About nature, the weather, and its changes.
About our body parts and their use. (demonstrate).
On what makes us feel happy or sad.

FREE CHOICE
Blocks:
Stack, lay, connect.
Observe differences in structures.

All Area Learning:
Begin to know areas and materials by use.
Make work/play choices.
Begin to plan the use of time.
Ask questions and use senses to gain information.
Negotiate turns with materials.
Explain wants and needs with words.
Match, sort, and tub materials.
Manipulate materials.
Examine computer.
Observe properties of sand, water, paint, playdough/clays.
Observe changes resulting in mixing colors.
Make playdough; measure, mix; see changes.

Dramatic Play:
Choose items for role-play and pretend.
Plan and carry out play.

Science and Math:
Observe and handle nature items.
Observe our plants and animals.
Measure and weigh ourselves.
Estimate in pouring and filling.

SMALL GROUP
Games:
Discuss play choices and plan one choice for next time.
Tub and sort items.
Count own body parts.
Count heads and noses of those in group.
Blow bubbles with individual cups/straws; observe and tell.

Meals and Snacks:
Set table with one-to-one match.
Help prepare snack when possible.
Problem-solve when using utensils.
Estimate in pouring, filling.

TABLE A.2 *Skill-Based Activities—My Expanding World Time Block 2 (October–November)*

MOTOR	PERCEPTUAL
LARGE GROUP **Body Movement:** Copy and/or create to music, songs, chants, rhymes. Act out prepositions. **FREE CHOICE** **Using Blocks:** Use unit and large blocks freely. **Active Play Inside/Outside:** Use varied locomotion, including wheel toys. Follow line with body or toy. Try balance beam, laid flat. Use steps/rocking boat. Use indoor climber. Use mats to jump and roll. Balance on one foot; try to hop. Toss/catch large, light items. Jump over a low rope; rake, jump in leaves. Use hammer and soft materials or pegs. **Clays and Playdough/Sand and Water:** Use freely; add variety. Pour, fill, float, sink, dig, mold. **Dressing and Undressing:** Outer wear, dress-up, and zipper/button toys. **Art Media:** Use crayons, markers, paper, scissors. Do varied painting, fingerpaint, collages. Try spray painting. Try dripped-glue designs. Try hole punch designs. Try rubbings from nature. **Manipulatives, Table Toys, Floor Toys:** Use all appropriate manipulatives freely. **SMALL GROUP** **Games:** Tear paper with purpose. Use simple templates with curves; one line. Fold paper; either one or two folds. Learn about eye dropper painting. String paper tubes, big pastas, or cereals. Snip or fringe with scissors. Practice any manipulatives. **Meals and Snacks:** Pour, pass, serve, and spread. Carry, clean up, brush teeth.	**LARGE GROUP** **Music and Circle:** Use instruments. Match sounds of like instruments. Identify other sounds. Compare ourselves; sizes and other characteristics. Guess hidden objects by touch alone. Notice what we wear. **FREE CHOICE** **Blocks:** Use all types. Handle, match, and find types. **Exploring with Senses:** Use clays, playdough, water, sand, mud. Match textures and recycled items. Mix and match paints. Do more smelling and tasting. Sort items found in nature such as leaves, stones, seeds. Use some musical instruments in play. **Manipulatives, Table Toys, Floor Toys:** Use materials fully. Use blocks, flannel pieces, beads, pegs, and parquetry to create own patterns. **Cleanup:** Use perceptual labels. Recognize sound cues. **SMALL GROUP** **Games:** Match primary colors, unnamed. Hum together; match a pitch. Recognize a voice. Identify familiar sounds on tape. Match familiar shapes. Match simple objects to their pictures. Reproduce easy three-part patterns with model in view using cubes, beads, or other objects. Find or match circles, ovals, squares. Guess objects by touch.* Match big and small objects. **Meals and Snacks:** Perceive and discuss tastes, smells, textures, colors. Perceive that some foods have shapes.

LITERACY

LARGE GROUP
Literature:
Hear stories and books.
Do fingerplays and rhymes.
Do songs and chants.
Use flannelboard and puppets.

Conversations:
About choices and plans.
On rules for our room and group.
About feelings and fears.
About friends and names.
About new toys and equipment.

Body Language:
Move to music.
Use gestures and imitations.
Try signing a simple word or phrase.
Add to actions with prepositions.

FREE CHOICE
Talk/Listen/Do:
Use books/pictures.
Use names of people and materials.
Use and talk about healthful ways.
Use friendly words.
Use and talk about safe ways/rules.
Use puppets and flannelboard.
Answer open questions.
Do artwork dictation.
Try new recipe cards.
Use the computer.
Tape record/listen.
Use play telephones.

Dramatic Play:
Use new props and materials.
Converse spontaneously.

Writing Center:
Create original communication.
Try new materials.

SMALL GROUP
Games:
Continue "me" book as a personal
  journal.
Discuss foods, health, safety.*
Discuss feelings of self and others.
Discuss visitors, trips, and walks.*
Discuss our plants and animals.
Begin simple dictation or experience
  stories.

Meals and Snacks:
Discuss and describe food. Talk with
  peers and adults.

MEMORY

LARGE GROUP
Remembering Together:
Copy adult modeling.
Imitate in simple games of "Do What I
  Do."
Hear stories and songs.
Do fingerplays/rhymes.
Know what comes next in schedule.
Try rote counting to 5 in nonstereotyped
  songs, rhymes.
See and discuss pictured sequence of
  routines such as fire drills, meals/
  toothbrushing.
See visual cues for limits/rules and
  helper jobs.
Know many names of friends and adults.
Recognize and name familiar sounds.
  See own name in print (name tag,
  creations).
Remember summer or past events.
Remember fun times with friends/
  family.
Recall name of a person hidden when
  adult gives clues.
Repeat simple oral or clapped rhythm.

FREE CHOICE
All Area Learning:
Know names of areas, equipment, and
  materials.
Know how to use these appropriately.
Use names of friends.
Know rules and expectations.
Remember helpers' jobs; use visual cues.
Practice health habits.
Practice safety habits.

Cleanup:
Remember light or sound cues.
Know where things go.

SMALL GROUP
Games:
Recall two things I did today.
See, match own name in print.
Remember walks, trips, visitors.*
Recall two or three objects removed and
  hidden.
Recall/do 1–2 tasks while seated.
Find one primary color when named.
Find circles and ovals.
Repeat a simple clapped or oral rhythm.

Meals and Snacks:
Remember the routine.
Use positive social language.
Begin to talk about food groups.
Talk about foods for healthy teeth.

PROBLEM SOLVING

LARGE GROUP
Conversations:
About work and play choices.
About the daily schedule.
About weather changes and how these
  tell us seasonal changes.
On rules developed by the group.
On "last time" or "next time."
On body parts and their use.
About ways we can relax.

FREE CHOICE
Blocks:
Stack, lay, connect, enclose.
See parts of whole.
Compare differences in structures.

All Area Learning:
Know areas by use.
Make work/play choices.
Ask questions and use senses to gain
  information.
Negotiate wants, needs, and turns with
  words.
See step-by-step process in use of media
  and manipulatives.
Begin to see parts of whole in puzzles,
  designs.
Match, sort, and tub materials. Use
  computer.
Try new multisensory media; colors,
  clays.

Dramatic Play:
Plan and carry out play.
Do safety and health habit role-play.

Science and Math:
Notice and handle new items; count
  some.
Observe/tell about nature and our plants
  and animals.
See changes mixing, cooking and
  grinding.
Use the balance scale and measuring
  tools.

SMALL GROUP
Games:
Use minilight and a magnifier to
  examine nature items found.
Blow bubbles with individual cups/
  straws; add drops of food color;
  observe and tell.
Sort nature items in two ways.
Graph selves by size or in other ways.
Guess, find out what floats or sinks in
  cup of water.
Match three or four items one to one.

Meals and Snacks:
Continue to help in set up and
  preparation.
See changes in foods experiences.

TABLE A.3 *Skill-Based Activities—Special Days in My World Time Block 3 (November–December)*

MOTOR	PERCEPTUAL
LARGE GROUP **Body Movement:** Copy and/or create to music, songs, chants, rhymes. Act out prepositions. Try simple pantomime. **FREE CHOICE** **Using Blocks:** Use all types. Use accessories. **Active Play Inside/Outside:** Use varied locomotion; roll, jump, dig in snow if available. Use jumpropes, hoops. Use balance beam *raised.* Use rotated indoor active equipment daily. Follow simple four-pan obstacle course: beam, jump, steps, mat. Balance on one foot; try to hop. Toss and catch big, soft ball. Hammer; try vise and short coping saw with Styrofoam or *soft* wood. **Clays and Playdough/ Water and Sand:** Add variety; accessories. Pour/fill, sink/float, dig. Wash dolls and chairs. **Dressing and Undressing:** Outer wear, boots, dress-up, and zipper/button toys. **Art Media:** Use variety of *open-ended* art media daily. Try new colors and materials. Try stamp printing. Try simple paper chains. **Manipulatives, Table Toys, Floor Toys:** Use all appropriate materials. Add smaller legos, beads, and pegs. **SMALL GROUP** **Games:** Use short Phillips screwdriver/screws in ceiling tile. Cut paper apart at random or folded once. Trace ovals or circles. Tear simple or random paper shapes. String smaller beads. Use easy lacing materials. Try three-dimensional constructions with tape and recycled items. **Meals and Snacks:** Pour, pass, serve, clean up, brush teeth. Help prepare foods whenever possible.	**LARGE GROUP** **Music and Circle:** Use instruments and identify their sounds. Compare and guess objects by touch. Notice what we wear. Talk about circles we see in room. Perceive gestures as words. **FREE CHOICE** **Blocks:** Use all types. Handle, match and find types. Name some shapes. **Exploring with Senses:** Try new variety in clays and playdough. Make play do prints by pressing against objects. Try new variety in sand and water. Examine earth from outdoors. Examine snow indoors if available. Look at animal, bird tracks in snow or earth. Observe/compare tracks of our boots. Sort and match textures, nature items, recyclables. Mix paint; try brown with pink and white for pastels. Enjoy taste and smell experiences. Use instruments in choice time. **Manipulatives, Table Toys, Floor Toys:** Use all appropriate items. **Cleanup:** Use perceptual labels. Recognize sound or light cues. **SMALL GROUP** **Games:** Match like pictures in simple lotto games. Continue reproducing simple patterns with pegs, flannel pieces, beads, and table blocks when model is seen; try four-part pattern if appropriate. Do easy sound-matching games with film containers or cans. Match familiar shapes and big and small shapes. Match primary colors and one or two secondary colors. See differences in items like our shoes.* Find and/or match circles, ovals, squares, triangles. **Meals and Snacks:** Perceive tastes, smells, textures, colors, shapes. Perceive "not full enough" and "too full."

LITERACY	MEMORY	PROBLEM SOLVING

LITERACY

LARGE GROUP
Literature:
Hear new, varied literature.
Try stories without words.
Try experience stories and a Big Book.

Conversations:
About choices and plans.
About adjusting rules made by the group.
About feelings and family.
About family traditions.
About friendships.
About new materials.
About health and safety.

Body Language:
Represent ideas with music
Imitate animals and nature.
Sign "I love you."
Safety and health role play.

FREE CHOICE
Talk/Listen/Do:
Use books/pictures.
Use and talk about healthy ways.
Use friendly words.
Use and talk about safe ways and rules.
Use puppets and flannelboard.
Dictation; art and constructions.
Dictation; science area observations.
Add new recipe cards.
Use computer.
Tape record and listen.
Use play telephones.

Dramatic Play:
Use "house" as a shop or restaurant.
Pretend "company" is coming.

Writing Center:
Use varied, recycled greeting cards.
Use other materials freely.

SMALL GROUP
Games:
Continue personal journal.
Discuss family traditions for special days.*
Discuss health and safety.*
Discuss special days and "company."*
Read a book together.
Answer open, what-if questions.
Discuss things I can do alone, or for others.

Meals and Snacks:
Discuss foods, some food groups, and simple nutrition.
Discuss foods for "special days" with peers and adults.

MEMORY

LARGE GROUP
Remembering Together:
Copy adult modeling.
Play simple games of "Do What I Do."
Participate in stories, songs, fingerplays, rhymes.
Count by rote up to 8 in songs, rhymes.
Try to count to 3 in another language.
Know what comes next in the schedule.
Know and state our group rules.
Know friends' and adult helpers' names.
Recognize own name in print.
Remember family fun and special days.
Remember special class events and visitors.
Repeat sounds and simple rhythms.
Act out familiar story or rhyme.

FREE CHOICE
All Area Learning:
Use names of things, friends, areas.
Know rules and expectations.
Know and do helpers' jobs.
Practice health habits.
Practice safety habits.
Pretend restaurant, "company," and shopping.

Cleanup:
Remember cues and know where things go.

SMALL GROUP
Games:
Remember two or three things I did today. *
Find circles, ovals, and squares when named.
Talk about summer, fall, past winters.*
Answer questions about a short story just heard.
Remember our walks and trips.*
Remember family traditions and/or special foods served.
Recall three objects or shapes removed and hidden.
Recall and do two tasks.
Furnish words omitted in familiar song or rhyme.*
Repeat a silly word or phrase.

Meals and Snacks:
Remember routine and positive language.
Remember some food groups; see food pyramid.
Remember foods we like or dislike.

PROBLEM SOLVING

LARGE GROUP
Conversations:
About work and play choices.
About weather and seasonal changes.
About the names *fall* and *winter*.
On what we do when a parent is "too busy."
About the holidays.
See pictures or symbols of the three most current holidays.
Discuss and help to sequence the holidays represented.
Represent ideas in creative movement.

FREE CHOICE
Blocks:
Sort/compare, see parts, connect, enclose.
Begin to bridge and repeat simple patterns.
Begin to use accessories.

All Area Learning:
Make work and play choices.
Ask questions and begin to discover answers.
Negotiate turns, wants, and needs with words.
Match, sort, and tub materials.
Experiment with manipulatives and constructions.
Use computer.
Use multisensory media fully; try new varieties.

Dramatic Play:
Plan and carry out play.
Do safety and health role-play.
Try new roles and ideas with new props.

Science and Math:
Observe nature and our plants and animals.
Observe and handle new items; count some.
Use new or different tools for measuring.
Use scales and magnifier.

SMALL GROUP
Games:
Repeat water experiments.
Arrange three items by size.
See snow or ice melt.
Sort objects two or three ways.
Give adult one to three items.
Discuss how to be safe when we go shopping.*
Discuss ways to feel better when sad.*
Graph holiday cookie cutter shapes.

Meals and Snacks:
Continue past experiences.
Try some different types of holiday foods.

TABLE A.4 *Skill-Based Activities—Learning More about My World*
Time Block 4 (January–February)

MOTOR	PERCEPTUAL
LARGE GROUP **Body Movement:** Copy and/or create to varied music and rhythms. Try side-to-side moves. Use pantomime to represent ideas, feelings, or nature's changes. **FREE CHOICE** **Using Blocks:** Use all types and use accessories. **Active Play Inside/Outside:** Use varied locomotion; include snow equipment if appropriate. Use balance beam *raised*. Use mats to tumble. Use jumpropes and hoops. Use varied four- or five-pan obstacle courses. Balance on each foot. Hop; try to gallop. Toss and catch; toss into target. Use hammer, saw, vise, Phillips screws. Add recycled embellishments to constructions. **Clays and Playdough/Sand and Water:** Add new variety, tools, accessories. **Dressing and Undressing** Practice with outerwear, dress-up, shoes/boots. **Art Media:** Use *open-ended* art media freely. Experiment with new colors/tools. Try string painting. Do more stamp prints. Tear and cut varied papers. **Manipulatives, Table Toys, Floor Toys:** Use all appropriate items; rotate as needed. **SMALL GROUP** **Games:** Trace circles, ovals, free forms, hearts. Cut paper folded twice. Tear simple paper shapes. String small beads. Use lacing materials. Practice tying one simple knot with shoelace or yarn. Cut paper apart on one thick, straight line. Do three-dimensional constructions with tape and recyclables. Draw own picture with marker or crayon. **Meals and Snacks:** Carry, pour, fill, pass, serve, spread, clean up. Help prepare foods; wash vegetables; pare a carrot.	**LARGE GROUP** **Music and Circle:** Use instruments and guess their sounds. Guess objects by touch. Guess a visible object or a person from visual clues given. Hear a special sound amid background noise. **FREE CHOICE** **Blocks:** Handle, match, and find all types. Perceive shapes and other attributes. See patterns created or repeated. **Exploring with Senses:** Experiment with new variety in clay, playdough, sand, water, and textures; include snow. Observe and compare tracks in snow or earth. Experiment with paint and painting tools. Continue to handle, sort, match. Make playdough prints; guess where from. Continue taste, smell, and foods experiences. **Manipulatives, Table Toys, Floor Toys:** Use all appropriate items freely. Use more complex parquetry designs. Use more complex puzzles. Use simple picture lotto cards. **Cleanup:** Use perceptual labels. Respond to sound and light cues. **SMALL GROUP** **Games:** Use easy picture and symbol lotto. Try reproducing simple five-part patterns with model seen. Match or find circles, ovals, hearts, squares. Match big, small, medium. Use sound-matching cans. Match three primary and three secondary colors. Guess a person's voice.* Guess where texture or object prints on playdough were made. Practice puzzle or parquetry skills. Perceive interesting similarities and differences among us. **Meals and Snacks:** Perceive and describe tastes, colors, textures, shapes. Observe a food and guess the method of cooking it. Sort and match cereal or cracker snacks.

LITERACY	MEMORY	PROBLEM SOLVING
LARGE GROUP **Literature:** Hear new and varied literature. Help tell story to group. Do experience stories and use Big Books together. Use sequenced pictures of day's schedule, seasons, holidays to tell about. **Conversations:** About play choices and plans. On getting along with friends and family. About the events of our holidays. About ways we learn with our senses and our questions. About staying healthy and healthy foods. About ways we stay safe in bad weather. About visual cues/pictures of our group rules. **Body Language:** Represent ideas and feelings in movement. Act out a story or rhyme. Try more words in sign. **FREE CHOICE** **Talk/Listen/Do:** Use friendly, safe, healthy ways. Converse with peers and adults. Use puppets and flannelboard. Continue dictation in art/science and/or other areas. Try dictation about block and other three-dimensional constructions. Use and add new recipe cards. Use computer and telephones. Tape record and listen. **Dramatic Play:** Add new prop boxes and props. Pretend vet, hospital, and other safety/health role play. Pretend bus, office, stores. **Writing Center:** Use all materials, including old greeting cards. **SMALL GROUP** **Games:** Answer "What if . . ." and "What do you think?" questions. Discuss/plan what to buy at store to make vegetable soup. Continue personal journal. Start a traveling journal that rotates among families. Sequence simple story cards. Write a thank-you letter using picture and dictation. Talk about learning with our senses and questions. Describe what I like about another person. **Meals and Snacks:** Converse sociably with peers and adults on foods/topics.	**LARGE GROUP** **Remembering Together:** Copy adult modeling. Help tell stories/rhymes. Sing favorite songs. Count by rote to 10 in songs and rhymes. Count to 5 in another language. Recall our group rules with the help of pictures/visual cues. Recall sequence of day using pictures of schedule. Play and sing name games. Recognize own name in print. Talk about holiday fun, trips, company. Repeat sounds and easy clapping rhythms. **FREE CHOICE** **All Area Learning:** Know names of friends, areas, materials. Know expectations for behaviors. Do helpers' jobs; help set up room. Practice health habits. Practice safety habits. Pretend with new props in new areas. Use flannelboard to tell familiar story. Use simple sequence cards. **Cleanup:** Remember the cues. Know where things go. **SMALL GROUP** **Games:** Talk about the holidays.* Find and/or match circles, ovals, squares, and hearts. Tell three things I did today. Recall three shapes when seen, then hidden. Recall and do two or three tasks. Recall holiday traditions and special foods served. Furnish words omitted in a familiar rhyme. Sequence pictures or symbols of the past three holidays. Repeat silly words or phrases. See and talk about photos taken of the group. **Meals and Snacks:** Remember positive language. Talk about some food groups. Recall having this food before. Talk about what is in vegetable soup. Talk about how to cook soup at school.	**LARGE GROUP** **Conversations:** About work and play choices. About weather and seasonal changes and their effects on us. About the sequence of summer, fall, winter; use pictures. See and discuss school days and at-home days; record them on a blank calendar with symbols (school bus and house). Represent ideas in creative movement. Plan how to cook vegetable soup. **FREE CHOICE** **Blocks:** Cooperate; use accessories. Repeat simple patterns. **All Area Learning:** Make work/play choices in all areas. Ask questions; try to find answers. Answer open questions. Negotiate with words. Reweigh and remeasure ourselves. Regraph ourselves and see changes. Work on a group art mural. Count things and people. Experiment with art, multisensory media, manipulatives. Tell about cause and effect in using materials and media. Try new tools with sand, water, paint. **Dramatic Play:** Plan and carry out new ideas, roles, and use of props. **Science and Math:** Observe nature, plants, animals; notice changes. Observe and handle new items; count and sort some. Use tools and methods for observing or recording. **SMALL GROUP** **Games:** Order three items by size; give adult three items. Introduce use of magnets. Count the eyes, ears, noses, feet of two people. Use food color or crepe paper to see color changes in water. Discuss something red and round from home. Prepare vegetables for soup; observe, describe. **Meals and Snacks:** Graph a cereal snack; count, discuss *more, less, most.* Eat soup; discuss preparation and changes that occurred.

TABLE A.5 *Skill-Based Activities—Learning More about My World*
Time Block 5 (February–March)

MOTOR	PERCEPTUAL
LARGE GROUP **Body Movement:** Copy and/or create to varied music. Represent ideas/feelings/nature in movement. Act out prepositions; move "sideways."	**LARGE GROUP** **Music and Circle:** Use and guess instruments by sound. Hear two sounds amid background noise. Guess visible object or person from clues. Guess visible shapes in room from clues.
FREE CHOICE **Using Blocks:** Use all types with accessories. Build sets for dramatic play w/big blocks.	**FREE CHOICE** **Blocks:** Handle, match, find, label, describe. Describe patterns in constructions. Use descriptors; tall, short, narrow, wide. Work cooperatively to build.
Active Play Inside/Outside*:* Use varied locomotion. Do parachute play. Use balance beam *raised;* carry object. Use jump ropes and hoops. Use mats; tumbling, obstacle courses. Varied four- or five-part obstacle courses, sometimes with slide. Practice hopping, galloping. Toss/catch; try using target. Use all woodworking tools; embellish/paint creations as option.	**Exploring with Senses:** Experiment with new varieties of media. Experiment with playdough prints. Experiment with painting; observe changes. Taste and smell experiences; match sweet/sour. Observe changes mixing, cooking, chilling foods. Observe/compare tracks in snow, mud or earth.
Clays and Playdough/Sand and Water: Add new variety, such as small hosing, wheels, syphons.	**Manipulatives, Table Toys, Floor Toys:** Use all appropriate items fully. Use more complex puzzles and parquetry. Use symbol and picture lotto cards. Use matching sound can games. Sort and find pictures of a given subject.
Dressing and Undressing Continue practice, including shoes/boots. Help peers with these tasks.	**Cleanup:** Use perceptual and printed labels. Respond to sound and light cues.
Art Media: Use *open-ended* art media freely. Experiment with new methods, materials. Work on an art mural with others.	**SMALL GROUP** **Games:** Use picture and symbol lotto. Match and/or find varied shapes, including square, triangle. Reproduce five part patterns with pegs/beads; model seen. Match real objects to symbols for numerals 1, 2, 3. Match and/or group big, small, medium items. Sort recyclables in three or more ways. Guess a voice, match a hummed pitch.* Match or find primary and secondary colors. Observe likenesses and differences among us.
Manipulatives, Table Toys, Floor Toys: Use appropriate items; and try more complexity. Work cooperatively with some materials.	**Meals and Snacks:** Discuss changes in foods after preparation. Describe tastes, textures, colors, shapes. Graph a snack by shapes or size; compare.
SMALL GROUP **Games:** Trace circles/ovals, hearts, free forms; try triangle. Tie a knot on top of one knot. String small beads, cereals, pastas. Cut thin paper folded three times at random. Cut folded paper on thick, simple curve; create heart. Tear paper shapes including heart shapes. Cut paper on one thick line with several curves. Use new lacing materials. Draw picture with marker or crayon. Do three-dimensional constructions (tape and recyclables).	
Meals and Snacks: Continue prior experiences; help in food preparation.	

LITERACY

LARGE GROUP
Literature:
Hear/help tell varied literature.
Experience stories based on interests, events.
Use more Big Books.
Hear entries from traveling family journal.
Hear dictation recorded about plants, animals.

Conversations:
About work and play choices.
About staying healthy.
About friends and helpers.
About how adults teach us about our world.
About helpers like ranger, garbage collector, snow plower.
About trips that teach us new things.
Plan for a field trip and how we travel there.

Body Language:
Act out simple story or rhyme.
Represent ideas, feelings in movement.
Sign the words *time, work, play.*

FREE CHOICE
Talk/Listen/Do:
Converse. Ask questions; answer open questions.
Use and talk about safe, friendly, and healthful ways.
Use puppets and flannelboard.
Continue dictation in art, science, blocks.
Dictate words to accompany art mural.
Use computer and telephones.
Tape record and listen.
Use recipe cards and add new ones.

Dramatic Play:
Try new role play, new props, new areas.
Continue safety/health role-play.
Pretend places: fire station, office, hospital, store.

Writing Center:
Use all materials, including recycled greeting cards,
Write valentines or notes to peers and/or family.

SMALL GROUP
Games:
Continue personal journal; hear some entries.
Continue traveling journal; hear some entries.
Discuss ways adults help us learn about our world.
Dictation: What I like best about a family member.
Write thank you with picture to adults after field trip.
Answer "what if" or "what do you think" questions.
Make up a new ending to a familiar story.

Meals and Snacks:
Converse sociably with peers/adults.

MEMORY

LARGE GROUP
Remembering Together:
Copy adult modeling.
Help tell stories, rhymes, fingerplays.
Sing familiar songs and chants.
Count by rote to 10 in songs and rhymes.
Count up to 5 in another language.
Recall/discuss adult visit or field trip.
Repeat chanted or clapped rhythms.
Correct familiar rhyme that adult says "incorrectly."
Tell the end of a familiar story.
Talk about names for school days and at home days.

FREE CHOICE
All Area Learning:
Know names of friends, areas, materials.
Name shapes of many blocks.
Know expectations for behavior.
Observe/discuss past events seen in photos.
Do helpers' jobs; help set up the room.
Practice health and safety habits.
Pretend in new ways with new props.
Recall and act out a past field trip.
Recall and act out other places we know.
Use simple sequence cards in play.
Use flannelboard to tell familiar stories.

Cleanup:
Remember the cues.
Know where things go.

SMALL GROUP
Games:
Tell how we used our senses to do something today.
Recall four objects or shapes when seen, then hidden.
Use picture sequence games.
Find circles, ovals, squares, hearts, triangles.
Use the names of colors.
Recall methods that keep us healthy or safe.
Recall what we like about a peer and dictate to make "… is special" poster.
Repeat several days until all children have posters.
Repeat a silly sentence.
Practice repeating home address.
Reproduce three- or four-part pattern; model hidden.
Recall "Who helps us when … ?" memory game.

Meals and Snacks:
Recall foods we have most or least often.
Recall healthy foods and food groups.
Recall how we made something to eat.

PROBLEM SOLVING

LARGE GROUP
Conversations:
On work/play choices.
On weather changes and their effects on us.
On sequence of holidays and approaching holiday.
Represent approaching holiday or trips with symbols on blank calendar with the school and at-home days.
Represent the *names* for school and at-home days on calendar.
Represent ideas and feelings in movement.
Plan a field trip together; discuss all aspects.

FREE CHOICE
Blocks:
Cooperate in building related structures.
Explain uses of parts of a structure.
Build/represent a place where adults help us.

All Area Learning:
Make work and play choices.
Use time effectively; work/play in all areas.
Ask questions and discover answers.
Experiment with computer.
Explain reasons for wants and needs.
Explain reasons for group rules.
Work on group art mural.
Count things and people.
Experiment with multisensory media and manipulatives.
Observe/tell about cause and effect during play.
Estimate/guess "what will happen" during play.

Dramatic Play:
Plan and carry out new ideas with roles, props.
Recreate a place where adults help us.

Science:
Experiment with new items and observation tools.
Make simple graphs of experiment results.

SMALL GROUP
Games:
Sort recyclable items in three or more ways.
Use recyclables to make sets of one to four; give adult four items.
Discuss something brought from home that is made of wood.
Count the eyes, ears, noses, feet of three people.
Graph various physical characteristics among group.
Order hearts by size, smallest to largest.
Play lotto Games: What's missing or does not belong.

Meals and Snacks:
Continue prior experiences and graph more snacks.
Discuss our thoughts about our own "cooking."

TABLE A.6 *Skill-Based Activities—Sharing My World
Time Block 6 (March–April)*

MOTOR	PERCEPTUAL
LARGE GROUP	**LARGE GROUP**
Body Movement:	**Music and Circle:**
Copy/create to varied music and rhythms.	Use our own homemade instruments.
Represent ideas, feelings, nature in movement.	Hear two special sounds amidst background noise.
Use prepositions combining movement with an object.	Guess visible object, person, or shapes from clues.
Practice ways to relax.	
FREE CHOICE	**FREE CHOICE**
Using Blocks:	**Blocks:**
Cooperate, using all blocks and accessories.	Handle, find, label, describe constructions.
Build "sets" for dramatic play with big hollow blocks.	Use descriptors: *wide, narrow, tall, short, heavy.*
Active Play Inside/Outside*:*	**Exploring with Senses:**
Use varied locomotion, including galloping.	Experiment with new varieties of media. Taste/smell experiences; match salty, sweet, sour.
Use jumpropes, hoops, wheel toys, parachute.	Perceive changes, cause/effect during cooking.
Fly a kite or blow and chase bubbles outside.	Cook eggs, see change from liquid to solid.
Walk on balance beam raised higher but securely at one end.	Perceive shoots, growth of new grass and plants.
Use balance beam raised securely at both ends.	Recognize last name when printed some of the time.
Use mats and tunnel in varied obstacle courses.	
Practice hopping, sliding, galloping.	**Manipulatives, Table Toys, Floor Toys:**
Catch a large bounced ball.	Use all appropriate items fully.
Toss and catch; toss into target.	Sort/group pictures of given subject.
Try brace and bit in woodworking with adult help.	Use puzzles and parquetry; simple to complex.
Continue use of other woodworking tools.	Use symbol and picture lotto cards/games.
	Match/find sets of items with numerals 1 to 5.
Clays and Playdough/Sand and Water:	Use matching sound cans; find identical pairs.
Continue to experiment with new media.	
Dig earth to prepare it for planting.	**Cleanup:**
	Use perceptual and printed labels.
Dressing and Undressing:	Respond to sound and light cues.
Continue practice; help peers with these tasks.	
	SMALL GROUP
Art Media:	**Games:**
Use *open-ended* art media fully.	Use picture and symbol lotto games.
Experiment with pastel paints and new materials.	Examine/sort small potatoes to see differences.
Work on an art mural with others.	Match and/or find varied shapes.
	Reproduce five-part patterns of items; model seen.
Manipulatives, Table Toys, Floor Toys:	Group items by size.
Use appropriate but more complex materials.	Group recyclables in three or more ways.
Make some simple musical instruments.	Match identical pairs of sounds in containers.
	Match and find colors.
SMALL GROUP	Use number lotto games.
Games:	Find numeral 1, 2, or 3 when adult shows corresponding set.
Trace circles, hearts, triangles, free forms.	See/discuss a "map" or floor plan of classroom.
Trace/cut out large paper ovals, circles.	Connect three to five dots when start and direction are shown.
Cut on one thick line that has several curves.	
Try cutting a line with a few zig-zags.	**Meals and Snacks:**
Tie one knot with a shoelace doubled into two loops.	Perceive/describe textures, colors, shapes.
Use yarn needle and yarn to sew at random on burlap.	Graph a snack by shapes or size.
Repeat prior small motor experiences desired.	Help prepare foods.
Do three-dimensional constructions with tape and recyclables.	
Meals and Snacks:	
Repeat prior experiences. Wash chairs/tables.	

LITERACY

LARGE GROUP
Literature:
Hear/tell varied forms of literature.
Experience stories based on interests, events.
Use Big Books; make new ones from own stories/journals.

Conversations:
About work and play choices.
About staying safe and healthy.
About friends and helpers.
About trips and walks that we take or plan.
About things I can do with pride.
About things I want to learn to do.
About seasonal changes in the weather and effects on us.

Body Language:
Act out simple stories or rhymes.
Represent ideas, feelings, nature in movement.
Talk without words; gestures or sign.

FREE CHOICE
Talk/Listen/Do:
Converse with peers and adults.
Answer open questions posed by adults.
Use, talk about safe, friendly, healthful ways.
Continue dictation in art, blocks, science.
Use flannelboard and puppets.
Use computer and telephones.
Practice calling 911 and telling my address on phone.
Use tape recorder and listening station.
Use recipe cards; add more.

Dramatic Play:
Continue safety/health role-play.
Continue new props; try "space," airplane, ship, train.

Writing Center:
Use many materials for communication; including invented ones.

SMALL GROUP
Games:
Continue personal journal; share some entries.
Continue traveling journal; share some entries.
Talk about things that happen in this new season.*
Talk about things I can do, things I want to learn to do.*
Do thank-you letters to adult helpers or places visited.
Make up our own group story.
Answer "What if . . . ?" or "What do you think?" questions.
Play rhyming games including real and silly words.*
Discuss something green brought from home.
Make a poster of a web; show a theme and units.

Meals and Snacks:
Continue prior experiences.

MEMORY

LARGE GROUP
Remembering Together:
Copy adult modeling.
Help do stories, rhymes, fingerplays, songs/chants.
Count to 10 by rote in nonstereotyped chants, rhymes.
Count in another language.
Try other words in another language.
Recall/discuss walks and changes seen outdoors.
Recall/discuss visits or field trips.
Practice remembering names of the days of the week.
Furnish the correct ending to a familiar story.
Correct words in rhyme that the adult says incorrectly.

FREE CHOICE
All Area Learning:
Use names of friends, helpers, materials, areas.
Name the shapes of many blocks.
Know expectations for behavior.
Observe/discuss past events seen in photos.
Do helpers' jobs; help set up the room.
Practice health and safety habits.
Pretend with new props; reenact field trips.
Use sequence games and cards.
Use the names of colors.
Use flannelboard to tell stories/rhymes.

Cleanup:
Remember the cues.
Know where things go.

SMALL GROUP
Games:
Tell some senses used today in work and play.
Recall four or more items when seen, then hidden.
Find circles, ovals, squares, triangles, rectangles.
Recall sequence of past holidays and approaching holiday.*
Discuss past family vacations and trips.*
Correct funny, incorrect endings to rhymes by adult.*
Reproduce three-part pattern when seen, then hidden.
Practice saying my home address. Remember ways we stay safe and healthy.*
Remember what plants need to be healthy.
Remember what seeds need to sprout. Recall/do three tasks that include movement.
Try to remember parents' first and last names.
Repeat sequence of three silly words or five numerals.

Meals and Snacks:
Remember positive social language.
Recall healthy foods and food groups.
Recall how we prepared a food.

PROBLEM SOLVING

LARGE GROUP
Conversations:
About work and play choices.
On weather/seasonal changes and effects on us.
Add words to blank calendar that represent days of week.
Plan for coming trip or event; discuss all aspects.
Talk about yesterday, last time, next time, and tomorrow.
Observe/discuss our growth; discuss things we need for growing.
Represent ideas, feelings, and "growing" in movement.

FREE CHOICE
Blocks:
Cooperate in building; use accessories.
Describe/explain construction; use descriptive words.

All Area Learning:
Use time effectively to work/play in all areas.
Ask questions, find answers; answer open questions.
Use words to negotiate, compromise, and explain.
Work together on group projects.
Note cause/effect in experiments.
Plant a garden; start plants from seeds or cuttings.
Note cause and effect in plant/seed experiments.
Count things and people; estimate quantities in play.
Guess "what might happen."

Dramatic Play:
Plan and carry out new ideas with props.

Science:
Experiment with new items, tools, and methods.
Experiment with seeds and plants.
Experiment with earth; see what disappears or remains over time in jar of earth. See whether earth dissolves.
Discover what plants/seeds need in order to grow.

SMALL GROUP
Games:
Sort items/recyclables in three or more ways.
Use items to make sets of 1 to 4; give adult 4.
Make sets; match them to numerals 1 to 5.
Introduce dry cell battery.
Experiment with battery and switch.
Dictate to make list of reasons we like plants.*
Read and discuss an appropriate book on the environment.*
Order items by size: biggest, smallest, middle-sized.
Match one to one up to seven or more.
Play "what does not belong," "what comes next."

Meals and Snacks:
Continue prior experiences.
Help in food preparation.

TABLE A.7 *Skill-Based Activities—Sharing My World Time Block 7 (April–May)*

MOTOR	PERCEPTUAL
LARGE GROUP **Body Movement:** Copy/create to varied music and rhythms. Represent ideas, feelings, nature in movement. Use prepositions combining body movement and object. Practice ways to relax. **FREE CHOICE** **Using Blocks:** Use all types and accessories; work cooperatively. Build "sets" for dramatic play with big blocks. **Active Play Inside/Outside:** Varied locomotion; gallop, duck walk, try to skip. Jump ropes, hoops, wheel toys, parachute. Balance beam; carry an object; turn around and return. Walk on balance beam set on its narrow edge. Use multipart obstacle courses; varied equipment. Toss and catch; use targets. Catch large bounced ball; bounce ball to peer. Bat a ball with plastic "big bat." Fly a kite; blow and chase bubbles outside. Dig and weed in garden or digging area. Use available woodworking tools; paint if desired. **Clays and Playdough/Sand and Water:** Use new and old varieties, tools, methods. **Dressing and Undressing:** Practice self-help and help peers as well. **Art Media:** Use *open-ended* art media indoors and outside. Use old and new methods, materials, tools and colors. **Manipulatives, Table Toys, Floor Toys** Use all appropriate materials; work cooperatively. Cut out magazine pictures if desired. Design with yarn needles/yarn on appropriate backing. Work with small beads. **SMALL GROUP** **Games:** Begin to print letters in name if interested. Tie bow by making one knot; then make a second, top knot with the two looped shoelaces. Draw picture with crayons or markers. Cut paper on one thick zig-zag line. Trace and cut large circles, triangles, or squares. Tear large paper circles and squares. Copy a circle or oval and an X or cross. **Meals and Snacks:** Continue all prior experiences.	**LARGE GROUP** **Music and Circle:** Continue to use music instruments. Guess visible persons, objects, shapes from clues. Begin to recognize first and last name in print. Begin to know left and right sides of body. **FREE CHOICE** **Blocks:** Find and label blocks; describe constructions. Use descriptive words; discuss repeated patterns. **Exploring with Senses:** Experiment with old favorites and new media. Continue foods, taste and smell experiences. Continue to perceive changes and cause/effect. Make and use universal visual symbols in play. Perceive changes/growth of plants, animals, and selves. Perceive changes in nature outdoors. **Manipulatives, Table Toys, Floor Toys:** Use all appropriate items fully. Sort and group pictures of a given subject. Use puzzles and parquetry simple to complex. Use symbol and picture lotto cards/games. Group sets of items matching numerals up to 10. Use matching sound cans; find pairs. **Cleanup:** Use perceptual and printed word labels. Respond to light and sound cues. **SMALL GROUP** **Games:** Observe/compare differences in visiting animal babies. Find/name circles, squares, triangles, rectangles. Use more complex picture and symbol lotto cards. Reproduce five or more part patterns with model seen. Group items; name them by size, shape, and color. Group sets of items that match numerals 1 to 7 Connect three to eight dots when start and direction are shown. Match and name letters in own first name. Examine simple map, adult-drawn, of a walk we took. Examine/discuss other shapes; diamonds, stars, octagons. Discuss something brought from home that is flat. **Meals and Snacks:** Perceive/describe textures, colors, shapes of foods. Perceive/describe attributes of dishes, bowls, cups.

LITERACY	MEMORY	PROBLEM SOLVING
LARGE GROUP	**LARGE GROUP**	**LARGE GROUP**
Literature:	**Remembering Together:**	**Conversations:**
Hear/help tell varied forms of literature.	Copy adult modeling.	About work and play choices.
See, hear, tell own experience stories and made up stories	Help tell stories, rhymes, fingerplays, songs/ chants.	On weather/seasonal changes and their effects on us.
Put stories in print and on tape.	Count rote to 10 or more in nonstereotyped songs/chants.	About the symbols on our calendar.
Conversations:	Count in another language.	About a way to show numbers for the days in a month; see these numbers placed on the
About work and play choices.	Practice other words in another language;	calendar for the first time.
About staying safe and healthy.	*hello, goodbye, please, thank you.*	Talk about today, yesterday, and tomorrow
About friendships and helpers.	Recall/discuss past events; see their symbols	and see them on our calendar.
About trips and walks we plan to take.	on calendar.	Talk about how we have grown since school
About weather/seasonal changes and effects on us.	Name days of the week and see their names on the calendar.	started.
About things I can do for myself and for others.	Remember past seasons and holidays and help sequence them.	Talk about plans for an event or trip.
About ways plants and animals help us.		**FREE CHOICE**
About the ways we can help plants and animals.	**FREE CHOICE**	**Blocks:**
About things I love about family or caregivers.	**All Area Learning:**	Cooperate in building; describe/explain constructions.
	Use names of friends, helpers, materials, areas.	
Body Language:	Name shapes of blocks and equipment in setting.	**All Area Learning:**
Act out simple stories or rhymes.	Know expectations for behavior.	Use time effectively to work in all areas.
Represent ideas, feelings, nature in movement.	Use the names of colors in play.	Ask questions/find answers; answer open questions.
	Observe/discuss past events seen in photos.	Use words to negotiate, compromise, explain.
FREE CHOICE	Do helpers' jobs; help set up the room.	Work together on group projects of interest.
Talk/Listen/Do:	Practice health and safety habits.	Note cause and effect in experiments.
Converse and ask questions of peers and adults.	Pretend/act out past experiences with props.	Harvest plants from garden; use in food experience.
Talk about ways we find our own answers.	Use flannelboard stories and other sequence games.	Count things and people and estimate quantities.
Answer open questions that require the use of imagination.	**Cleanup:**	Guess "what might happen" in play.
Use safe, friendly, healthy ways; explain reasons.	Remember the cues.	Reweigh and remeasure ourselves; graph results.
Continue dictation; include comments about trips.	Know where things go.	Use computer.
Continue use of literacy materials, including computer.	**SMALL GROUP**	**Dramatic Play:**
	Games:	Carry out new ideas with new and old props.
Dramatic Play:	Tell some things I did today and who I did them with.	Pretend going to new school and riding the bus.
Continue safety/health role-play; pretend picnics, 911, campfires, swimming, fishing, boating.	Recall four or more shapes seen, then hidden.	**Science:**
Continue to use props; re-create places visited.	Find and label circles, squares, triangles, rectangles, etc.	Experiment with dry cell battery, switch and mini-light.
Incorporate water and camping safety in play.	Reproduce four or more part pattern when seen, then hidden.	Experiment with new and old materials in all areas.
Writing Center:	Practice saying my home address and parents' names.	Use words, graphs, and dictation to record observations.
Use all materials for creative communication.	Correct funny, incorrect ways adult says my address.	**SMALL GROUP**
Encourage "invented" spelling and writing.	Practice saying my telephone number.	**Games:**
SMALL GROUP	Recall/do 3 tasks that require movement.	Sort/group items and recyclables in four or more ways.
Games:	Recognize and name numerals 1 to 7 or higher.	Use items to make sets of 1 to 5. Give adult five items.
Continue personal and traveling journals.	Remember some things we have learned about animals.*	Order items first, second, last.
Talk about ways we can take better care of plants and animals in our world; dictate to make ongoing list over several days.	Remember summer and the things we do on vacation.*	Match one to one up to eight or more.
Talk about the animals we have seen; homes, ways they get food, and "clothes" or coverings.	**Meals and Snacks:**	Act out prepositions by using two objects.
Discuss something from home that you use to help animals.	Remember positive social language.	Begin to talk about opposites.
Write a special note to mother, grandmother, or caregiver.	Recall healthful foods and food groups.	Over several days, talk about why we like animals; dictate to make ongoing list.
Do group or individual thank-you letters with drawings.	Recall foods we have prepared or cooked.	Talk about what animals need; dictate/add to list or web.
Meals and Snacks:		Read/discuss appropriate book on the environment.*
Continue prior experiences and conversations.		Play "what does not belong," "what is missing."
		Help plan a special end of the year event.*
		Meals and Snacks:
		Continue all prior experiences.

Program Curriculum Examples

"Early Discoveries" of the YMCA of South Hampton Roads, Norfolk, VA, is part of the Virginia Preschool Initiative and serves over 900 at-risk 4-year-olds in multiple centers. It has many community partnerships with local resources, including the public school system. This program used the first edition of this book, *A Practical Guide to Early Childhood Planning; Methods, and Materials: The What, Why, and How of Lesson Plans,* to develop their own unique curriculum for daily and monthly learning experiences throughout the year. Led by the director, Linda Lloyd Zannini, and teachers Rachel Johnson and Ann Marie Alexander, the staff worked for over two years to complete and fine-tune their written curriculum, which is for 4- and 5-year-old children.

"The Curriculum That Works" is divided into three sections. "The Workings" includes narrative information on philosophy, goals, objectives, learning experiences, roles, the setting, the daily schedule, assessment, and lesson plans. The second and third sections contain "Tools to Support the Curriculum" and "Curriculum Experiences." These sections provide themes, a planning guide, a lesson plan format, observational checklists, progress reports and many suggested resources (songs, rhymes, books, and so on) to support thematic, emergent, and skill-based planning. "The Curriculum That Works" skill-based planning system—using developmentally sequenced and scaffolded activities to help children reach outcomes in the language/literacy, motor, perception, memory, and problem solving learning domains—is based on the original system and the seven time blocks in Appendix A of this book.

In this appendix you will see a "Skill Planning Guide," weekly planning guides that mesh with themes, and monthly "centers" guides that provide teachers with suggestions for materials in each learning center. The "Skill Planning Guide" breaks out the examples of skill-based learning domain objectives for the entire year. Based on Appendix A in this book, it is similar to the time blocks, but in a different format. The weekly forms show how the examples in the Skill Planning Guide are broken down into the weeks of the year. This is an effective way to ensure that teachers plan a full balance of already developmentally sequenced skill activities from week to week as the year proceeds, which is the goal of the curriculum planning system discussed in this book.

Although space prohibits including more excerpts from "The Curriculum That Works," this curriculum has been copyrighted (with a possible name change) and is available for sale as a guide to curriculum development for other programs. Contact Linda Lloyd Zannini, Director and Vice President of Children's Services at Llloyd-zannini@ymcashr.org or write to the Early Discoveries Program, YMCA of South Hampton Roads, 312 W. Bates Street, Norfolk, VA 23510.

TABLE B.1 Skill Planning Guide

	Language	Perceptual	Problem Solving	Memory	Fine Motor	Large Motor
September	1. Use and talk about safe ways and rules. 2. Conversations about plans and routines. 3. Discuss work and play choices. 4. Discuss health and safety, including brushing teeth.	1. Use pictures and perceptual labels. 2. Notice what we are wearing. 3. Match simple objects to the picture. 4. Recognize body parts.	1. Discuss play choices and plan one choice for the following day. 2. Make play and work choices. 3. Match, sort, and tub items. 4. Notice likeness and difference.	1. Learn daily schedule, limits, and routines. 2. See own name in print. 3. Imitate simple games of "Do What I Do." 4. Use names of friends in songs, rhymes, and games.	1. Use crayons, markers, chalk, and paper. 2. Use tongs and pinch clothespins. 3. Tear paper at random. 4. Manipulative materials to pick up and insert objects with ease.	1. Follow line with body. 2. Use varied locomotion. 3. Copy and/or create to music, songs, chants, and rhymes. 4. Practice climbing and rolling.
October	1. Start a "me" book. 2. Do fingerplays and rhymes. 3. Read and discuss picture books. 4. Discuss me, my home, and my family.	1. Compare sounds; discuss *loud* and *soft*. 2. Guess hidden objects by touch alone. 3. Match primary colors. 4. Examine and match circles and ovals.	1. Graph selves by size or in other way; discuss short/ tall, large/small. 2. Ask questions and use senses to gain information. 3. Tub and sort materials. 4. See changes (mixing, cooking, and grinding).	1. Recall today and what I liked best. 2. Note when objects are changed, added, or removed from a group. 3. Use healthful habits during snack, mealtimes and in bathroom. 4. Recognize first name in print.	1. Trace simple template or free form with fingers or crayons. 2. Practice spooning and pouring. 3. Tear paper with purpose. 4. Use eye droppers.	1. Use varied locomotion 2. Toss, catch, pass with big, soft beanbags or paper-stuffed pillow ease 3. Try flat balance beam 4. Jump with both feet
November	1. Use puppets and flannelboards. 2. Begin simple dictation or experience story. 3. Try new recipe cards. 4. Discuss things I can do alone or for others. 5. Try stories without words.	1. Match secondary colors. 2. Examine and match circles, ovals, squares, and rectangles. 3. Reproduce simple pattern using objects. 4. Play visual matching games. 5. Do simple sound-matching games.	1. Repeat a Simple pattern. 2. Notice and handle new items; count some. 3. Experiment with manipulatives and constructions. 4. Give adult 1–3 items. 5. Arrange items by size (large, medium, and small).	1. Find and name primary colors. 2. Try rote counting to 5 in songs and rhymes. 3. Find and name circles and ovals. 4. Recall/do one or two tasks while seated. 5. Find and name circles, ovals, squares, and rectangles.	1. Snip or fringe with scissors. 2. Use easy lacing and stringing materials. 3. Tear simple, random paper shapes. 4. Practice self-help skills. 5. Cut on a given line.	1. Use varied locomotion. 2. Copy and/or create to music, song, chants, and rhymes. 3. Act out positional words like over, under, in, out, above, below, etc. 4. Jump over low rope. 5. Follow simple 4-part obstacle course.
December	1. Discuss food for special days with children and teacher. 2. Give dictation about art and construction. 3. Give dictation about science area observations.	1. Reproduce simple patterns. 2. Match primary colors and secondary colors. 3. Examine and match triangles, hearts, diamonds, stars, and octagons.	1. Use new or different tools for measuring. 2. Graph a variety of items; discuss quantities like most, least, more, less. 3. Ask questions and begin to discover answers.	1. Fine and name secondary colors. 2. Count to 10 by rote. 3. Recall 3 objects or shapes when removed or hidden.	1. Use different tools to create designs. 2. Make simple construction using a variety of fasteners. 3. Trace variety of objects.	1. Try traditional dances. 2. Toss and catch a variety of materials. 3. Copy and/or create to music, songs, chants, and rhymes.

(continued)

TABLE B.1 Continued

	Language	Perceptual	Problem Solving	Memory	Fine Motor	Large Motor
January	1. Use sequenced pictures to talk about day's schedule or the seasons. 2. Use a new recipe card. 3. Write a symbol or representation of name. 4. Talk about learning using the senses. 5. Give dictation about science area observations.	1. Handle, sort, and match items. 2. Perceive similarities and differences. 3. Repeat a chant or clapped rhythm. 4. Use matching sound game. 5. Demonstrate curiosity about materials.	1. Order items from first to last. 2. Classify objects into two or more categories. 3. Note cause and effect relationships in experiments. 4. Recognize differences in musical tones. 5. Make simple graph of experiment results.	1. Retell familiar story. 2. Play simple games of things I do. 3. Recognize last name in print. 4. Find and name primary and secondary colors. 5. Find and name triangles, hearts, diamonds, stars, and octagons.	1. Use paintbrush and paint. 2. Manipulate clay or dough. 3. Trace circle, oval, and free forms. 4. Cut materials apart on wide, straight line. 5. Use items that twist and turn.	1. Use pantomime to represent ideas, feelings, or natural changes. 2. Copy and/or create to varied music and rhythms. 3. Balance on each foot. 4. Use jump ropes and hoops. 5. Use varied locomotion.
February	1. Use materials for communication. 2. Discuss and understand that materials can be reused, recycled, and reduced. 3. Tell story using pictures. 4. Use puppets, flannelboards, and other props.	1. Observe changes from mixing, cooking, or chilling foods. 2. Use instruments and guess the sounds. 3. Generate questions and seek answers. 4. Compare and graph a snack by shape, size, and color; discuss quantities like most, least, more, less.	1. Observe, tell, or guess what will happen during play. 2. Make sets and match them to numerals 0–5 or more. 3. Graph a snack; count and discuss more or less. 4. Experiment with new items and observation tools.	1. Practice home phone number. 2. Use sequence games and cards. 3. Recall/do 2–3 tasks. 4. Recall and/or discuss the basic needs of humans and animals.	1. Practice self-help and safety skills. 2. Make 3-D constructions with tape and recyclable items. 3. Use writing and/or drawing materials with control. 4. Use different tools with a purpose.	1. Move along a raised balance beam. 2. Practice hopping and galloping. 3. Toss and catch; try using target. 4. Use a parachute.
March	1. Play rhyming games, including real and silly words. 2. Use big books; make up new ones. 3. Act out a story or rhyme. 4. Dictate words to go with art mural.	1. Guess hidden object, person, or shapes from clues. 2. Distinguish a variety of different tastes and state preferences about differences. 3. Sort and group pictures by given subject. 4. Make comparisons.	1. Make sets; match them to numerals 0 to 9 or more. 2. Graph various physical characteristics of a group; discuss shortest/tallest, heaviest/lightest, etc. 3. Try rhyming and silly word play. 4. Measure using nonstandard units.	1. Tell end of familiar story. 2. Begin to know left and right side of the body. 3. Practice home phone number. 4. Recall/do 3 tasks that include movement.	1. Cut paper on thick line with several curves. 2. Use plastic knife for spreading and cutting. 3. Use needles and yarn to sew designs. 4. Do 3-D constructions.	1. Play traditional games. 2. Use jump ropes and hoops. 3. Carry object across raised balance beam. 4. Represent ideas and in movement.
April	1. Discuss things I want to learn. 2. Make a poster of a web; show a theme and units. 3. Make up a class story.	1. Perceive changes in nature and the outdoors. 2. Use picture and/or symbol lotto games. 3. Use homemade instruments. Recognize loud/soft, high/low, fast/slow.	1. Sort and/or group items in 3 or more ways. 2. Make sets; match them to numerals 0 to 9 or more. 3. Dictate a list of reasons why we like something	1. Recall 4 or more items when seen and then removed. 2. Practice saying home address. 3. Arrange events in sequence.	1. Work on art mural with others. 2. Use scissors to enhance cutting skill. 3. Use open-ended art media outdoors.	1. Fly a kite; chase bubbles. 2. Practice hopping, sliding, and galloping. 3. Dig earth to prepare for planting.

232

	Language	Perceptual	Problem Solving	Memory	Fine Motor	Large Motor
May	1. Answer open-ended questions that require use of imagination. 2. Write a special note to mother, grandmother, or caregiver. 3. Talk about/dictate ways we can take better care of plants and animals. 4. Read and retell fingerplays, poems, and stories.	1. Examine and manipulate pennies, dimes, nickels, and quarters. 2. Examine simple maps. 3. Arrange items in a series rough/smooth, heavy/light, long/short etc. 4. Group items and name groups.	1. Act out positional words. 2. Play with rhyming words. 3. Estimate quantities and count things. 4. Experiment with different forms of measurement.	1. Recognize and name numerals 0 to 9 or higher. 2. Practice saying home address. 3. Reproduce four or more part pattern when seen. 4. Remember some things we have learned.	1. Cut paper on thick zig-zag line. 2. Use plastic knife for spreading and cutting. 3. Work with small manipulatives. 4. Use new materials to develop precision grip.	1. Copy/create to varied music and rhythms. 2. Move in varied locomotion—gallop, duck walk, or skip. 3. Carry object across balance beam and turn around. 4. Catch large ball and bounce it to friend.
June	1. Act out simple stories or rhymes. 2. Discuss ways to stay safe and healthy. 3. Discuss things that are fun to do in the summer.	1. Guess visible person, object or shape from clues. 2. Continue to perceive changes and cause and effect. 3. Experiment with old favorites media.	1. Help plan a special end-of-year event 2. Talk about how we have grown since school started. 3. Explore relationships.	1. Observe/discuss past events seen in photos. 2. Remember some safety rules. 3. Remember things we do in the summer.	1. Use old and new methods, materials, tools and colors. 2. Make favorite snacks/cooking experiences from the year 3. Use hands as a tool to clean classroom.	1. Toss and catch; use targets. 2. Use an obstacle course. 3. Create a variety of movements using music.

TABLE B.2 My Environment: Fall Harvest   November (Week 2)

Language: Begin simple dictation or experience story.

Try a "Mystery Bag." Put harvest items (farmer, fruit, vegetables, etc..) in a bag. The number of items should equal the number of children plus one. Teacher pulls an item out of bag to start the story and then passes bag on to a student. Record and illustrate story.	After visiting a farm or pumpkin patch, have the children dictate what they saw and did. Alternately, each child can draw a picture of the trip and then have a teacher write down all children's stories.	Make an apple book. Have the children taste, touch, listen, smell, and look at apples. Cut paper in the shape of an apple. On each page have children dictate a description of the apple.	Make a harvest book. For the cover and shape create a cornucopia. Discuss the harvest. Use magazines and grocery store ads for the children to cut or tear Out pictures of foods that are harvested.	Invite a farmer to visit the class. After discussing the farmer and what he/she does, the children can dictate a story about life on the farm.

Perceptual: Examine and match circles, ovals, squares, and rectangles.

Play "I Spy." Holdup and identify a shape (e.g., circle). Give a clue using the shape as a descriptor: "I see something circle- shaped." Children try o find the circle-shaped object the teacher is describing.	Play the game "Guess What's Missing." Display a group of different shapes on a tray. Cover the tray and remove one shape. Take off the cover, and have children guess which shape is missing.	Put shapes in a "Feely Bag." Have children feel and describe the shapes. Children can try to guess what the shape might be. When they are removed from the bag, shapes can be matched to other identical shapes.	Create a path game. Make a path from the farmer to the store with a shape in each space of the path. Using a die with shapes on each side, children roll and move to the next space with that same shape.	Make a game board that looks like a pumpkin patch. On each pumpkin put a pumpkin shape. Make matching pumpkin cards. Children choose a pumpkin card, and place it on the matching pumpkin in the patch.

Problem Solving: Notice and handle new items; count some.

Sort and count a variety of nuts. Try both shelled and unshelled nuts. Enjoy them for snack.	Sort and count leaves of different colors and shapes.	Sort and count different types of pinecones.	Staple a cut out squirrel to a paper cup. Number squirrels 1–5. Children count appropriate number of acorns into each cup.	Ask parents to visit the supermarket produce aisle with their children to see what new foods have recently been harvested.

Memory: Try rote counting to 5 in songs and rhymes.

Place a bag of nuts in the snack area. Have children count out nuts in groups of five. Have children shell and eat.	Sing the song "Five Little Turkeys" found in resource book *Transition Tune* by Jean Feldman.	Read and act out the fingerplay "The Apple Tree" found in resource book *Transition Time* by Jean Feldman.	Sing the song "Ten Little Pumpkins."	Sing the fingerplay "Five Little Pumpkins."

Fine Motor: Use easy lacing and stringing materials.

Use posterboard to cut out leaf shapes. Punch holes along edges. Have children lace leaves. Hang leaves from ceiling to make a seasonal tree.	Practice lacing shoes in dramatic play.	Use shoestrings to lace beads or pasta.	Provide string, lace, ribbons, etc. to lace through strawberry baskets. Have children fill with seasonal items found on a nature walk.	Use craft foam to cut out animal or shape puppets. Children lace together puppets and decorate as they wish.

Large Motor: Copy and/or create to music, songs, and rhymes.

Sing apple songs found in resource book *Creative Resources for the Early Childhood Classroom* Herr and Libby (Theme— Apples).	Sing autumn songs found in resource book *Creative Resources for the Early Childhood Classroom* by Herr and Libby (Theme— Fall).	Play the game "The Farmer in the Dell."	Adapt the song "Teddy Bear, Teddy Bear" to reflect a seasonal character. Try "Scarecrow, Scarecrow" or "Farmer, Farmer."	Sing and create movements to poem *Fall Fun*.

TABLE B.3   *Centers for November: My Environment*

Library/Writing/Listening	Dramatic Play	
Props for retelling *The Little Red Hen* Magazines with fall, harvest pictures Shape books (apple, leaf, pumpkin) Fall stencils (apple, leaf, pumpkin, foods) Stamping with fall and food stamps Flannelboard sets with accompanying fingerplays and poems Books about fall, harvests, family celebrations, etc.	Scarecrow clothing Farm clothing Fall clothing Baskets for harvesting	Grocery store Fruit and vegetable stand Paint box for farmhouse
Art	**Science/Discovery**	

Leaf rubbing   Easel painting with paper cut in
Fall collage materials   Fall shapes
Twig sculpture   Hole punch
Printing using variety of fruits and vegetables
Bread dough sculpture
	Scale for weighing vegetates and fruits
	Fall objects for sorting, counting, observing (leaves, seeds,
	    pine cones, acorns)
	Seeds and berries for measuring and weighing
	Poster of food pyramid
	Guessing box of fall objects
	Corn in a variety of different forms (corn meal, corn starch,
	    popcorn, kernels)
	Variety of nuts and nutcracker	

Manipulatives	**Sensory**	
Lotto games Path games Matching games for color discrimination Lacing materials Sorting kits with foods	Box of leaves Rice Oatmeal Beans Hay or straw Mashed potatoes Dirt (allow children to bury and dig up potatoes, etc.)	
Blocks	**Cooking/Food Experiences**	
Food boxes to build with Farm props (animals, tractors, farm building) People to support family life play	Dried apples Fruit kabobs Peanut butter Applesauce Pumpkin muffins and butter Scarecrow faces No-bake pumpkin custard Skeleton snack	

TABLE B.4 Animals Pond/Forest   March (Week 2)

Language: Use big books; make up new ones.

Listen to song "Frogs, Tadpoles and Toads" from musical tape *Q'd Up* by Betsy Q. Make a "baggie book." Place items related to ponds and forests into plastic bags. Attach bags to large pieces of paper and have children draw a picture around the items. Combine pictures to create book.	After reading *Over in the Meadow*, have the class dictate its own version of the story.	Read the story *Have You Seen My Duckling?* by N. Tafuri. Re-create the story using props brought from home or collected on a walk. Hide a cut-out duck.	Write a cumulative story about the pond or forest Read the story *Jump Frog Jump* by E. Kalan is a good example to follow.	Read *In the Small, Small Pond* by D. Fleming. Make up a different version using animals the children think they would see in a pond.

Perceptual: Distinguish a variety of different tastes and state preferences about differences.

Bring in creamy and chunky peanut butter. Ask the children to taste the two and tell which they prefer. Graph their preferences or record their reasons for their choices.	Allow the children to taste salty and sweet foods and state preference. Make a graph of their favorite or a chart telling why they prefer their choice.	Taste white, strawberry, and chocolate milk. Ask the children to state their preference and why they feel the way they do.	Sample a goldfish mix for snack. Ask the children to tell which flavor goldfish they like best and why and graph responses.	

Problem Solving: Graph various physical characteristics of a group. Discuss shortest / tallest, etc.

Ask the children to generate a list of their physical traits (hair, eye color, etc.). Select one or two to measure and graph.	Ask the children to generate a list of physical activities they can do. Graph which ones they like to do best.	Ask the children to generate a list of animals that live in the pond or forest. Graph the animals by the number of legs they have.	Using pond and forest animals, graph the animals by the type of skin they have: fur, feathers, scales.	Place plastic fishing worms into a tub of water. Using tongs have the children fish out the worms. Graph worms by color.

Memory: Begin to know the left and right side of the body.

Move to the song "Boogie Walk" from musical tape *We All Live Together Volume II* by Greg and Steve.	Have the children sing and move to the musical dance "Hokey Pokey."	Play the song "Left and Right" from musical tape *Getting to Know Myself* by Hap Palmer.	Play the game "Simon Says" using left and right direction.	Play the game "Follow the Leader."

Fine Motor: Use a plastic knife for spreading or cutting.

Make a fishpond by tinting cream cheese blue, spreading it on crackers, and topping it with goldfish.	Make a forest scene by spreading tinted cream cheese on a cracker and standing animal crackers on it.	Make a pond snack. Spread a spoonful of cream cheese (colored blue) on ½ English muffin. Add 3 cucumber slices for lily pads and gummy frogs on pads.	Toast bread and spread with butter. Sprinkle cinnamon and sugar on toast.	Make peanut butter and jelly sandwiches. Cut them in half or use cookie cutters shaped like fish, frogs, or trees.

Large Motor: Use jump ropes and hoops.

Use hoops to represent ponds. Have the children pretend to be frogs jumping in and out of ponds.	Pair the children up. Have one child hold a hula-hoop on its side, while the other child tries to throw a beanbag through the hoop.	Lay a jump rope on the ground. Make slow waves in it by gently moving your arm. The children can jump over the rope.	Use a jump rope and play the Limbo. The children may need to bend forward rather than backward for safety.	Play "Leap Frog."

TABLE B.5   Centers for March: Animals

Library/Writing/Listening Props for *The Three Billy Goats Gruff* Shape books cut out in animal shapes Rhyming books and rhyming Word Wall Soundtracks tapes Tapes of ocean, river, rainforest Class books (Big Books, baggie books, contributions from parents) Charts of poems and songs Copies of children's addresses Tape recordings of each child's address	**Dramatic Play** Veterinary office Forest Ranger office Farm props Zoo props Address book with all of children's addresses and pictures
Art Easel paper cut out in animal shapes Materials for string painting Animal stencils Needle and yam Materials for mural Materials for 3-D constructions	**Science/Discovery** Levers Magnifying glass Pulleys and rope Bug cages PVC piping and materials to roll through pipes Test tubes Sensory bottles made by children Water experiments
Manipulatives Mother and Babies puzzle Nuts and bolts Graphs (physical attributes, class favorites, etc.) Seashell collections Super Sorting Kit Unifix Cubes Number sets (materials to make sets to match numerals) Materials for measuring (pennies, Unifix Cubes, Legos) Pattern cards and materials to complete patterns	**Sensory** Playdough and animal cookie cutters, materials to make animal track imprints Water and props for fishing Materials for sink and float experiments

Blocks
Animal sets
Insect sets
Zoo props
Trees, barns, vines, etc. to support pretend play about various
    terrains
	Cooking/Food Experiences
	Taste preference tests (salty/sweet, white/chocolate/
	    strawberry milk, creamy/chunky peanut butter, goldfish)
	Fishponds Forest scenes
	Lily pad pond snacks Cinnamon toast
	Peanut butter and jelly sandwiches Apple sailboats

APPENDIX C
Developmental Profiles: Birth to Age Eight

All children grow and develop at their own pace, and there are many individual differences. Individual differences in children are interesting, worthy of watching intently, and require individual attention from adults. The indicators listed here for each age group, however, are not based on differences but on national averages for most children, on observations of children, and on basic child development such as is taught in colleges.

All skills are actually learned bit by bit, in a sequence of small events. It is more important to note the sequence of events or milestones of growth in each area (physical, intellectual, social, emotional) than the exact age at which the milestone occurs. Natural sequences of growth and development are an integral part of learning skills. For example, babies learn to lift their head and then sit up. They creep or crawl before they pull themselves up to stand, and walk with assistance before they walk alone. They walk before they run, jump, or hop.

Growth sequences like this can be seen in any developmental checklist or profile by following the development of a particular skill from one age group to the next. If a child is continuing to follow the steps of the developmental sequences at about the same time as most other children, or if, whether slower or faster, the child is still moving along the sequence of steps of growth and development, he or she is probably developing normally.

However, when certain children lag far behind the others in moving through the developmental milestones or outcomes in an area of growth, teachers should discuss the need for more information with the child's parents. Parents may need assistance in arranging for in-depth observation or screening by a qualified diagnostician. They should be reassured that there may not be a problem at all, but that the earlier a problem is identified, the more quickly it can be addressed successfully.

Infant to Age 6 Months
Physical
- Grasps objects, rattles, or hair
- Wiggles and kicks
- Turns toward bright lights or sounds
- Rolls over

Source: Evelyn Petersen. *Parent Talk: The Art of Parenting Video Series; Leader's Guides,* Volume 1, "The Young Child," pp. 48–54 and Volume 2, "The School Age Child," pp. 50–58. Traverse City MI: Platte River Printing, 1990.

- Reaches for objects
- Sits with support

Intellectual
- Knows crying will bring attention
- Carries hand to mouth
- Watches and listens to surroundings and people
- Enjoys splashing in bath with supervision
- Relies on senses and nonverbal communication to learn

Social
- Coos and smiles; recognizes familiar faces
- Responds to familiar voices, smells, and sounds
- Babbles at adults: enjoys people talking to him or her
- Babbles to self; laughs
- Cries to communicate discomfort

Emotional
- Expresses emotions; anger, fear, hunger, joy, sadness
- Holds out arms or legs to assist in being dressed
- Wants to feed self; finger foods
- Loves to be touched and held

Ages 6 Months to 1 Year

Physical
- Follows moving object with eyes; sits alone; crawls
- Pulls self to standing
- Transfers objects one hand to another, and rolls ball in imitating adult
- Drops and picks up objects
- Walks around furniture, using it for balance
- Develops first teeth

Intellectual
- Amuses self for short periods
- Drops things to observe what happens
- Observes people and surroundings carefully
- Attempts to imitate sounds
- Responds to body language, gestures, and simple words and commands ("Stop," "Hi," and "Bye-bye")
- Puts things in container and takes them out

Social
- Smiles and laughs; babbles and squeals
- Cries when interrupted from play
- Plays pat-a-cake and peek-a-boo; imitates adults
- Responds differently to familiar people or strangers
- Responds to "No"

Emotional
- Drinks from cup
- Begins to use spoon
- Pays attention to own name
- Feeds self finger foods
- Knows own name and responds to it

Ages 1 to 2

Physical
- Stands alone for longer periods
- Climbs as much as possible
- Learns to walk alone, forward and backward
- Pulls and pushes toys; moves to music
- Lacks depth perception; runs clumsily, often falls
- Begins to try to turn book pages
- Scribbles; likes painting
- Throws ball and turns knobs

Intellectual
- Very curious; explores, pokes, tastes, probes, opens things
- Does not understand danger; explores with all senses; loves water play
- Learns by trial and error and by experimenting
- Points to objects named by adult
- Builds tower with 2 or 3 blocks; puts rings on stick
- Says first words; vocabulary grows; begins naming body parts and objects
- Initiates own play; very short attention span
- "Talks" to self

Social
- Recognizes "no-no"
- Imitates adults and repeats actions that get a response
- Imitates adults in his or her play; plays alone
- Helps put things away sometimes
- Responds to simple directions and questions
- Can find self in picture of small group; names familiar people
- Learns "please" and "thank you"
- Understands rituals like hellos and good-byes
- Claims things as "mine"

Emotional
- Continues to show wide range of emotions
- Reacts to emotions of adults; may have tantrums
- Impulsive; moves quickly; rapid shifts of attention
- Thinks world revolves around self; loves mirrors
- Awareness of ownership; refers to self by name; uses "mine"
- Learns to feed self and remove clothing; may indicate toilet needs
- Says "no" to establish own identity

- May cling to parents and fear strangers

Ages 2 to 3

Physical
- Scribbles; enjoys using new finger skills and simple art media
- Much body activity and climbing
- Walks, runs, falls easily, jumps, rolls
- Needs help in dressing; dawdles
- Begins to toilet self (frequent accidents)
- Drinks from a cup, uses spoon (many spills)

Intellectual
- Uses 2- to 3-word sentences; usually hard to understand at age 2
- Very curious; likes to examine and explore with all senses
- Good observer, listener; understands more than is communicated
- Interest in books; turns several pages at once
- Names familiar objects people and pictures; can associate functions of familiar objects
- Asks names of things; vocabulary grows to hundreds of words
- Begins to organize and classify objects

Social
- Often watches other children, but plays alone or near another
- Little interest in peers; hits, pushes, grabs
- Is very possessive but shares sometimes
- Begins to "play house" or pretend; imitates others
- Watches and copies family and caregivers' modeling

Emotional
- Suspicious of new situations
- Power struggles and tantrums are common
- Needs security of consistency in routines and guidance
- Shows independence of spirit
- Loves praise and hugs

Ages 3 to 4

Physical
- Helps dress self/undresses fairly well
- Toilets self; accidents still common at age 3
- Climbs steps alternating feet
- Runs well; pulls, pushes, or steers wheel toys; jumps
- Throws, catches, and begins to be able to balance on 1 foot, then hop; can walk balance beam or line by age 4
- Can do simple puzzles and stack blocks or rings
- Enjoys using dough, clay, paint, etc., and moving to music
- Has all teeth

Intellectual

- Listens to and repeats stories, rhymes, songs
- Talks in simple sentences; can be understood
- Knows age and name
- Begins to recognize, sort, and name objects
- Begins to ask many "why" questions
- Understands *today* and often, *tomorrow,* but lives in the NOW
- Learns through hands-on activity and the senses
- Can sit on adult's lap at PC and begin to use mouse to see cause and effect; skills increase by age 4 to use of mouse and software
- Better memory; attention span grows to 15 minutes
- Confuses fact and fiction

Social

- Plays well with 1 or 2 peers sometimes, and participates in group activity for short times; wants to have friends
- Learning to tell own wants or needs with words to others
- Plays with same toys as others in a small group; sometimes will take turns or share; sharing increases by age 4
- Watches and copies adult modeling; begins to show sympathy
- Pretends; plays house or imitates family and other adult roles
- Notices sex differences
- Enjoys own birthday and simple celebrations, especially at own home

Emotional

- Still fears new things; likes rituals and consistent routines
- Wants to please; generally cooperative with adults
- Can become jealous and revert to babyhood for attention
- Wants to try to do things independently (self-care)
- Thrives on praise, hugs, and positive reinforcement
- Sense of pride in accomplishments
- Still possessive about belongings, toys

Ages 4 to 5

Physical

- Handles blunt scissors and simple tools safely with adult guidance
- Very active; uses slides, climbers, tunnels, and balance beams in many ways
- Hops, gallops, begins learning to skip; pumps swing
- Toilets self; washes self; helps clean up toys; helps with "jobs"
- Enjoys using variety of open-ended art media, and creative movement to all kinds of music
- "Workaholic" about learning through play; often becomes overtired
- Handles crayons easily; begins to use scissors
- In all physical areas, 5-year-olds progress easily; eye hand coordination is not complete, may spill or knock over things; establishes handedness

Intellectual
- Talks a lot; compound sentences and increased vocabulary; the "age of questions"
- Loves to experiment; wants to know how and why; learns by doing; can tell others her or his observations
- Can increasingly use simple computer software with parents and peers; do simple searches; and use software to express ideas in print or illustration
- Likes books, stories, and acting them out; can make up own stories, songs, and "jokes"
- Designs and constructs; uses original ideas with art and blocks
- Still somewhat confused about "real" or "pretend"; understands *yesterday, today,* and *tomorrow.*
- Can match and sort; makes many associations; enjoys nature and cooking activities; likes simple science
- Begins to grasp the idea of numeracy and counting
- *Note:* In all areas above, 5-year-olds become more skillful and more verbal. They become curious about birth and death; start to use invented writing; and can recognize some words and letters.

Social
- Enjoys peers, makes "friends" and plays cooperatively; often plays or builds with a purpose and delegates roles; interested in world outside the family
- Can share and take turns, but sometimes teases or calls names
- Enjoys participating as member of group; enjoys "jobs" and holidays
- Enjoys imitating adults and using positive social language and manners (copies "bad" words too)
- Empathy, sensitivity, and conscience start to develop
- *Note:* Five-year-olds can play simple group games and can accept group rules and experiences. They play cooperatively most of the time, taking turns easily, and they like rules, especially for others.

Emotional
- Four-year-olds show many emotions, most of them loudly
- Four-year-olds can separate from parents fairly easily for child care
- Four-year-olds are impatient and change moods often; test limits; five-year-olds are more even tempered and cooperative
- Four-year-olds want to be more independent than they are able, and still resist unpredictable changes; five-year-olds can accept change more easily, and are comfortably independent
- Four-year-olds still need lots of praise and reassurance.
- Four-year-olds may brag or boast; five-year-olds do less "showing off" and begin to have a comfortable sense of who they are and what they are able to do
- Both four- and five-year-olds begin to learn how to give and receive; both groups sometimes develop fears and nightmares.

Now let's look at the profiles for school-age children. Each child will grow in all these areas at his or her own pace. However, the following milestones are generally accepted in the fields of health, human development, and education as "normal" expectations for growth in school age children.

Age 6

Physical

- Bursts with energy, always on the go, overtires easily
- Loses baby teeth, molars erupt
- Can skip, hop, ride a bike easily; tie shoes; jump rope
- Growth slackens at age 6; needs 11 to 12 hours sleep a night
- Boisterous; likes to wrestle but doesn't know when to stop
- Demonstrates more activity than actual accomplishment
- Is awkward at some fine-motor tasks but very interested in manipulating
- Is self-conscious about work being done, often tries too hard

Intellectual

- Likes to work, especially likes to begin something new, but often gets confused and needs help and praise to finish
- Not ready for purely formal abstract instruction in reading, writing, and mathematics
- Works best through creative activity, life experiences, and hands-on learning
- Can do simple math with concrete objects and learns to read and write
- Interested in reading, likes to recognize words, and enjoys printing letters
- Span of concentration is still short
- Creates stories, does projects, searches, and art at the PC; uses computer to support school curriculum

Social

- Can play with one playmate best; inconsistent with relationships
- May find it hard to fit into the group; daydreaming is common
- Likes social routines that provide a sense of security; plays with both sexes, though beginning to prefer same gender
- Needs guidance in deciding what to do in school but often responds slowly and negatively to direct demands; very sensitive to criticism
- Cannot distinguish between good and bad clearly; still needs much practice in critical thinking skills

Emotional

- Not moderate; does nothing by halves, demonstrates much emotional intensity
- Wants to cooperate, but at times wants own way and is often bossy
- Success and a sense of achievement are of utmost importance
- Always wants to win and be first; begins to like rules, especially for others
- Needs to feel loved; wants much attention

- Feels guilt about own negative feelings
- Jealous of anyone becoming between him or her and mother
- Unable to easily consider compromises
- Takes criticism badly; thrives on praise; is possessive
- Lives intensely in the present and might worry about problems in the family
- Begins to understand and accept reality
- Dramatic play and block play help to organize thoughts and feelings
- Has an inner-self, which he or she keeps secret and in which grievances are hidden
- Has nightmares about wild animals, darkness, fire, thunder, monsters, lightning, etc.

Age 7

Physical

- Activities come in spurts; generally calmer than at age 6
- Must constantly be manipulating things
- Physical skills are imperfect and inconsistent
- If pushed into physical activity before ready, may become stubborn and may never try again; organized sports may cause undue stress
- Needs balance of rest and activity

Intellectual

- Good understanding of time; "easy" to teach
- Makes generalizations (sometimes incorrect) based on own observations
- Has an almost scientific interest in causes of things
- Becomes absorbed in classroom work; likes to debate
- Able to concentrate harder
- Logic and reasoning still based on personal and real hands-on experiences.
- Becomes very computer literate, and begins to use the PC to support school curriculum as well as to communicate with friends

Social

- Begins to be more detached from mother; forms peer friendships
- Enjoys "clubs" and buddies; may try to "buy" friendships
- Learning laws of group living; very loyal to group
- Sensitive to attitudes of others
- Begins to discriminate between good and bad in others and self
- Tries to settle question of authority "who is boss."
- More companionable, likes to do things for adults, is a very good helper if tasks are not solitary or too hard
- Becomes very fond of teachers

Emotional

- Often calm and self-absorbed; resents intrusions on thoughts
- More inhibited, more controlled, and more aware of others

- Gets angry with self if cannot do something
- Often lacks confidence; withdraws from new or unsure situations
- Very sensitive to being laughed at; ashamed of fears
- Has difficulty starting something, but once started, becomes overpersistent
- Assumes responsibility and takes it seriously
- If under too much pressure, may exhibit regressive behaviors

Age 8

Physical
- Looks more mature; seeing and hearing should be very well developed; eye exams are very important
- Nervous habits are common in children under pressure or trauma
- Athletic games and skills are of high interest, but child is often a poor loser
- Wants to excel in skills and works at it
- Loves computer and video games

Intellectual
- Books have meaning; reads for pleasure and for information
- Can obtain information both directly and indirectly
- Continues many avenues of active curiosity; loves hands-on learning activities
- Beginning to have historic perspective of self and behavior
- Interests are often short-lived; shifts from one thing to the next, but is very creative
- Enjoys school, has good attendance, enters with enthusiasm
- Is interested in babies, origins of life, marriage, and reproduction (especially own birth)
- Begins to see fundamental differences between the impersonal forces of nature and the psychological forces of humans
- Growing conscious of own cultural or ethnic status and heritage
- Impatient; wants to get things done fast; does not enjoy long demonstrations
- Becoming an expert computer user and does research easily

Social
- Has accepted parents' prejudices and attitudes towards others
- Feels more at home with adults and talks with them freely; likes to ask riddles they cannot answer
- Shows strong admiration for parents in words and actions; hero worship begins.
- Discovers teacher can be a friend; likes teacher involvement and feedback
- Conscious of belonging to his or her school group; understands responsibility to this group
- Likes to work with and to be with other people
- Sees self more clearly as a person participating among other persons

- Wants to be "good," is aware of good and bad forces, is willing to take consequences but often apt to pass the blame
- Admits wrong doings, but rationalizes the reasons; has aversion to falsehoods; tall tales usually have some truth in them
- Much dickering and bickering in games
- Interest in barter, exchange, and collecting; value is less important than numbers and quantity
- Likes to argue; is aware of other's mistakes; is self-critical
- Exaggerates and uses slapstick humor; gets excited and often interrupts adults

Emotional
- Susceptible to jealousy and still can be easily hurt
- Begins to doubt the infallibility of parents and adults in general
- Sensitive to criticism, whether actual or implied
- Does not like to be criticized about short-comings, even humorously
- Self-conscious; may feel impelled to assert scorn of demonstrative affection when around peers
- Begins to desire to stand alone; judge for one's self; to "be somebody"
- Does everything in "high gear"; courage and dare are characteristics

Index